Theodor W. Adorno and Alban Berg
Correspondence 1925–1935

THEODOR W. ADORNO
AND ALBAN BERG

Correspondence 1925–1935

Edited by Henri Lonitz
Translated by Wieland Hoban

polity

This translation copyright © Polity Press, 2005. First published in German as *Briefwechsel 1925–1935* by Suhrkamp Verlag, Frankfurt am Main, © 1997.

The publication of this work was supported by a grant from the Goethe-Institut.

First published in 2005 by Polity Press

Polity Press
65 Bridge Street
Cambridge CB2 1UR, UK

Polity Press
350 Main Street
Malden, MA 02148, USA

ISBN: 0-7456-2335-2

A catalogue record for this book is available from the British Library and has been applied for from the Library of Congress.

Typeset in 10.5 on 12pt Sabon
by Servis Filmsetting Ltd, Manchester
Printed and bound in Great Britain by TJ International Ltd, Padstow, Cornwall

For further information on Polity, visit our website: www.polity.co.uk

Contents

Editor's Note vii

Translator's Note xi

Correspondence 1925–1935 1

Appendix I: Letters from Adorno to Helene Berg 1935–1949 231

Appendix II: Other Correspondence 243

Bibliographical Listing 253

Index 261

Editor's Note

Adorno was twenty-one years old when he travelled to Vienna at the start of March 1925, to continue with Alban Berg the studies in composition that he had begun with Bernhard Sekles before entering university. He had first met Berg at the Frankfurt premiere of *Drei Bruchstücke aus der Oper 'Wozzeck'* in June 1924, and immediately felt drawn to Berg both musically and personally: 'If I try to recall the impulse that drove me spontaneously to him, it was certainly a very naïve one, but still based on something important for Berg: the Wozzeck fragments, in particular the introduction to the march and the march itself, struck me as both Mahler and Schönberg at once, and this is what I imagined true new music to be like at that time.' For Adorno, continuing his compositional studies above all meant moving away from the quietly academic and uncritically retrogressive dictates of his first teacher. Bernhard Sekles, with whom he had studied since 1919, was not able to provide him with the guidance he was searching for. The liberation that Adorno experienced with Berg of 'not having to write tonally' any more fulfilled a musical need that he had already recognized, but which, according to his own verdict, he had still not succeeded in dealing with practically. In his first letter to Berg, of 5 February 1925, he formulated his reason for coming to Berg quite clearly: 'Meanwhile, I am dissatisfied with all of these [works], and in order to fulfil my new plans I would first of all like to entrust myself to your guidance and supervision. There are quite specific technical problems at issue, ones which I do not feel equal to; I think that I can tell you quite precisely what help I require from you.'

In addition to various songs, a set of variations for string quartet, and the second of the *Six Short Orchestral Pieces* op. 4, Adorno composed an unfinished string trio during his time with Berg in Vienna;

this was no mean feat for a little under six months' tuition – twice a week in Berg's Hietzing apartment, Trauttmansdorffgasse 27 – if one considers that the lessons seem not always to have taken place regularly. By his own account of this part of his life, Adorno would get up early each day, devote the morning to composing, and the afternoon to critical work, at the same time reading Kierkegaard in the evening. His first essay on musical interpretation, 'Zum Problem der Reproduktion', was written in March 1925 at the guesthouse Luisenheim, where he was staying during this period. Very soon he began his piano studies with Eduard Steuermann; through Berg he also came into contact with Arnold Schönberg, Anton Webern and Alma Mahler-Werfel. In his capacity as a *postillon d'amour* between Berg and Hanna Fuchs-Robettin, Adorno travelled to Prague several times, and there made the acquaintance of the musician and writer Hermann Grab.

*

What was more important for Adorno than the official and semi-official life in Vienna, however, which he examined critically in his letters to his friend Siegfried Kracauer, was the aesthetic presence of the unity of reflection and compositional practice in Berg's works, the unique combination of strict construction and a lingual, non-formulaic quality to the music, which Adorno later spoke of as the 'epic element' in Mahler. A passage from Adorno's letter to Berg of 23 November 1925 reveals the early influence of Berg's tuition and works, also upon Adorno's critical ideal of a dialectical representation. Writing about his first essay on *Wozzeck*, he states that the essay, 'unlike earlier ones, is not disposed according to "surface relations", but rather finds its balance in the continuity of the underlying thinking, the conceptual simultaneity and factual equality of intentions; so not "sections", themes to be grasped in isolation. My most secret intention was to make the essay's use of language correspond directly to the way in which you compose, for example in the quartet. This gave rise to a curious encounter between your manner of composition and my current intellectual stance.'

*

In a note from the end of 1944, Adorno writes: 'How much of my writing will remain is beyond my knowledge or my control, but there is one claim I wish to stake: that I understand the language of music as the heroes in fairy tales understand the language of birds.' It was no less than the desire to learn to speak this language that drew him to Berg. Adorno already knew what he wanted to compose before he came to Berg; the aim of his stay in Vienna and the following years was to learn to put this into musical practice. His correspondence with this composer who was soon to be world-famous is thus partly defined by his engagement with the compositional problems posed for the musical avant-garde by Schönberg's discovery of the twelve-tone technique, for which Adorno supplied much propaganda, not least in Vienna and through Berg. This correspondence not only documents how he wrote numerous essays on Berg, Webern and Schönberg during this time, and tried in vain to establish a platform for the Second Viennese School against 'moderated modernity' in the journal *Anbruch*, where he exerted considerable editorial influence from the start of 1929 onwards; it also shows how much Adorno – continually admonished by Berg to compose – strove to reconcile his academic duties, the *Habilitation*, and his literary and journalistic work with the constant wish to compose, only to compose.

*

For the present edition of the correspondence, the editor was able to draw on a transcription of the Berg letters with a first commentary made in the second half of the 1980s by Prof. Dr Rudolf Stephan and his student Dr Werner Grünzweig. When in doubt, the transcription proved invaluable for consultation; the editor takes sole responsibility for any possible errors, however. Beyond this, Rudolf Stephan supported the editorial work in the most generous manner with his advice. The editor also owes a great deal to Frau Dr Regina Busch in Vienna, who subjected the manuscript to critical reading and suggested numerous improvements.

The originals of Adorno's letters form a part of the Berg archive in the Musiksammlung der Österreichischen Nationalbibliothek, there guarded by Dr Josef Gmeiner, whom the editor would like to thank for his valuable support, while Berg's letters survived among Adorno's belongings and are now preserved in the Theodor W. Adorno Archiv in Frankfurt.

The surviving letters and cards have been reproduced in full and in chronological order. Two letters written by Maria Wiesengrund, Adorno's mother, have been included, as they pass on to Berg news of Adorno's car accident and his welfare in Adorno's name. A first appendix contains a number of letters written by Adorno to Helene Berg after Berg's death, which focus particularly intensely on the memory and works of his friend. The second reproduces letters by Berg to Bernhard Sekles and Hans W. Heinsheimer that played as important a part in the correspondence between Adorno and Berg as a letter from Heinsheimer to Adorno concerning the editorial policy of *Anbruch* and a letter sent to Berg in November 1933 by Edward Dent, concerning Adorno's prospects of finding a place in musical life in England.

*

The notes serve the purpose of explaining names and events mentioned or alluded to in the letters; in addition, they list the relevant works – both musical and literary – of the correspondents. The notes attempt neither a commentary upon the correspondence nor a discussion of the research so far; they are intended merely as an aid to reading.

Translator's Note

While translation always involves a balancing act between faithful rendition and an idiomatic use of language, historical documents such as letters raise particular issues. The implicit aim of published translations is generally to create and maintain the fiction that the text in question was actually written in the target language; in a correspondence, however, with countless references to external life and the respective proper names, this fiction is particularly unconvincing. Rather than attempt to translate all names of institutions, classifications of musical works or other references of this kind, I have sought to retain the German where I felt the original could be regarded as a proper name, as opposed to a straightforward categorial classification; one thus finds Frankfurter Kammermusikgemeinde in German, but 'Berlin State Opera' in English. With names of works, this principle has also been extended to the parameter of italics; standard terms such as 'Piano Sonata' or 'String Quartet' are thus not italicized, while more idiosyncratic classifications such as *Six Short Orchestral Pieces* are. German titles have been retained where I felt that their idiosyncratic nature exceeded this, as with *Drei Bruchstücke aus der Oper 'Wozzeck'*.

Besides this, I have also sought to retain any unevenness, clumsiness or stilted language found in the original letters, as well as erroneous or, as in the case of *Schönberg* rather than *Schoenberg*, historically authentic spellings of names. While this cannot excuse any shortcomings of the translation, it was considered the primary stylistic aim to reproduce as faithfully as possible the individual tone of each letter, rather than exerting any editorial influence upon the formulations used in the originals.

Wieland Hoban
April 2005

Correspondence 1925–1935

5 February 1925.
Frankfurt a. M. – *Oberrad*
19 Seeheimer Straße.

Dear Herr Berg,

you may perhaps remember me: at the Tonkünstlerfest[1] in Frankfurt in 1924, I had Scherchen introduce me to you, and told you of my intention to come to Vienna and study with you. The plan has now become ripe for decision, and I would like to ask you if you would be willing to accept me.

Allow me to relate to you in brief my curriculum vitae: I was born in Frankfurt in 1903, completed secondary school in 1921, and received a PhD from the university in 1924 for an epistemological study.[2] – I have played music since my earliest childhood, first playing the violin/viola, later the piano. My first compositional attempts were also made at an early age; I taught myself harmonic theory, and in 1919 came to Bernhard *Sekles*[3] with songs and chamber music. I have been his student since; most recently, I have been composing five- and eight-part vocal counterpoint and double fugues for voices. Independently of this tuition, I have also been composing for myself; six 'Studies for String Quartet' (1920)[4] were given a private performance in 1921 by the Rebner-Hindemith Quartet,[5] and my First String Quartet (1921)[6] was performed in 1923 by Hans Lange. In addition I have written two string trios[7] and songs with differing instrumentation. The last years have been devoted largely to scientific, pianistic and technical work; I have managed to compose only three four-part songs for female chorus a capella (1923)[8] and three piano pieces.[9] Meanwhile, I am dissatisfied with all of these, and in order to fulfil my new plans I would first of all like to entrust myself to your guidance and supervision. There are quite specific technical problems at issue, ones which I do not feel equal to; I think that I can tell you quite precisely what help I require from you.

A by-product of my philosophical and musical activities has been some work as a critic: I was music critic for a Frankfurt journal[10] from 1921–22; since 1923 I have been the Frankfurt correspondent for the 'Zeitschrift für Musik'; since 1925 I have also reported for the Berlin journal 'Musik'.

For information concerning me, you would perhaps best consult Sekles (director of the Hochsches Konservatorium), or Dr. Karl Holl[11] of the Frankfurter Zeitung. I will gladly send you articles of mine, if you wish; it would probably suit your needs better to send you compositions,

3

but as I am not content with my work, I am loath to send you anything. At least my writings on music could give you an idea of how I think. – I hope to bring you something when I come to Vienna, some work I can stand by in some measure. – I would also like to continue my piano studies there, and hope you can offer me some friendly advice in this matter. But the deciding purpose of my stay would be your tuition alone.

I would be grateful if you could respond soon, and tell me your conditions. – I need hardly add that my powerful impression of your works compels me to call upon your services.

My thanks to you in advance for your efforts

yours in sincere admiration

Dr. Th. Wiesengrund-Adorno.

Original: manuscript.

1 On 16 June 1924, Hermann Scherchen (1891–1966) conducted the premiere of the *Drei Bruchstücke aus der Oper 'Wozzeck'*.

2 Adorno's doctoral thesis, 'Die Transzendenz des Dinglichen und Noematischen in Husserls Phänomenologie', remained unpublished in its author's lifetime; see Theodor W. Adorno, *Gesammelte Schriften*, ed. Rolf Tiedemann in collaboration with Gretel Adorno, Susan Buck-Morss and Klaus Schultz, vol. 1: *Philosophische Frühschriften*, 3rd edn, Frankfurt am Main, 1996, pp. 7–77 (the *Gesammelte Schriften* [1970–86] will henceforth be referred to with the abbreviation GS and the number of the volume).

3 The composer Bernhard Sekles (1872–1934) taught at the Hoch'sches Konservatorium in Frankfurt from 1896, and was its director from 1923 until the Nazis seized power; he was also Paul Hindemith's teacher.

4 The premiere of the yet unpublished work was given on 12 September 1994 in Frankfurt by the Neues Leipziger Streichquartett.

5 The quartet founded by the Austrian violinist Adolf Rebner (1876–1967), who also taught at the Hoch'sches Konservatorium; Hindemith played in the quartet until 1921.

6 The premiere took place on 24 April 1923 in Frankfurt; besides this, the Lange Quartett (H. Lange, R. Itkes, G. Graf, W. Lange) played the String Quartet op. 28 by Ernst Toch – also a premiere – and *4 Gesänge für Tenorstimme mit Violine und 2 Bratschen* by Ludwig Rottenberg (1864–1932).

7 The first of these – dedicated to Adorno's former German teacher 'Reinhold Zickel in friendship' – is dated 'June 1921–February 1922'; the second, composed immediately after it, follows the model of Schönberg's First Chamber Symphony op. 9 in its single-movement form, and is signed: 'Fair copy completed 18.IV.1922: on Gustav Mahler's birthday'. Both trios are as yet unpublished; the first was premiered by Trio Recherche on 30 July 1994, during the International Summer Course for New Music in Darmstadt.

8 These are the *Drei Gedichte von Theodor Däubler für vierstimmigen Frauenchor* op. 8, which Adorno revised in 1945.

9 These as yet unpublished pieces – dedicated to Maria Proelss – were premiered by Maria Luisa Lopez-Vito on 18 September 1981, during the seventh Festival of Contemporary Music in Bolzano.

10 The reference is to the *Neue Blätter für Kunst und Literatur*, edited by Albert Dessoff, which was published from 1918 to 1923.

11 Karl Holl (1892–1975), who worked for the *Frankfurter Zeitung* from 1922, had taken over Paul Bekker's post there in 1925.

2 WIESENGRUND-ADORNO TO BERG
   FRANKFURT, 17.2.1925

Frankfurt a. M. – Oberrad,
19 Seeheimer Straße
17 February 1925.

Esteemed Herr Berg,

many thanks for your cordial letter,[1] which compels me to come to you as soon as possible, if possible still in February, otherwise in the first days of March. I shall give you the precise date,[2] or call you directly in Vienna. – I also look forward to following you to Berlin in May,[3] if this meets your approval. In June you would be back in Vienna, I daresay.

It gives me particular satisfaction that you were sympathetic to my articles,[4] as they caused me some frustration in Frankfurt. I should think that I will find a somewhat conveniently situated room with a grand piano. I have already asked friends in Vienna[5] to look for quarters for me.

Devoted greetings
Yours Th. Wiesengrund-Adorno.

Original: manuscript.

1 Berg's letter of reply does not seem to have been preserved.

2 Adorno arrived in Vienna on 5 March.

3 That is to say: to the premiere of *Wozzeck* originally scheduled for early 1925, which took place only on 14 December 1925.

4 In Berg's library, an issue of the journal *Neue Blätter für Kunst und Literatur*, dated 18 September 1922 (vol. 5, no. 1), has survived, containing two articles by Adorno: 'Bartók-Aufführungen in Frankfurt' (see *GS* 19, pp.

16–21) and 'Zeitgenössische Kammermusik: erster und zweiter Abend im Verein für Theater- und Musikkultur' (see *GS* 19, pp. 21–4).

5 Unknown.

3 WIESENGRUND-ADORNO TO BERG
   VIENNA, 19.5.1925

fuchs robettin[1]
for berg

arrive wednesday lunchtime
blauer stern[2] wiesengrund

Original: telegram.

1 At the time, Berg was staying in Prague, where Alexander von Zemlinsky (1872–1942) performed the *Drei Bruchstücke aus Wozzeck* on 20 May. Berg was the guest of the industrialist family Fuchs-Robettin; Herbert Fuchs-Robettin (1886–1949) was married to Franz Werfel's sister Hanna (1894–1964); the invitation most probably came about on the initiative of Alma Mahler-Werfel. Hanna Fuchs-Robettin, with whom Berg fell in love, was the addressee of the 'secret programme' of the *Lyric Suite* (see George Perle, 'Das geheime Programm der Lyrischen Suite', in *Musik-Konzepte*, ed. Heinz-Klaus Metzger and Rainer Riehn, 4: *Alban Berg, Kammermusik I*, Munich, 1978, pp. 49–74). Berg's letters to Hanna Fuchs-Robettin were published for the first time in 1995; see Constantin Floros, *Alban Berg und Hanna Fuchs: Briefe und Studien*, in *Österreichische Musikzeitschrift*, special fiftieth anniversary issue, Vienna, 1995, pp. 30–69.

2 The hotel *Zum blauen Stern* in Prague. Adorno was also invited to the Fuchs-Robettins' house.

4 WIESENGRUND-ADORNO TO ALBAN
   AND HELENE BERG
   MARIENBAD, 9.6.1925

Mariánske Lázně, 9 June 25.

Dear Herr Berg and dear lady, as proof of the fact that I, in spite of the irate Steuermann,[1] am truly relaxing for a few days, I send you, from the idyllically languid Marienbad, this card, which is not particularly beautiful, and would certainly not have immortalized your friend P. A.[2] But the air is good, and the colonnade is full of tempta-

tions to literature. I hope that one part of you is fever-free, and the
other part composing, yours in faithful devotion Teddie W.

Best wishes

Anna v. Tolnay.[3]

Original: postcard: Marienbad, full view; stamp: Marienbad, 10.VI.25.
Manuscript with an additional note by Anna von Tolnay.

1 The pianist and composer Eduard Steuermann (1892–1964), who had
studied with Ferruccio Busoni and Arnold Schönberg and went on to become
one of the most important performers of the Second Viennese School, was
Adorno's piano teacher during his Vienna days, and a close friend until his
death; see Adorno's 1964 obituary 'Nach Steuermanns Tod' (*GS* 17, pp.
311–17) and 'Die Komponisten Eduard Steuermann und Theodor W.
Adorno: aus ihrem Briefwechsel' (in: *Adorno-Noten*, ed. Rolf Tiedemann,
Berlin, 1984, pp. 40–72).

2 The Austrian poet Peter Altenberg (1859–1919), whose real name was
Richard Engländer, owned a sizeable collection of postcards; Berg composed his
Fünf Orchesterlieder nach Ansichtskartentexten von Peter Altenberg as op. 4.

3 Unknown.

5   BERG TO WIESENGRUND-ADORNO
SÖLLHUBEN, NEAR ROSENHEIM, 18.6.1925

Post office:

Söllhuben, near Rosenheim ⎤	sufficient	$^{18.}/_{6.}25$
Upper Bavaria, c/o v. Klenau ⎦	as address!!![1]	

My dear Wiesengrund I come to you with a few requests:
I wish to give the lady of the house[2] 'Die letzten Tage der Menschheit'
by Karl Kraus as a farewell gift. Could you please obtain a linen-
bound copy for me at Lányi's (Kärntnerstraße extension) & send it to
me post haste. Perh. you can let Lányi send it to me after *you* pay for
it (with postage). When I come to Vienna (which should be at the end
of the month) I will reimburse you for the sum.

    2.) I need for my fair copy,[3] which is progressing slowly but surely
(often when asthma torments me I already sit at my desk at 5 in the
morning!), a few more *quills* matching the sample I have enclosed.
Please insert a few into your next letter to me! But to be on the safe
side, buy a few dozen right away, and I shall take them off you after
my return (I believe *Soennecken* has a special Vienna branch, in case
you cannot find the quills in any larger 'city' stationer's!).

7

3. Please tell me what size of tips I should give here in your opinion (& maybe ask around a bit). & send 2 maids to take care of everything for us

    I. Clearing up
      serving
      etc
    II. Cooking

It would be for about 3 weeks & according to *German* terms, which are about twice the size of Austrian terms!

Re. 1.) should 'Die letzten Tage der Menschheit' be unavailable, then please the two volumes 'Weltgericht'[4] by Kraus

---

I expect you have by now received my letter of the 16th with newspaper cuttings.[5] Since then, nothing has changed. I am quite content with my work. And aside from this I soak my nerves – which are improving daily – in water & air. *Reading:* after long *vain* attempts (Ossendovski: People, Animals & Gods)[6] Döblin[7] [what do you think and know of him??] Meyrink (Golem!)[8] *finally* landed with a poet: *Flaubert* 'Bouvard & Pécuchet'.

    So in July I am sure to be in Vienna. –

Fond regards, also from my wife.
Yours Berg

What's the matter with you, my dear Wiesengrund? *No* news from you since your postcard from Marienbad!

Original: manuscript.

1 Written by Berg along the bracket.

2 Annemarie von Klenau (1878–1977), sister of the editor of the *Frankfurter Zeitung*, Heinrich Simon, was married to the Danish composer and conductor Paul August von Klenau (1883–1946) until 1926.

3 Berg completed the fair copy of the *Kammerkonzert für Klavier und Geige mit 13 Bläsern* (Chamber Concerto for Piano and Violin with 13 Wind Instruments), which he had begun composing in early 1923, on 23 July 1925.

4 The two volumes were published in Leipzig in 1919.

5 Not preserved.

6 The travel book *Animals, People and Gods* by the Polish writer Antoni Ossendovski was published in Frankfurt 1923–4.

7 Possibly *Wallenstein* – as mentioned in the following letter – which was published in 1920 in two volumes.

8 Gustav Meyrink's novel first appeared in 1915.

> Vienna, 21 June 25.
> (– Café Museum)
> (I got the quills together
> here through begging;
> as I did so, a waiter spilled
> milk on the letter –
> of human kindness?)

Dear Herr Berg,

yesterday evening I found your letter awaiting me at home, and will make my way to Lányi and Soennecken first thing tomorrow. I already received your card[1] and the Krull fragment[2] (which is wonderful, I once heard Thomas Mann read it) a few days earlier, and am most grateful to you. The fact that I am writing only now is the fault of a heavy depression which has rendered me incapable of any utterance; no unfounded one, as so often, but rather one stemming from events. *Everything* I begin ends in failure, and it need not surprise you if I soon borrow some Strindberg off you. To start with my journey to Czechoslovakia was a dead loss. Not only was there not a trace of recovery; this time I did not even find my lady friend (who signed the card), and went angrily on to Prague, where I could at least give vent to some philosophizing with dear Grab,[3] admittedly without thus finding a substitute for my friend. In Vienna I immediately got into a discussion with the Marxist thinker Lukács[4] (arranged by Morgenstern),[5] whom, as you know, I greatly revere; he made a strong impression upon me on a personal level, but in intellectual terms communication proved impossible, which of course pained me particularly in the case of Lukács, who has had a more profound intellectual influence on me than almost anyone else.

Now the sensation, the tragedy or the satyr play, however one chooses to see it: Heinsheimer[6] approached me and, to my utter amazement, offered me the chief editorship of 'Anbruch' to replace Stefan,[7] whom he felt unable to work with any longer. I cannot tell you how sorely I missed you: at Universal Edition I felt like a virgin in a dissolute men's club. I consulted with Morgenstern, who is a reliable and valuable person, with Stein,[8] who encouraged me vigorously, and with Steuermann, who, despite Krausian reservations, did not discourage me. I conferred with Heinsheimer for an entire morning on the nature of my position, and already conceived a (detailed) programme for him.

On the day of the deciding meeting, Heinsheimer explained to me briefly and cordially that he had – only now, after extensive negotiations! – spoken to Hertzka,[9] and that the bearded one could not decide at present to let Stefan go.

You can imagine my displeasure! Only think if I had undertaken further efforts to acquire the position! But I certainly had no desire to challenge poor Stefan's income; all the initiative came from the other side, only to be overturned in a manner that forced me into the vile situation of the unsuccessful entrepreneur, which is as little suited to me as, shall we say, loyalty is to Herr Hertzka. That evening, in the museum and then in the Reichsbar, the same society gathered from which you received the card,[10] which I hope you did not take offence at on account of its tone, for it was sincerely meant, but simply as strained as the mood that evening! Eisler,[11] incidentally, who is truly attached to you, and speaks of you with warmth and veneration, asks your permission to visit you before his final departure to Berlin.

As for me, I play Beethoven from morning until evening. Also compose, albeit somewhat sporadically. But now I hope: ça ira.[12]

It is good to hear that you are making progress with the fair copy, on account of the concerto, which is, and the quartet, which is to be; it is less pleasing that your asthma has returned; I had hoped that it had faded with time; but I suppose that the things we suffer have their own temporality, and all that remains is the desperate belief that it is all for the sake of eternity. Forgive my theological digression, which certainly does little to alleviate concrete suffering; I only venture it because I know that you, like me, can only gain mastery over suffering by interpreting and *forming* it! And as, I think, we have no alternative, you will not find my symbolic excursion unkind. I hope that the woods offer you more palpable help.

Is Flaubert the right thing for you at present; and his most terrible book at that? Do you know the education sentimentale?! – Döblin is a difficult case, very talented (coming intellectually from the circles of Bloch and Lukács), but truly degenerate, and without conscience in the aestheticizing manner in which he appropriates religious elements. I suspect that Karl Kraus is right in his opposition to him.[13] What is more, I find his attempt in Wallenstein to take control of history once more shaky, not least in its conceptual foundations. More on this when we speak.

And how are you, dear lady? Do you still have a fever, or did the cure you took enable you to recover properly and take your fill of verdure, so that you can now return to Vienna fit for music making? And is Germany, southern Germany not delightful after all? It is you who should now read Gottfried Keller, as I so long to do.

– To the baser life once more; 10, *at the very most* 15 gold marks

10

will surely suffice for each of the maids, probably it is much too much by rural standards.

I look forward more than I can express to seeing you both once more. Devotedly yours

Teddie Wiesengrund

Original: manuscript.

1 The card seems not to have survived.

2 See Thomas Mann, *Bekenntnisse des Hochstaplers Felix Krull: Buch der Kindheit*, Berlin and Leipzig, 1922 (*Der Falke*. Library of Contemporary Novellas, volume 10).

3 The Prague-born Hermann Grab (1903–1949), who, after doctorates in philosophy and law, as well as a brief subsequent career as a lawyer, worked primarily as a writer and musician, was a student of Alexander von Zemlinsky.

4 Adorno writes at length about his visit to Lukács in the Isbarygasse 12 in Hütteldorf in his unpublished letter of 17 June 1925 to Siegfried Kracauer.

5 The writer Soma Morgenstern (1890–1976) worked as the Vienna culture correspondent for the *Frankfurter Zeitung*. He had been a friend of the Bergs since 1923; see Soma Morgenstern, *Alban Berg und seine Idole: Erinnerungen und Briefe*, ed. Ingolf Schulte, Lüneburg, 1995 (in the following, abbreviated to Morgenstern, *Berg und seine Idole*).

6 Hans Heinsheimer (1900–1993), who had studied with Julius Weismann and Karol Rathaus, was director of the opera department at Universal Edition from 1921 to 1938; he emigrated to the USA in 1938.

7 From 1923, Paul Stefan (1879–1943) was editor of the *Musikblätter des Anbruch*, which was published by Universal Edition; it was only in 1929 that Adorno became the unofficial editor of *Anbruch*, as the journal was called from that year onwards, while Stefan remained the official 'editorial director' (*Schriftleiter*).

8 The music writer and conductor Erwin Stein (1885–1958), who had studied with Schönberg, was editor of the journal *Pult und Taktstock* (Podium and Baton), which he had founded, and which was also published by Universal Edition, from 1924 to 1930. See also Adorno's essay 'Erwin Stein: zu seinem Tode' (*GS* 19, p. 463f.).

9 The Budapest-born Emil Hertzka (1873–1932) was director of Universal Edition from 1909.

10 The card seems not to have been preserved.

11 Hanns Eisler (1898–1962), who took private lessons with Schönberg from 1919 to 1923, may already have made Berg's acquaintance in 1919 through the *Verein für musikalische Privataufführungen* (Society for Private Musical Performances).

12 Also a reference to the French revolutionary song *Ah! ça ira!*, which Adorno had arranged some weeks previously as part of the *Sept chansons populaires françaises arrangées pour une voix et piano* (Seven Popular French Songs Arranged for Solo Voice and Piano), which Adorno is likely to have shown Berg; see Theodor W. Adorno, *Compositions*, ed. Heinz-Klaus Metzger and Rainer Riehn, vol. 1: *Songs for Voice and Piano*, Munich, 1980, p. 94f. (the volume will henceforth be abbreviated as Adorno, *Compositions 1*).

13 It could not be conclusively ascertained what Adorno is referring to here; the only statement made by Kraus about Döblin from the mid-1920s concerns the latter's review of the Berlin premiere of *Traumtheater* and *Traumstück* on 25 March 1924 on the occasion of the twenty-fifth anniversary of his journal *Die Fackel*; see *Die Fackel*, no. 649–656, early June 1924, p. 40f.

7 WIESENGRUND-ADORNO TO BERG
   MADONNA DI CAMPIGLIO, 23.8.1925

Madonna di Campiglio, Hotel Campo di Carlo Magno, 23.VIII.
   Dear esteemed Herr Berg,
after a strenuous journey[1] I have arrived here, and am already quite captivated by the indescribably beautiful and impressive natural surroundings, and am taking pains to devote myself extensively to all holiday duties. Yesterday we went motoring at length, and after Schönberg's latest turn[2] I felt I was entitled to drive over the Tonale pass, not least because there is no Atonale pass. Many thanks for your card; the quotation,[3] it seems, to me, is from Götterdämmerung; but what does it mean?! More soon. Fond regards to both of you devotedly yours Teddie W.

Original: picture postcard: Gruppo di Brento 3476 Rifugio Stoppani verso Groste e Cima Brenta; stamp: Campo Carlo Magno, 24.VIII.25. Manuscript.

1 With his departure from Vienna on 19 August, Adorno also ended his lessons with Berg.

2 Presumably a reference to Schönberg's Suite op. 29 for piano, E flat clarinet, clarinet, bass clarinet, violin, viola and cello, about whose third movement – *Thema mit Variationen* – Adorno wrote in 1928: 'The third movement is a set of variations on *Ännchen von Tharau*. The theme, the unchanged E major melody, is adapted in the most artful manner to the vertically disposed note-row and its inverted and retrograde forms, being retained and henceforth contrasted with the other row-material – which is also retained – as an exceptional note-row, but at the same time also treated thematically in the traditional variational sense' (*GS* 18, p. 361). This movement was completed in

August 1925 – the complete Suite only in early May 1926 – so it is possible that Adorno learned of Schönberg's procedures by word of mouth while still in Vienna.

3 Berg's card with the Wagner quotation seems to have been lost; in the preface to his book on Berg of 1968, Adorno writes: 'Bidding farewell for a longer time, Alban Berg wrote the author a postcard with a quotation of the Hagen passage in Götterdämmerung: "Sei treu" [be faithful]' (*GS* 13, p. 324). See Richard Wagner, *Götterdämmerung*, act II, scene 2 (piano reduction by Felix Mottl, p. 159); the words are spoken by Alberich to his son Hagen.

8 WIESENGRUND-ADORNO TO ALBAN
AND HELENE BERG
CAPRI, 12.9.1925

HÔTEL DES PALMES
CAPRI
12 September 25.

Dear esteemed Herr Berg,

I am sincerely troubled to hear nothing from you. Did you not receive my cards from Madonna and Genoa?[1] Or did I offend you somehow: by not understanding the quotation? Or what else can it be? Is your wife sick? Are you stricken with asthma once again? I ask with all my heart that you send me a reply and, if you have something against me, to tell me rather than shrouding yourself in silence. I am myself too much inclined to silence not to understand it entirely on your part. But for this reason I also know, better now than I once did, of its danger. So allow me to chance this attack, at the risk of being objectively unqualified to do so.

Are you composing? And what has it become? Symphony or suite,[2] and indeed a quartet? Or songs after all? At any rate, it will no doubt be more correct a priori than the theory with which, bore that I am, I rather molested you, and which must be incorrect a priori, but was not actually meant a priori, rather with reference to a current matter, at the time that I pronounced it. And I had long known that the problem of the *turn* towards the objective was a considerably more complex matter than I had indicated when I inveighed against *beginning* with the objective without any personal investment, that is, against Křenek and in part also against Eisler, and I hope that this came to the surface in the essay on Schönberg[3] (has that been published yet?). I would like to repeat this with emphasis, as it is conceivable that you may have taken offence at the rigidity of my attitude – a rigidity that can be smoothed out entirely by any one note of your music. But you will concede that in a situation whose points of orientation have shifted as far as they have today, any intention that hopes to preserve itself must continually overstep the limits imposed on it by the dialectic of reality, as otherwise the chaos around it will break its already insecure boundaries. That, despite metaphysically charged terminology, is probably all that I was endeavouring to communicate with my proclamation of 'subjectivism'.

For my part, I am currently pursuing an unconditional – albeit not without some wanton advance interpretation – apperception of reality. The mountains would be the right thing for me, I realized this once again in Madonna, and I think I need not fear any loss of originality if I should plan later on to divide my time between South Tyrol and Vienna. Would you still be in accord? I consider it likely that I shall return to that particular city which cannot decline far sooner than I had supposed, as I am concerned with decline in particular – my own, of course. – In the meantime Italy, in particular southern Italy, has taken up a rather skewed position among my categories. A land in which the volcanoes are institutions, and the swindlers are saved, goes against my public spirit just as fascism conflicts with my inflammatory tendencies. And yet I am very well here. Though one does not get around to composing, as the external distractions are too strong and too alien, and whereas I could spend entire nights sketching in Madonna, I now lie beneath the zanzariera,[4] relishing my protection from the mosquitoes.

Your demonic taste for civilization and illusion would find ample sustenance here, for nowhere is civilization more glassy than in Italy, and intense, though in a different, more positive sense than with us, for the whole of life, lived as it were to the point of destruction, resists constant stabilizations and mirrors its own transience in illusion.

Being together with my friend[5] is in every sense exciting and important: in personal terms it demands full relaxation, in factual terms it forces a revision of the very basis. Indeed, in the six months of separation, we have both developed in the same sense – a sense that would also be fitting to you. He is no cheerful fellow, to be sure. We spent yesterday afternoon commenting on sports reviews in the B.Z.,[6] that was enjoyable. – I shall send you an essay by my friend which I identify with (I once spoke to you of it) entitled 'Der Künstler in dieser Zeit'.[7]

When is the Wozzeck premiere? I shall most certainly come, and would ask that you inform me of the relevant details in good time. I can take care of accommodation for Klein;[8] I need only know the date. Probably with Herzberger,[9] Berlin N, Prinzenallee 58. Or in Dahlem. But without any doubt. – My Webern endeavour[10] has not yet borne tangible fruits.

For the time being I am remaining here, then we will take a look at Pompeii and Paestum, also Naples once more, and hope to gain a few days for Sicily; for it would be a sin to visit Rome in passing. At the start of October I shall be in Frankfurt, and intend to stay in Amorbach for a few weeks in order to compose there – assuming that Wozzeck does not call me to Berlin.

Do you know that I still have your Altenberg?[11] I will send you the volume as soon as I am within a secure postal district. From Capri it strikes me as too unsafe.

You, dear Frau Helene, should not work too much, today it is my turn to preach this to *you*. And you are not to have any fever. But rather take walks and sing: those songs op. 2,[12] these op. 15,[13] and those by Zemlinsky from which I only ever heard you sing 'wohin gehst du'.[14]

I must ask you once again, o master of secret configurations, for the solution to your card that appears to have eluded me.

With my very fondest wishes.

Devotedly yours

Teddie W.

Original: manuscript with printed letterhead.

1 Adorno's card from Genoa appears not to have reached Berg.

2 It is possible that Berg had spoken to Adorno of his early – ultimately fragmentary – symphonic plans (see Alban Berg, *Sämtliche Werke*, ed. Alban Berg Stiftung, department: symphonic fragments. Facsimile edition with transcripts, supplied and introduced by Rudolph Stephan, Vienna, 1984), and speculated in conversation on returning to them. The question regarding the 'suite' most probably refers to the *Lyric Suite* for string quartet; Adorno, as letter 42 reveals, preferred the formal classification 'quartet'.

3 See Adorno, 'Schönberg: Serenade, op. 24', in *Pult und Taktstock*, 2 (1925), pp. 113–18; *GS* 18, pp. 324–30.

4 Ital.: mosquito net.

5 This is Siegfried Kracauer (1889–1966), with whom Adorno, coming from the Dolomites, had met in early September in Genoa, and with whom he travelled to southern Italy.

6 This is the *Berliner Zeitung*.

7 Kracauer's essay 'Der Künstler in dieser Zeit' (The Artist in Our Time) was published in the journal *Der Morgen* (vol. 1, 1925–6, pp. 101–9); see Siegfried Kracauer, *Schriften*, ed. Inka Mülder-Bach, vol. 5 [1]: *Aufsätze 1915–1926*, Frankfurt am Main, 1900, pp. 300–8.

8 The composer Fritz Heinrich Klein (1892–1977) was a student of Alban Berg; he edited the piano reductions of *Wozzeck* and the Chamber Concerto.

9 This means in the apartment of the Berlin branch of the Herzberger family. Whether or not the wealthy businesswoman Else Herzberger (1877?–1962),

a long-standing friend of Adorno's parents, was also living in Berlin at the time could not be ascertained.

10 Unknown.

11 It is unknown which volume by Peter Altenberg Adorno had borrowed from Berg.

12 See Alban Berg, Four Songs for Voice and Piano op. 2, on poems by Hebbel and Mombert.

13 See Arnold Schönberg, 15 Gedichte aus 'Das Buch der hängenden Gärten' von Stefan George op. 15.

14 The quotation is from the last of the Maeterlinck songs – 'Sie kam zum Schloss gegangen' – the Six Songs for Voice and Piano op. 13 by Alexander von Zemlinsky.

9   BERG TO WIESENGRUND-ADORNO
    TRAHÜTTEN, 21.9.1925

ALBAN BERG C/O NAHOWSKI
TRAHÜTTEN IN STEIERMARK   21./₉ 25
POST OFFICE: DEUTSCH-LANDSBERG
A./D. GRAZ-KÖFLACH RAILWAY

Dear Theddy, for the last month I had received only your card from Madonna & was therefore genuinely a little peeved*. For this reason, & because I could not know how long you would be reachable there, I did not write. Now, however, I have been reassured by your letter from Capri & I hope that you too shall be once you have received mine.

I have had – externally – a rather busy time. When we bade each other farewell at the Südbahnhof on the 17./8., I little suspected that I would that same evening – instead of finding the country house in Trahütten empty, for me to rest my weary nerves, find an entire family there: the husband of my wife's sister[1] had suffered a terrible lung haemorrhage the previous night, and could of course not be moved, leaving this family of four: a severely ill man, a severely hysterical wife, a severely ill-behaved, noisy child & a servant suffering from severe religious delusions in the house & the 3 of us[2] squashed together into 2 small rooms in the middle of this wasps' nest.

We bore this for 8 days, then we fled. Back in Vienna 8 days [where

---

* And after leaving you with that rather pregnant Wagner quotation to boot. Perhaps you shall one day find someone who knows his Wagner well enough (as you know your Schönberg) that he can reveal to you the missing words of the text. I should think that there are still – 'thank God' – a few such people!

we also saw Morgenstern, who should have found good quarters with Reinhardt by now][3] and now out for the 2nd time c. 14 days ago. Only now have I been able even to think of working. For the moment just bear in mind: I was in very poor health & am only now beginning to recover slowly. Alongside this I wrote an article [response to the call for papers from U.E. 'Perspectives for the next 25 Years'] for the U.E. yearbook coming out in November. And now I am composing a song: an occasional composition. For a collection in honour of Hertzka being published on the occasion of 25 years of U.E. 2 songs on the same text[4] printed on 2 facing pages. The first composed in C major almost 25 years ago, the 2nd composed today in the strictest 12–tone style [note-row!]. *So 25 years of U.E.!* But the latter is giving me little joy, although it is progressing relatively easily. *Too easily*, I fear!

Then, however, I want to return to real composing. & scnd I am still thinking a great deal about the quartet suite.[5] [but next perhaps indeed a symphony, as I will surely never find an opera text!] For I would like to remain here a while yet – & work. Wozzeck being only in *November*(!) Before that: *Sept*: Fidelio; *Oct.* Afrikanerin, Zigeuner-baron; *Nov.* Palestrina & Wozzeck, *Dec.* Boris Godunov.

With my opera, I hope to wake up the audience put to sleep once and for all by *Palestrina*.

I am thus genuinely up in the air during the month of October. If you were to ask me whether I would not like to travel to Vienna to give lessons, I should reply: 'Not for a "Schloss"' (who incidentally wrote to me not long ago).[6] On the other hand, the climate here is so rough that I cannot inflict it on my wife in the long term, while living with my paranoid brother-in-law is so unbearable that my nerves would not put up with it for long either.

But for the time being (1, 2 weeks), it seems we shall remain here.

And now you know all my news. [yes: in between all this I am also preparing F.H. Klein's piano reduction of the *Concerto* for engraving. In a few days the prints he has duplicated will come out, and they look splendid: 116 pages]

And now my thanks for your kind letter, which I found *most* interesting & pleasing. Your comments on the various problems, especially that of Italy, are bona fide Wiesengrunds once again & already as such they gave me a most homely feeling. This is what I have been lacking most this past month. So your silence troubled me all the more. But all the more pleasing was the news of your decision not to be entirely unfaithful to Vienna. You must always keep me informed as to where you can be reached. It is with great concern that I give up this letter to Capri; Kraus would say: 'give it up!' But perhaps it will reach you after all, and then with many warm regards from us both.

Your old Berg

My wife is not feeling much better than before. But she continues to work and knows only one thought: those around her!

You must ask U.E. for the issue of Pult & Taktstock with your (fine!) article.[7]

Original: manuscript with sender stamp.

1 Arthur Lebert was married to Anna Nahowski, Helene Berg's sister.

2 The Bergs often took Helene's mentally ill brother, Franz Josef Nahowski, with them on summer trips; see also below in the letter.

3 Further details unknown.

4 The two settings of Storm's poem 'Schließe mir die Augen beide', composed in 1905 (–1906) – on this dating, see Nicholas Chadwick, 'Berg's unpublished songs in the Österreichische Nationalbibliothek', in *Music & Letters*, vol. 52/2 (April 1971), pp. 123–40; here p. 125 – and 1925, are dedicated to Emil Hertzka on the occasion of the twenty-fifth anniversary of Universal Edition; first published in *Die Musik*, 22 (1929–30), musical supplement (issue 5, February 1930). Berg sent a duplicate copy of the songs to Adorno on 22 April 1926 (see letter no. 29). Adorno also set this poem by Storm in 1918.

5 Berg worked on the *Lyric Suite* for string quartet from September 1925 until October 1926.

6 An allusion to Berg's student Julius Schloss (= Germ. *castle*) (1902–1972), who had, like Adorno, come to Berg in 1925. Before that, Schloss had studied composition at the Hoch'sches Konservatorium in Frankfurt.

7 Adorno's essay on Schönberg's Serenade op. 24 (see letter no. 8, note 3).

10   BERG TO WIESENGRUND-ADORNO
     TRAHÜTTEN, 21.9.1925

$^{21.}/_{9.}$25 Dear Teddy. As your letter of the $^{12.}/_{9.}$ arrived here today on the 21st, I dare not send the letter I have just written you to *Capri*. You are surely no longer there! I will therefore merely send you best wishes & refer you, incidentally, to my extens. letter, which I am sending to Frankfurt-Oberrad with the same delivery.

fond wishes from your
Berg

Best wishes,

yours,
Helene Berg

Original: picture postcard: Villa Nahowski, Trahütten, 1000 m above sea level, near Deutsch-Landsberg, Steiermark [and added in Berg's hand:] *via Graz Austria*; stamp: Graz, 25.9.25. Manuscript with an additional note by Helene Berg on the picture side.

11 BERG TO WIESENGRUND-ADORNO
TRAHÜTTEN, 12.10.1925

ALBAN BERG C/O NAHOWSKI
TRAHÜTTEN IN STEIERMARK
POST OFFICE: DEUTSCH-LANDSBERG
A./D. GRAZ-KÖFLACH RAILWAY

$^{12.}/_{10.}25$

Did you, dear Wiesengrund, receive the letter I sent to you in Frankfurt? I wrote to you there on the $^{21.}/_9$ & at the same time sent a card to Capri. What are you doing these days? What plans do you have? – We are remaining here for another c. 2 weeks, then Vienna, where we shall await being called to Berlin. But it seems that the premiere there is to be rather delayed. I have heard nothing good about it. My work is coming along slowly. How are you & your esteemed mother & aunt?[1] Fond regards to all of you from us both. Yours Berg

Sekles has seen fit *not* to reply.[2]

2140 m. I was up there[3] not long ago. You know that I have to come to this 2000 m region every 1, 2 years. Even if it far exceeds my constitution. But I did return home alive. –

Original: picture postcard: Koralpe, Schutzhaus d. Sekt. Wolfsberg d.D.ö.A.V.; stamp: Deutsch-Landsberg, 13.X.1925. Manuscript.

1 Maria Wiesengrund (1865–1952), who had, during the 1885/6 season in Vienna, sung the part of the wood-bird in Wagner's *Siegfried*, among others, and her sister Agathe Calvelli-Adorno (1868–1935), who was a pianist, had made Berg's acquaintance in March 1925 when staying in Vienna before moving on to Salzburg.

2 Berg's letter of 27 July 1925; see appendix II, p. 243.

3 The entire postscript is written along the edge of the picture side.

Frankfurt a. M. – Oberrad
19 Seeheimer Straße, 15 October 25.

Dear esteemed Herr Berg,

upon my return here – I was with my mother and aunt in Amorbach[1] until 12 October; I had left Italy on 30 September – I found, to my greatest pleasure, your letter. My joy came above all from the fact that it was there, and that you were not angry with me; for what you relate in it, and the manner in which you relate it, certainly does not sound pleasing, and after reading also your most recent card, I am under the impression that you are not doing so very well. It is a good thing, at least, that you are now able to compose, after the ordeal of the first weeks in Trahütten, and, after all, the plan to write a symphony closes the horizon in a friendly manner, even if it should become a tragic one. –

Concerning my silence: it certainly did not result from disloyalty, for to whom could I feel more loyal than to you! –, but merely from a profound exhaustion which made me incapable of writing a single decent word; and you will no doubt understand that I was loath to write to you half-heartedly. In addition to this there was the ongoing confrontation with my friend,[2] which was in every respect a difficult matter, and which gave me no opportunity for repose. In Naples we met with Benjamin shortly before our return, and engaged in a philosophical battle with him in which we were able to control the field, albeit not without finding it most necessary to regroup our forces; a strategic opening which has not yet been concluded. – Incidentally, Italy still held many fine things in store; the countryside in Positano is one that one knows only from one's dreams, and the people there adapt themselves to this; the Byzantine Ravello – above Amalfi – offers a glance of the East for an evening, before closing in Italian fashion once more with its fountain, cool upon its hill. In Paestum, near Salerno, I had my first view of Greek temples, which remained mute and alien in the solitude of this feverish region; they seemed, in the way that they stand there on their own, more needy of attention than disposed towards speaking themselves. Then Naples was initially a threatening chaos, the roads there look like forests, melons are sold among heathen cult symbols, stuffed cats' heads are considered a delicacy, animal brothels an erotic speciality, and even the kitsch of the buildings, which purport to be classical in style, excessively ruptures all civilizatory security. Admittedly, this chaos soon changes into order, a non-rational order between the stubbornly elemental and an irregularly and heretically intruding transcendence. Much of the baroque has become, if I may be allowed an interpretation, paradoxically immortalized; and we came to wonder whether the confirmed and incomprehensible reality of this city is not ultimately more normal than the abnormal, self-asserted reality of our world.

Nonetheless, we departed from Naples in some confusion. I travelled on the train for 36 hours without interruption, which is a pleasure of its own kind. In Amorbach we celebrated my mother's birthday, 2 days later my Prague friend Hermann Grab (who is a student of Zemlinsky) visited us there; we indulged in endless music-making and philosophizing, and he sought, in his Jewish manner, to convert me to Catholicism, but theology did not impair our enjoyment of the radiantly beautiful autumn, which now made my return to Germany bearable. Grab would like to visit you when he is in Vienna again, though he is reluctant for fear of seeming intrusive. I have therefore taken it upon myself to introduce him to you. I consider him a very special person, and also think that you will not have cause to take exception to him. As far as I understand your economy in the choice of personal relationships, I can readily take responsibility for asking you in this case to receive a friend who will not be a burden to you.

It was the day before yesterday that I arrived here, in this dreadful city, and have so far spent my time being annoyed at the crass, ugly people on the street, at Hindenburg, at a chamber music society[3] which has been thrown together under an absurd directorship, at the letter of an estranged lady friend, who now remembers me because she is in need of reviews, at an immorally stupid article by Karl Holl[4] in the Frankfurter Zeitung, in which he praises the unimpaired nature of Messrs. Korngold, Casella, Labroca, Rieti and company at length, while there is only one sentence on Schönberg's Serenade, born of a misunderstanding of my essay, and Eisler, who has no luck (he seems to be having a terrible time in Berlin!), is disdained in the most impudent manner. – I am homesick for Vienna, the city one complains of as long as one is there, and which one only learns to appreciate once more in exile. I am convinced that I shall surface there again soon. Grab gave me the good idea of qualifying as a professor in Frankfurt and applying for the venia legendi in Vienna or Prague. If this were to prove feasible, it should be a good solution. – In the meantime I am planning either to visit you in Vienna in November and attend the Berlin premiere with you (and if possible also some rehearsals) or to meet you directly in Berlin and then perhaps follow you to Vienna for a few weeks. I cannot yet quite say what will be; it depends primarily on the date of the premiere, and on which of these options would enable us to spend more time together. You can no doubt determine this better than I can. At any rate, I shall consider it certain that we will see each other in November.

I am quite especially pleased that you enjoyed the Schönberg essay, which of course went without response. Did the strict one himself read it? And was the Eisler analysis[5] printed in Anbruch? – Here is a suggestion: as far as I know, the state theatres in Berlin (under the direction of Julius Kapp, if he is still alive) are publishing newsletters, and Wozzeck too will not escape being announced to the Berlin Jews in this context. But if it must be: would it not be better for me to write about it, rather than some dreary critic? Please inform me of your thoughts on the matter. What I would especially like, of course, is the chance to write the paper for Anbruch.[6] Do you think I have a chance to receive the commission if I make an effort? It would spare Herr Hertzka the travel expenses for Herr Stefan. But I expect he will favour Herr Weissmann,[7] who will ultimately do more harm than good. – Incidentally, I have asked Heinsheimer to place me in charge of the Frankfurt office of Anbruch.

I am now beginning to work again, will first of all conclude the songs (in 'Mußt du bei Tag und bei Nacht',[8] a number of things will now turn out rather differently), then trio. Meanwhile I am studying Wozzeck, your quartet,[9] which appeals to me more and more, and which – unlike Webern – anticipated all the problems of today as otherwise only Pierrot[10] did, and this moreover shows quite exceptionally the connection to chromaticism, and as a document of the *path* offers a strong apologia for atonality. Then the Wind Quintet,[11] which I have fully unravelled; of the Suite[12] I have so far only obtained the Intermezzo and, of course, the Minuet; but these two pieces are themselves outstanding.

Have you replied to Stein's questionnaire?[13] You are humorous enough to do so, and I shall myself presume to contribute something to its destruction, which is Stein's aim. – I shall study a great deal of Wagner.

Dear Frau Helene, are you living in a manner that would satisfy Peter Altenberg (– for your husband struggles in vain against your altruism!)? Or do you dip your fair hands in glacial waters to clean the dishes which should clean themselves?! Ah well, Zemlinsky is right,[14]

ver - irrt   sich   die   Lie - be   (if love goes astray) then it consumes itself in work that dissolves the subject for the sake of the object of love, so that nothing remains but the memory – whereas it would be better to sing the song than to live too closely by it. In Berlin I hope to be with you without household worries once more – if my eager friends allow it!

Until then fond regards to both of you
from your faithful Teddie W.

My mother and my aunt send their warm greetings.
Please: tell me at greater length about your new quartet!

Original: manuscript.

1 Adorno's family stayed in the small town in the Odenwald, not far from Frankfurt, several times a year; Maria Wiesengrund celebrated her sixtieth birthday there on 1 October 1925.

2 Siegfried Kracauer.

3 The Frankfurter Kammermusikgemeinde, founded in 1925 by the pianist and painter Maria Proelss (1892–1962), a friend of Adorno; for Adorno's obituary see *GS* 19, pp. 465–7.

4 See *Musikfeste 1925: Donaueschingen und Venedig*, in *Frankfurter Zeitung*, 15.10.1925 (vol. 70, no. 768), p. 1f.

5 Adorno's essay on Hanns Eisler's Duo for Violin and Violoncello op.7, no. 1, had appeared in the *Musikblätter des Anbruch* in September 1925; see *GS* 18, pp. 519–21.

6 Adorno indeed wrote his essay *Zur Aufführung des 'Wozzeck'* for the December issue of the *Musikblätter des Anbruch* (see *GS* 18, pp. 456–64).

7 The music critic Adolf Weissmann (1873–1929).

8 This is the first song from Adorno's op. 1: *Vier Gedichte von Stefan George für Singstimme und Klavier* (see Adorno, *Compositions 1*, pp. 8–12), whose first line should read: *Darfst du bei Nacht und bei Tag*.

9 Berg's String Quartet op. 3, which he had completed in 1910.

10 Schönberg's *Pierrot lunaire* op. 21.

11 Schönberg's Wind Quintet op. 26.

12 Schönberg's Piano Suite op. 25.

13 This refers to the *Drei Rundfragen* from *Pult und Taktstock* of September 1925 (vol. 2, issue 7, p. 123):

1. We know from music history that the audience in general does not possess sufficient judgement to appreciate the qualities of a musical

work of art. How is it that important composers have nonetheless always established themselves in the end, if often after going for a long time without recognition?

2. Furthermore: do success or failure tell us anything about artistic merit, be it of a composition or a performance?

3. And finally: can the audience be trained to develop a better understanding of art? If so, how?

A response by Adorno has not been found.

14 Adorno notates the vocal part (bars 22 and 23) of the third song – the *Lied der Jungfrau* – of the *Maeterlinck-Gesänge* op. 13 by Alexander Zemlinsky.

13   BERG TO WIESENGRUND-ADORNO
     VIENNA, 3.11.1925

ALBAN BERG VIENNA XIII/I
TRAUTTMANSDORFFGASSE 27 $3 \cdot /_{11} 25$
TELEPHONE: 84831.

My dear Wiesengrund, I am now in Vienna again, and can finally reply to your questions. First of all, many thanks for your letter. Its beauty and wealth of detail offered ample compensation for the scarcity of our summer exchange.

Now it is clear that we shall meet again before long. The Wozzeck premiere is (as I have meanwhile heard *un*officially) fixed for 14 December. Colossal difficulties in filling the roles have proved surmountable. One singer (the doctor) has even gone insane. Now, however, each part is to have an understudy. Until the premiere (or 1, 2 weeks before it), I suppose I shall remain in Vienna. Though I (& U. E.) certainly expect that I shall be called to Berlin for 2 or 3 days before then, around mid-November. I hope I shall be well enough; for I have been close to a nervous breakdown these last days. After increasing physical decline (I have lost over 10 kg since May), I was struck down in the first days here by a terrible series of asthma attacks. But now *that* at least is better & I hope I have overcome it. Please no mention of my health in your letters: my wife is understandably distressed by *my appearance*, though I have managed to keep the matter of my 10 lost kilos from her. And as far as the other matter is concerned, I am now seeking medical treatment. –

U. E. will write to you concerning an essay on Wozzeck for the December issue of Anbruch; I spoke with Heinsheimer yesterday for that reason.

I am greatly looking forward to it. But one request!! Do not write anything *difficult*! You no doubt have so much to say about it, & I want those who read it to *learn* all that from you. But they can only do that – as they are mostly just musicians & music-lovers, – and entirely uneducated in philosophical matters – if you express yourself in *generally comprehensible* terms. I am sure this will pose no problem for you. It would mean a great deal to me if you could expand on why I set this book in particular & had already decided to do so early in 1914 at a time when Büchner's ideas were not yet en vogue (as e.g. *after* the war) What seems less important to me is this wittering on about what musical forms I used there. Everybody knows about that nowadays. – That would only be useful if – in 1 or 2 cases – one were to go into *greater detail*; about the hexachord in the suicide scene, for example [connection to Schönberg's 12–note row principle] or the rhythmic variations of the last scene in the tavern, or the doctor's passacaglia or equally the chorale arrangement (journeyman's sermon) Do you know e.g. where the *chorale* is from?[1]

But that is not supposed to be an order, rather merely a *suggestion*, or in the best case a *guideline*.

The various Anbruch and Taktstock fellows[2] will no doubt insist on reporting on the performance. And a preliminary article from your pen strikes me as more important. At least the reporters will then have something decent to copy from. Nonetheless, I shall do my best for you in this respect.

I should naturally be most pleased to see Grab, to whom I also took a considerable liking,[3] in my house. He should call me on the telephone whenever he is in Vienna. Perhaps he will come to Berlin for the premiere! Please write to him!

Your reports of *Italy* were *most agreeable*. Those of *Frankfurt* less so, but interesting. Are you still there? Do you ever see Sekles?

Do you know yet whether you shall 'apply' for the 'venia legendi' (if I only knew what that is!) in Vienna or Prague. Seems a very good idea, dear Herr Professor [that is not ironic, but merely intended to demonstrate my good humour to you].

An article from you in the Berliner Staatstheater Blätter (Kapp) would naturally be *very much* to my taste. But I have no access *in this case*. And *can* hardly arrange that myself in any case. You understand!

How are your songs faring? The trio?

My wife's health is a little better.

Unfortunately, I have not composed a great deal. The only part of the quartet suite to be entirely finished is one movement an Allegretto giojoso[4] composed in the 12–tone note-row style (very strictly!). Perhaps I can continue it here (we have only been in Vienna for three days).

I have not yet seen Morgenstern. Once again, he has *failed* to reply to a long letter we sent him (from Trahütten).[5]

Pass on our warmest greetings to your dear esteemed lady mother & aunt. Fond regards from me & from my wife

your Berg

Schönberg after the Stravinsky concert[6] in Venice: well, who's drumming away there?[7] It's Stravinsky, he's grown himself a lad's ponytail!

Schönberg is composing diligently: chamber suite and choral pieces[8] (own and Chinese texts)

Original: manuscript with sender stamp.

1 Willi Reich writes on this: 'The first trio represented by the journeyman is repeated (bars 615–50) in such an altered form that its underlying harmonies (456ff.) are taken apart, producing a chorale melody in minims which, presented by Bombardon (604–35), forms the basis for the melodramatic parody of a sermon. (This melodrama, then, is on the one hand the repetition of the first trio, and on the other hand an outright – albeit parodied – five-part chorale arrangement!)' (Willi Reich, *Alban Berg: Leben und Werk*, Zurich, 1963, p. 128).

2 Translator's note: Berg's original words contain a punning elision of the two publications' names (*Musikblätter des Anbruch* and *Pult und Taktstock*): he writes *die angebrochenen Taktstöckler*, which (alongside the obvious reference) would translate approximately as 'the broached batonists'.

3 Berg will have made Grab's acquaintance on the occasion of his Prague visit in May 1925.

4 The original marking for the first movement of the *Lyric Suite*, which Berg changed to *Allegretto gioviale*.

5 In the published correspondence between Berg and Morgenstern (see Morgenstern, *Berg und seine Idole*, pp. 141–281) there is no such letter from Berg to Morgenstern from this time.

6 Stravinsky performed his piano sonata during the International Chamber Music Festival, which took place in Venice from 3 to 8 September.

7 See the second of Schönberg's Three Satires for Mixed Choir op. 28.

8 Schönberg's op. 29 was completed in 1926; the choral pieces composed in 1925 are the Four Pieces for Mixed Choir op. 27.

ALBAN BERG VIENNA XIII/I
TRAUTTMANSDORFFGASSE 27
TELEPHONE: 84831.

Dear Wiesengrund, what is the matter with you? Did you receive my letter? Today only the message that the premiere is on 14 December. Start of December I'll go there. I have just been there for 2 days (stopping for 24 hours in Prague on the way there and back) and have the impression that it shall be a truly wonderful performance. Kleiber[1] colossal. Anbruch is awaiting an article from you. Will you write it? We shall now see each other soon enough! When will you come to Berlin? Fond regards from your Alban Berg, who has become c. 10–12 kg lighter in the last 6, 7 months,
which sorely troubles me with warm greetings yours
Helene

Original: postcard; stamp: Vienna, 20.XI.25. Manuscript with sender stamp and an additional note by Helene Berg.

1   The conductor Erich Kleiber (1890–1956) was chief musical director of the Berlin State Opera from 1923 to 1934.

15   WIESENGRUND-ADORNO TO ALBAN
     AND HELENE BERG
     FRANKFURT, 23.11.1925

Frankfurt, 23 November 25.

Dear master and teacher,
   your intelligible being is to blame that I have so long offered nothing empirical: for since receiving your letter, I have until now done nothing else but work on the essay, which will now hopefully be in Vienna for the 20th. May it give you a little of the joy that it gave me: it is really the first that I am quite satisfied with, and certainly the first to develop my new stylistic ideal with some degree of purity. But what seems most important to me is the fact that it *came to be* at all. I have asked Heinsheimer to pass it on to you, so that you still have time to voice any reservations or suggestions for changes – and radically so, I would ask, I am here without sensibilities and desire nothing other than to be useful to you.

27

On the matter itself: I followed your directives, in so far as it was possible within the overall framework; I thus refrained from going on about the forms in 'Wozzeck', instead seeking to account for the choice of text (reread much Büchner for this purpose: what a writer!); referred to Wozzeck's death scene in connection with twelve-tone music; had to abstain from detailed musical analyses, on the other hand, as they would have made the essay disproportionately more difficult to read; and I truly took pains to write plainly; this admittedly made the essay rather long on account of one or other necessary explanation. It undertakes two things that I would still like to bring to your attention:

1) Attempt to draw a clear line between the work and Schönberg, in a manner to which Schönberg must himself consent; namely by deducing the impossibility of forming a 'school' from his own stance (my aim: this prattling on about the 'Schönberg pupil' must stop).

2) 'Theory of variation' in Schönberg's works and yours, intended to target the connection and the typical differences. Your relationship to Mahler will also be mentioned here.

I ask you, then, to note these two things. I am emphasizing this because the essay, unlike earlier ones, is not disposed according to 'surface relations', but rather finds its balance in the continuity of the underlying thinking, the conceptual simultaneity and factual equality of intentions; so not 'sections', themes to be grasped in isolation. My most secret intention was to make the essay's use of language correspond directly to the way in which you compose, for example in the quartet.[1] This gave rise to a curious encounter between your manner of composition and my current intellectual stance. You can imagine how eagerly I await your opinion.

Berlin: I do not yet know *when* I shall be there, but am naturally seeking to be there as soon as possible. It is truly a great joy to me that you are satisfied with the performance. I should think I am now sufficiently prepared for it. I shall inform you regarding Klein's accommodation as soon as I know myself how the matter stands. My original plan was thwarted by the fact that my friend,[2] who is in hospital, will be at home for a few weeks at the very time of the premiere. It would therefore hardly be feasible for her parents to receive a guest at the same time. But I am hoping to find another solution. (Dahlem, where it could easily be arranged, is very far outside.)

Those 10–12 kg will no doubt restore themselves to you soon enough. 'Wozzeck', in which I have the greatest faith – also *externally* – will contribute to that. After all, external success is a fact that can still be reckoned with mentally, even when one has lost faith in the immanent justice of the art industry to the extent that you have. I generally believe that, in a particular layer of suffering and inwardness, the manifest empirical knowledge represented by reality has a great and lasting power. It is this power that I place my hope in.

I can tell you about Sekles. I did not, of course, go in search of him; but he came to me repeatedly, told me of your letter, explained that the praise conferred upon him is undeserved, as he has no understanding of my music, though was clearly very flattered, apologized for his negligence, which he attributed to lack of time, and asked me if he could still write to you without it being ridiculous. As I heard from Holl that his position as director of the conservatory is very difficult, as he runs about dejectedly, and already depends for his very self-respect on having been introduced to Hindenburg as the head of the institution – in short, because I feel sorry for him, I did not snub him, and told him that I did not think you would mind his still writing to you. At some point I shall also play him some of my things. – I assume you do not object. Of course, a real personal relationship can no longer develop. But a form of contact may be upheld, partly out of respect, partly out of pity.

I am finally finding time for music again. I am quite serious about my intentions regarding a reception of Wagner (nothing in the world but you could have enabled me to do so once more!). I have been studying Parsifal very closely, and found Mahler's 'Der Lenz ist da'[3] note for note at the start of act III, at Kundry's awakening, as well as various more important things, especially in the scene with Kundry and Parsifal in act II and Titurel's funeral music in III, the birth of the 3rd Symphony,[4] which is admittedly still finer (I heard it recently with the most profound emotional shock. How truly the composer's ear has probed the stuff of our existence, how fully we are joined with it, despite the rupture!). I heard Rheingold and Walküre under Kraus,[5] not at all bad, likewise studied them. Now I am taking up Siegfried and Götterdämmerung, where the quotation[6] must surely be located: for I cannot imagine that I could have missed it in Parsifal. Or is it bewitched?* I would like to discuss Wagner most thoroughly with you. Perhaps I shall write a few fragments on the Ring.[7]

I will now also have more time for composing once more. And I am practising the piano systematically again. Chopin and Debussy. – The songs will now truly be finished by the time we meet in Berlin, I should think. – I should be able to inform you within the next few days as to when I shall be in Berlin.

What is Morgenstern up to? Is he roaming or well behaved, and by the way: is he a dramatic adviser? If he comes to you, you must greet him most heartily from me. If not, I should be cross with him – then his Ahasverian manner is too 'Jewish' for me.

* nor do I yet know where the cantus firmus of the journeyman's sermon in Wozzeck is from.

I hope to return to Vienna for longer soon. I hope to see you, dear Frau Helene, in peace in Berlin at last. Perhaps the commotion of Berlin can manage what the seclusion of Hietzingen could not: to remove you a little from your circle of duty. And perhaps, during the one hundred and eighty-seven rehearsals, and while you are unable to relieve your husband of all his authorial burdens, we could find an hour or so for some quiet music-making.

Fond regards from your ever devoted Teddie W.

Original: manuscript.

1 Berg's op. 3.

2 Presumably Gretel Herzberger, related to Else Herzberger; further details concerning her and her hospital stay could not be found.

3 See Gustav Mahler, *Das Lied von der Erde*, fifth movement: *Der Trunkene im Frühling*, 2 bars after figure 8; the passage from Richard Wagner's *Parsifal* extends from the final bar of p. 214 to the first bar of p. 215 in Felix Mottl's piano reduction (Gurnemanz sings: 'und Lenz ist da').

4 By Gustav Mahler.

5 Spelled thus in Adorno's handwriting; he means the conductor Clemens Krauss (1893–1954), who was director of the Frankfurt Opera and the Frankfurt Museumskonzerte from 1924.

6 See letter no. 7 and note 3 there.

7 The plan was not taken any further during this time.

16   WIESENGRUND-ADORNO TO BERG
     FRANKFURT, 7.12.1925

Frankfurt, 7 December 25.

Dear esteemed Herr Berg,

I was almost prevented at the last moment from reaching Berlin in time for the premiere. At the start of last week I was struck by a very severe throat infection which even the aspirin was powerless to alleviate, and was forced into bed. Today I am up again for the first time, still faint enough, and must remain on my feet for a few days yet. But I will no doubt arrive in Berlin in the course of this week, probably on the 11th, and would be most grateful if you could inform me of your address – perhaps by telegraph.

Have you received my letter, which was extensive? And did Heinsheimer or some other slave bring you the proof copy of my essay? As I have heard nothing from you, I am concerned on both counts, not least because Anbruch sent me the corrections without any accompanying comments.

My hope of finding accommodation for Klein has been thwarted by an unhappy quirk of circumstances. The situation is such that I myself cannot stay with friends, but must rather depend on a hotel or guest-house. What would you recommend? I naturally wish to be near you.

I cannot tell you how I look forward to seeing you again – and to Wozzeck! Especially because I hope, once the matter of my *Habilitation*[1] has been sorted out to a degree, to come to Vienna for longer once more – so our encounter this time will not have that hopeless exceptionality which one must normally fear so much with such occasional meetings.

Would it be possible for the two of you to spend a few days in Frankfurt on the return journey to Vienna? My parents would be overjoyed, and you would be well taken care of, despite the cold and the people of Hindenburg.

Fond regards to both of you

Yours,

Teddie W.

During my illness I studied your quartet thoroughly once again, and am now living fully within it. It is a match for the F sharp minor![2] I can say no more than this. The end of the 1st movement – from about 160 onwards – is among the most beautiful chamber music I have encountered!

Original: manuscript.

1 Adorno was preparing for his *Habilitation* (qualification as a professor) with Hans Cornelius (1863–1947), who had already been his doctoral tutor. The first *Habilitation* thesis, 'Der Begriff des Unbewussten in der transzendentalen Seelenlehre' (The Concept of the Unconscious in the Transcendental Doctrine of the Soul), which Adorno worked on from early 1926 until autumn 1927, was published only after his death (see *GS* 1, pp. 79–322). Adorno ultimately had to withdraw his application in order to pre-empt an impending rejection. Only the second attempt, which Adorno later undertook with his study on Kierkegaard, succeeded with the help of Paul Tillich.

2 In the analysis of Berg's String Quartet op. 3 that Adorno wrote in 1937 for the book *Alban Berg: mit Bergs eigenen Schriften und Beiträgen von Theodor Wiesengrund-Adorno und Ernst Krenek* (Vienna, Leipzig and Zurich, 1937), edited by Willi Reich, he likewise placed it alongside Schönberg's F sharp minor quartet op. 10; he included it in his 1968 book *Berg: Der Meister des kleinsten Übergangs*: 'It certainly has its stylistic-historical background, as much as any other. Schönberg's F sharp minor

quartet is the most evident: the cadential group model in the first movement, for example (bar 58), touches on an important motive from it, and is also treated in a similar manner. But the similarities are evident only in the details. Its invention and execution are entirely Berg's own; there is no model that could ever be found' (*GS* 13, p. 391).

17 MARIA WIESENGRUND-ADORNO TO BERG
FRANKFURT, 15.12.1925

most heartfelt congratulations and greetings = wiesengrund adorno[1]

Original: telegram.

1 Note of congratulation sent by Maria Wiesengrund-Adorno in the name of the whole family on the occasion of the premiere of *Wozzeck*.

18 BERG TO WIESENGRUND-ADORNO
VIENNA?, AFTER 15.12.1925

Please take good care of this!!
The voice of the people   is the voice of God
Frankfurt a. M.
Excerpt from the edition of December 15th 1925

The Viennese composer Alban Berg had supplied the Prussian State Opera with a setting of Büchner's 'Wozzeck' that was performed for the first time on Monday. According to reports from Berlin, the work was applauded vigorously by the majority of listeners, albeit not without objection from some quarters. 'Wozzeck', or more correctly 'Woyzeck', is the well-known story of a poor soldier who, tormented by his superiors and betrayed by his wife, becomes a murderer and meets his fate. It was to be expected that this play would also be gripping on the operatic stage; but Berg managed in several passages to heighten and increase this effect yet further through his music, which was reminiscent of Seckles and Schönberg.[1] Chief musical director Kleiber and the chief stage director were called out repeatedly at the end.

Original: newspaper cutting stuck onto writing paper, with handwritten additions from Berg.

On the dating: It could not be ascertained whether Berg handed Adorno this cutting taken from the 15 December edition of the newspaper *Volkstimme*

[People's Voice, hence the statement at the top of the letter], which had been passed on to him by the Berlin office ZAS Adolf-Schustermann-Ausschnitte, while he was still in Berlin, or rather sent it later from Vienna without an accompanying letter.

1 Underlined by Berg; the incorrect spelling of the name *Seckles* has been retained from the newspaper cutting.

Frankfurt, 27 December 1925.

Dear master and teacher,

when I heard on Saturday last week that the follow-up performance of Wozzeck[1] had been postponed, I decided to wait for it nonetheless. It took place on Tuesday; I arrived here Wednesday night, then the turbulent days of Christmas followed, and so I am only now finding the peace to report to you.

So: the performance went ahead without without disturbance, to increasing acclaim, and at the end the applause seemed as if it would never end. The audience – subscription audience! – had some difficulties at first, but was noticeably drawn in, and in act III one could already sense the resonance before it became manifest. The greater confidence with which the scene-changes were carried out helped: leaving aside Wozzeck's death scene, all images were in place a tempo. The performance itself: Miss Johannsen[2] had been announced as indisposed, but sang much better than before, in particular more correctly, but also *sang*, such that one could gain an impression of how much sensuous and melodic substance Marie has, which is the deciding factor for that part. Bible scene excellent (like the whole of act III), the Adagio also good and the jewellery scene – also in its acting – substantially better than before. Schützendorf[3] good; all rough edges smoothed out, everything more secure. Big tavern scene very clear this time: I do not know whether it is through Kleiber's doing or my own insight, but I genuinely see the centre of the work in this central scene today; it is a uniquely inspired act of daring, and convincing for the manner in which it grasps what is baser and diffusely elemental and takes it up: the singing of wrong notes as a constructive motivic element is a metaphysically cryptic discovery, and outdoes Mahler's most secret intentions. I can find no other words for it than these great ones, and for Benjamin,[4] who may seem to you less dubious a witness than myself – he incidentally understood the true meaning of your

33

work better than any musicians – for Benjamin it was no different. So it is then no coincidence that the scene comes where it does: it is the caesura in Hölderlin's sense, through which the 'expressionless'[5] can invade the music. And what a source of hope it is that precisely here, between the shreds of the exiled soul and truly malgré elle, the grand form asserts itself! That you had to do away with the symphony for the sake of the symphony! And how fitting it is that this German tragedy, which is the closest to Marx, was destined to be captured by your music, for your music has captured it in its history instead of depicting it compositionally. – But enough, I should return to the performance; would truly love to find an opportunity to speak apologetically and demonstratively on many aspects of Wozzeck which were not, I readily admit, evident to me before the performance, and which could no doubt be spoken of more truthfully at a later point, but which – in their timeliness, which feeds off the incredible timeliness of the work – would have their own particular truth today. Do you know of an occasion on which this could take place at an adequate level? Pult und Taktstock, much to my amazement, asked Herr Stuckenschmidt for a review of Wozzeck.[6] I am too 'profound' for Herr Heinsheimer, it would seem – the quotation marks are his, from a brochure[7] located between the pages of 'Anbruch' which you should not miss!

The only thing that concerned me about the performance was that Kleiber, knowing he need no longer fear your vigilant ears, is allowing himself one or two primadonna airs, underlining some things (the violin glissandi in the sonata theme of the jewellery scene; the ritardando and the D minor reprise in the long interlude), and takes the dance pieces with rather too much untainted 'verve'. But he is a professional conductor, after all, not a Schönberg, and I am certainly grateful to him for his knowledge and his clear, consistently musical direction. It is understandable enough at this stage of the work's history (and there will certainly be a history of Wozzeck interpretation, just as Büchner's drama had its history!) that conductors, as long as it still pounces upon them in all its foreignness and immediacy, will cling to its expressively temperamental aspects, and it is only through its sensual nature – i.e. through the conductors, who may miss the mark! – not freely and ahistorically – i.e. through composers and aestheticians of my sort! – that the work's truth can become visible. One therefore has all the less reason to be cross with Kleiber. Although I am a trifle jealous that he is allowed to conduct Wozzeck, whose beauty transcends his sphere.

Did you send a correction citing press law to the Berliner Tageblatt? Leopold Schmidt *falsified* the theme of the passacaglia![8] – I am not polite enough to think that he did so out of stupidity.

I still spent much time with your friend Schmid,[9] and got on *very* well with him. And immediately so; alone for the reason that he is the first to know you in depth. He is a very pure, clear and existent man and has that dose of despair without which, it seems, one cannot live.

Aside from this, Berlin also gave me many moving moments. On Sunday I was with my friend[10] in Nikolassee. She recognized me, and was pleased. It is possible that, if I were to stay very close by, I could help her. So I am now once more thinking a great deal about moving to Berlin. Of course, the matter of my *Habilitation* would have to be clarified first. As soon as the two sets of songs, which are to be called op. 1 and op. 2,[11] are finished, I shall come to Vienna. Perhaps there will also be occasion in January. We can discuss all future plans then.

And what of *your* intentions regarding Berlin?[12]

A further small matter. The pianist Hirschland,[13] friend of Rathaus,[14] mentioned a statement by that Yiddish composer to me: he claimed you had said to him that I was very talented, but 'my head plays tricks on me'. It is naturally out of the question that you could have stated anything in this form, and the whole matter dim-witted and jealous gossip. But in order that such things should not impinge upon us, it seems better to inform you immediately.

How would Webern be disposed towards an essay from me?[15] It would not, I should add, be a credo like the one about you – and Webern in particular would set great store by a credo. But every critical word could only serve to measure the tragic depth of his position. And *tactically* it would certainly be of advantage to him. Please inform him, and then me. I promise a 'Theory of the Miniature' in the essay.

Farewell, and relate to me, if you so please, what has been happening with you. Fond regards to you both from your faithful Teddie: who is no more and no less Hagen than you are Alberich: that is, not at all: but faithful nonetheless. And for that very reason.

Original: manuscript. The original of the letter is among Adorno's documents in the Theodor W. Adorno Archiv, Frankfurt am Main; Adorno probably had Berg return this letter to him in order to draw on it for the second essay on *Wozzeck*, which Berg had suggested, but which was not written until later.

1 The first performance after the premiere took place on 22 December 1925.

2 Sigrid Johanson also sang the part of Marie in the premiere.

3 Leo Schützendorf (1886–1931), who sang the title role, was a member of the Berlin State Opera from 1920 to 1929.

4 Adorno had apparently attended the performance of *Wozzeck* together with Walter Benjamin; Benjamin recalled the evening immediately after Berg's

death in a letter to Adorno: 'You know how his work is the only one regarding which our conversations, in this field that I am otherwise less attuned to, reached the same level of intensity as those on other matters, and you too will recall in particular the one after the Wozzeck performance' (Theodor W. Adorno and Walter Benjamin, *The Complete Correspondence 1928–1940*, ed. Henri Lonitz, Cambridge, 2003, p. 119).

5 Benjamin used this term in his essay 'Goethes Wahlverwandtschaften' regarding the Hölderlin-like aspect of the caesura; see Benjamin, *Gesammelte Schriften: Unter Mitwirkung von Theodor W. Adorno und Gerschom Scholem*, ed. Rolf Tiedemann and Hermann Schweppenhäuser, vol. 1.1, 3rd edn, Frankfurt am Main, 1990, p. 181f.

6 See H. H. Stuckenschmidt, 'Bergs "Wozzeck" und die Berliner Aufführung', *Pult und Taktstock*, 3 (1926), pp. 1–5 (issue 1, January).

7 The text of this brochure could not be traced.

8 The critic, who was also the Berlin correspondent for the Viennese *Neue Freie Presse*, had written: 'The reader cannot imagine the inconspicuous nature of the thematic invention!' (cited from 'Alban Bergs "Wozzeck" und die Musikkritik', *Pult und Taktstock* 3 [1926], pp. 17–48; the quotation is from p. 21). Schmidt's alleged evidence is the rhythmicized E flat in the cellos that begins in act I, scene 4; in fact, the E flat in question is simply the first note of the twelve-tone passacaglia theme.

9 Josef Schmid (1890–1969), one of Berg's first students, was Erich Kleiber's conducting deputy at the time.

10 This is probably the same friend mentioned in letter no. 15; nothing could be ascertained concerning Gretel Herzberger, the friend mentioned there in the notes.

11 The second of these became op. 3, while the opus number 2 was reserved for the Two Pieces for String Quartet.

12 Unknown.

13 Unknown.

14 The composer Karol Rathaus (1895–1954), who had studied with Franz Schreker, taught composition at the Musikhochschule in Berlin at the time.

15 Adorno published his first essay on Berg's friend in 1926 in the June/July issue of the *Musikblätter des Anbruch*: 'Anton Webern: Zur Uraufführung der Fünf Orchesterstücke, op. 10, in Zürich' (see GS 18, pp. 513–16). Nothing has been discovered concerning Webern's reaction to this suggestion.

Frankfurt, 6 January 1926.

Dear master and teacher,

as soon as I received your letter[1] I cabled U. E. and set to work, my head and limbs already afflicted with pains which, in the manner of influenza, became so intense that I had to retire to bed and could only get up once more, by no means recovered, for a few hours today. There will therefore – regrettably! – be an inevitable delay of a few days. I have now begun once more, but with severe inhibitions. I am seeking to free myself of you in defending myself against the grave charges which your letter, albeit implicitly, but clearly enough to me, levels at me – charges which, to anticipate this point immediately, appear to arise from tactical-literary concerns, but which, according to their objective final intention, are of a more radical and moral nature.

For if we all – Schönberg and you and Webern and I – agree with Karl Kraus on one point: it is beyond doubt that 'objectivity' in every sphere of objectification and the inseparable reciprocal relation between 'content' and 'form' (whose mere disjunction is already problematic, and problematic in a historico-philosophical sense!) are the true *moral* criteria for the connection between creation and creator. Kraus's critique of language, Schönberg's statement[2] that art (and surely also a product – such as my essay – intended to provide insight) should not adorn, but rather be truthful, your argument in the fine article on the D minor quartet:[3] that the mode of compositional expression is, *like the language of any work of art* (and did you not even term my essay thus? – I cite this not out of vanity, but with objective intentions!), the only one adequate to the object of representation – all these thoughts concur on that one point. So if you do not assign my efforts from the start to the sphere of second-rate pen-pushing, and posit that branch's relative standards as immanent to my manner of writing – which you certainly do not! –, then that same principal criterion of adequation that I first of all apply to *you* and Kraus, although it seems less naturally secured to me than it does to him, must certainly also be applicable to *me*. In this case, however, the 'too difficult' objection would strike my *project* at its very heart. It would declare that I had not represented the matter purely, to the level of its linguistic shadings, but rather inappropriately tainted it, as an untalented pupil brazenly defaces harmonies with ornamental counterpoint. If, judged by the standard of the matter itself, a single sentence of my essay[4] were truly too difficult, then Schönberg would be quite right in his indignation at me, and the essay would belong in the flames. But this is admittedly to be judged according to the matter, not the public. One should not, if one disdains Herr Stefan, suddenly elevate Herr Stefan to the norm. And what do you think that the master Arnold Schönberg would say if a short-eared person demanded of him that he should compose a bar more simply than he had heard it and it must objectively be heard? He would send him to Marx,[5] and rightly so. As little as I am entitled to compare my achievement to even the least of Schönberg's, I must all the more decidedly demand the same dignity: that the measure of all my intellectual endeavours is truth, not effect in its arbitrariness. There are two clear options here, as Schönberg so rightly claims in his rigour. I can therefore draw no comfort from your conclusion that Schönberg's objections are 'exaggerated'. The slightest shadow of truth would damn the essay toto genere. The question is merely whether it can apply itself to the content.

And I would challenge this. I will not hide from you that the attacks from Schönberg – whom I had imagined, as it were, as the ideal reader of my essays, which are so very close to his concerns – soon came to vex me to the same degree that they initially injured me. If Schönberg the terrorist, himself terrorized by his twenty-five-year Fackel readership, presumes to detect the whiff of the hack as soon as he merely reads 'to speak of . . .' and 'truth', then this is perhaps a Viennese fate which even a man of his calibre is powerless against. But if, after the first few lines, he does not realize that he is dealing with a literature that treats words meaningfully, and if he persists heedlessly in jovially chastizing this supposed journalist who is in turn nurtured by the intention of such inanely directed pedagogy – then this fits more into the horizon of the Mödling family life,[6] and is certainly not from that other planet[7] which, even without second-inversion chords, I still do suppose Schönberg to inhabit. I certainly do not wish to argue with him over the depth and the problems of Kraus's nominalism, over his intention to eradicate the great universals in our language, which are no more than 'grand words' today. I would be happy to discuss this with you in Vienna if it is important to you. May it suffice here for me to show briefly that the words to which Schönberg takes exception are not used as vague quantities, but precisely. 'Talking about A. S.'s school' cannot be replaced by something else, for the reason that this 'talking' genuinely refers to the usual *talk* of the Schönberg school, that same talk which could take over Wozzeck with its empty phrases and which the entire essay levels its polemical barb at. And now even 'truth'! It is the same truth which, heavily altered, may constitute the theme of Schönberg's criticism, this truth which 'emanates from him', whose musical measure he has found, is the adequation not only of content and form, but rather within it that of the person and the total situation, or, to say it (– which I find very difficult on account of pro-

found considerations of an epistemological nature) in all its naked-
ness: truth is the theological reality-content of Schönberg's works *and*
teaching. You see what should be clear anyway from a close reading*:
that the word carries the heaviest of baggage and really, in its application to your work in the category of 'free choice', is the constructive
centre of the whole essay. The difficulty – this I admit – lies in locat-
ing it as such. But it could not be avoided, as the involvement of theological words was not permitted. And everywhere that I have used
the word 'truth', there is a manner of intellectual cavity around it from
which it stands out, foreign and accentuated. Werfel will no doubt
testify to all of this. – I need hardly add after all this that Schönberg's
interpretation, or rather translation, is completely *nonsensical*. In presuming to give the idea a solid footing, he in fact turns it on its head.
The *key statement* of the first section, which can admittedly be understood from the first sentence as little as the Eroica (– as unheroic as it
is!) can be grasped from its opening chords, yet could not be understood *without* them – the key statement reads:[8] being A. S.'s pupil
means not being his pupil. For the truth that emanates from him is that
of personal aloneness, and precludes the amalgamation of a 'school'.
This lies in the *teaching*, which places the isolated craft in the stead of
the crumbling tradition, just as it does in the *works*. Both thus have
one and the same sense (not, as Schönberg interpreted my words:
Schönberg's works teach, not his teaching. Rather the teaching in particular, in its reduction to craft, testifies to Schönberg's aloneness and
demands it of the student). Your relationship to Schönberg, therefore,
is – precisely as a *strict* 'pupildom' – free choice. – Thus are the
thoughts of the first section in raw, inexact form. They are stated more
responsibly in the essay.

What follows unfolds from the musical material, and can no longer
be difficult. At least, no more difficult than the things in question.
Concerning the cleanness of the language (which seems here to be at
issue everywhere), I would calmly await the judgement of Kraus, from
whose sphere I garnered my ammunition. I could not bow with a clear
conscience to a school of language presided over by Schönberg.
Whatever Herr Pringsheim[9] might be obliged to tolerate from Jens
Quer,[10] it is nothing I approve of from the beloved composer. I am too
grateful to the agitator to submit to him.

Dear, dear Herr Berg, this letter has been written mostly in bed, to
where I have been confined on account of a heavy throat infection and
a high fever. The apologia is turning into scribble. Nonetheless, I am
certain that it has convinced you, and thus restored to me the moral
right to conclude the Wozzeck essay soon, which I am greatly enjoying.

* see the expression 'truth which commands aloneness'!

39

If, admittedly, the first was too esoteric for Webern, then the new one will be too Bolshevistic for him. But if I can satisfy you and consider it decent myself, then this is as great an effect as I could hope for. In any case, I wish to reduce my practice of music criticism, which is so ruinously confounded with effect, to the minimum of private necessity, would most like to write only about you and the indignant Schönberg. Or legitimate philosophical matters. And perhaps a 'better opportunity' will soon be found for me: music, thanks to you, for my composing is proceeding well. Fond regards to both of you your faithful Teddie.

'Blatt issue III' to follow![11] Thank you for the questionnaire.[12] I can answer it with the quotation.

Please: notify Stein of my illness, and contain his hunger for essays with promises. You know that I will complete it once I am able! – What is the state of the Rathaus affair?

Original: manuscript.

1 Berg's letter, which has not survived among Adorno's documents, appears to have contained a favourable response to Adorno's suggestion to write a second essay on *Wozzeck*; it was, as the end of the letter indicates, to appear in the journal *Pult und Taktstock*, which was edited by Erwin Stein. At the same time, Berg evidently voiced in his letter a series of reservations – in particular Schönberg's – about Adorno's first *Wozzeck* essay, which the author defends himself against in his reply. On the unwritten essay, see also letters 23 and 27.

2 The statement – 'music should not be decorative, however, it should merely be truthful' – was reported by his student Karl Linke (1884–1938); see *Arnold Schönberg: mit Beiträgen von Alban Berg, Paris von Gütersloh, K. Horwitz, Heinrich Jalowetz, W. Kandinsky, Paul Königer, Karl Linke, Robert Neumann, Erwin Stein, Ant. v. Webern, Egon Wellesz*, Munich, 1912, p. 77.

3 See Alban Berg, 'Warum ist Schönbergs Musik so schwer verständlich?' (Why is Schönberg's Music so Difficult to Understand?), *Musikblätter des Anbruch*, 6 (1924), pp. 329–41 (special issue: *Arnold Schönberg zum 50. Geburtstag*, 13 September 1924). Adorno cites the *argument* from the start of the essay: 'I am concerned only with the musical events within Schönberg's works: with the compositional mode of expression that, like the language of any work of art (though this assumption is admittedly a precondition), must be considered the only one adequate to its object of representation.'

4 The essay on *Wozzeck* that appeared in the December issue of the *Musikblätter des Anbruch* (*GS* 18, pp. 456–64), from which the quotations defended by Adorno against Schönberg in the following are taken.

5 Joseph Marx (1882–1964) taught music theory and composition at the Akademie für Musik und darstellende Kunst in Vienna.

6 Schönberg had lived with his family in this town, located half an hour's train journey from Vienna, since 1918, before moving in January 1926 to

Berlin, where he was placed in charge of a master class for composition as Busoni's successor at the Berliner Akademie der Künste. In August 1924 he had married Gertrud Kolisch (1898–1967). Schönberg's first wife, Mathilde (*née* Zemlinsky), had died in 1923.

7 An allusion to the fourth movement of Schönberg's Second String Quartet (with soprano voice) op. 10, which includes a setting of Stefan George's poem 'Entrueckung' from *Der siebente Ring*, containing the words 'Ich fühle Luft von einem anderen Planeten' (I feel air from another planet).

8 'To be Schönberg's student out of choice, and this more decidedly than simply in loyalty to his craftsmanship, means: not being his student, but rather, like him, beginning in the breach with all predefined objectivity and under the sign of aloneness, and letting the power of affirmation remain alone in that truth which commands aloneness' (*GS* 18, p. 457).

9 The conductor Klaus Pringsheim (1883–1972), a brother-in-law of Thomas Mann, was employed at the Viennese Court Opera from 1906 to 1909 as Gustav Mahler's assistant; from 1918 until his emigration he worked under Max Reinhardt at the Grosses Schauspielhaus in Berlin.

10 Schönberg wrote glosses and small articles for *Pult und Taktstock* under the pseudonym of Jens. Qu. (Jenseitiger Querdenker [maverick from beyond]). Klaus Pringsheim had published a contribution in issue 7 of *Pult und Taktstock* (November 1924, pp. 118–20) – 'Marschiert die Normalpartitur? Beitrag zu einer Diskussion, die verhütet werden soll' – to which Schönberg responded under his pseudonym in the following issue (December 1924, p. 137f.):

> Through his response to the question 'Does the normal musical score march?' (I say: no; one would first have to get it moving), Klaus Pringsheim wishes to prevent a discussion; the matter is to be voted on without discussion. I agree with him, for one will soon be able to distinguish this with the naked eye, and I am meanwhile looking forward to the image. I am more interested in a different question. In the 'cry' for a normal score, the author sees a 'symptom of the current anti-artistic mentality.' Our poor times are in very poor shape once again! But I would like to inquire: if, for example, Herr Pringsheim or some other figure of influence were to succeed in preventing not only this discussion and the march of the normal score and the reform hidden behind it: then this mentality would perhaps not be quite so current and anti-artistic? I am only asking for the sake of our poor times, which are once more being blamed for everything. Might I take the liberty of putting in a word in their favour? It would then be this: Certainly these are bad times in which so many people are permitted to say this, although there are so many others, so many whose achievements would be much better off belonging in better times. No one can deny, therefore, that the former persons are right if they say something like the following to themselves: what times are these which the likes of us live in?!

11 Berg had evidently asked Adorno in his letter to obtain for him the first issue of the *Illustriertes Blatt* of January 1926, which contained a short article

on the premiere of *Wozzeck* and some photographs of Berg, Leo Schützendorf and Sigrid Johanson.

12 On p. 88 of the March/April 1926 issue of *Pult und Taktstock* there was a list of questions on metronome markings, the answering of which is here being referred to:

1. What are the advantages,

2. What are the disadvantages of metronome markings?

3. Are the advantages or the disadvantages predominant, and decisive for musical practice?

4. How can the composer avoid misunderstandings that could arise from the excessive exactitude of metronome markings?

5. Are detailed metronome markings for tempo inflections, for example ritardandi or accelerandi (as in Reger's scores), to be recommended?

6. Do precise metronome markings render any further tempo indications unnecessary?

7. The abstractness of the numbers is one of the primary arguments against metronome markings. Could this abstractness not be reduced by giving the terms that are intelligible to every musician, such as Largo, Adagio, Andante etc., an at least somewhat fixed metronomic value, respective to the different metric units, such as minims, crotchets, quavers etc.?

In the same issue there were responses by Bernhard Paumgartner, Albert Bing and Franz von Hoesslin. Adorno's reply – 'Metronomisierung' – appeared only in late summer that year, in *Pult und Taktstock*, 3 (1926), pp. 130–4; see *GS* 17, pp. 307–10. It could no longer be traced which *quotation* Adorno originally intended to answer the questionnaire with; it is not inconceivable that Berg's Chamber Concerto, which is 'quoted' at the end of 'Metronomisierung', could be meant.

21   BERG TO WIESENGRUND-ADORNO
     VIENNA, 11.1.1926

ALBAN BERG VIENNA XIII/I
TRAUTTMANSDORFFGASSE 27
TELEPHONE: 84831.

Dear Wiesengrund, Morgenstern advised me to set 'Und Pippa tanzt'.[1] What do you say to that? Request an opinion as soon as possible.

The news that you are to write about Wozzeck for *Pult und Taktstock* is very pleasing to your warmly greeting

Berg

Please do not forget the 5 copies of the Frankfurt 'Das Illustrierte Blatt' № 1/1926 Eschenheimerstr. 31

Yesterday 4th Wozzeck perf. with Schönberg present[2]

Original: postcard; stamp: Vienna, 11.1.26. Manuscript with sender stamp.

1 In his memoirs of Berg, Morgenstern writes about this as follows:

> For some reason I reread a number of Gerhart Hauptmann's dramas. Among them also *Und Pippa tanzt*. This fairy tale play struck me as a suitable operatic text for Alban. Thereupon I read it once more, and reached the conclusion that one would have to compress the four acts into three. I suggested this to Alban at the next opportunity. He knew the play. He reread it at once, and his mind was made up. Unfortunately, the Fischer Verlag behaved as if it had a priceless jewel in its possession. After many negotiations and letters, Alban gave up the plan, disgusted by the publisher's shameless demand: to be given fifty percent. (Morgenstern, *Berg und seine Idole*, p. 133)

See also the account of Thomas F. Ertelt: *Alban Bergs 'Lulu': Quellenstudien und Beiträge zur Analyse*, Vienna, 1993, pp. 25–33 ('Pippa oder Lulu?', *Alban Berg Studien*, ed. Rudolf Stephan, vol. 3).

2 Schönberg had informed Berg of this in his postcard of 11 January 1926 (see *The Berg–Schoenberg Correspondence: Selected Letters*, ed. Juliane Brand, Christopher Hailey and Donald Harris, New York and London, 1987, p. 342).

22   BERG TO WIESENGRUND-ADORNO
VIENNA, 28.1.1926

ALBAN BERG VIENNA XIII/I
TRAUTTMANSDORFFGASSE 27 $28/_126$
TELEPHONE: 84831.

My dear Wiesengrund, I wanted to reply to your wonderful letter of 6 January *immediately*, but was so busy & heavily burdened on all fronts that I forever kept postponing it. Finally I contented myself with an *overall* letter that I wanted to write after looking at your new Wozzeck article, which U. E. awaited daily. But, as it did not arrive (which N.B. does not matter, as Pult & Taktstock will just as readily print it in a later issue), and as you did not reply to my urgent post-card question as to whether I should set 'Pippa tanzt', I am *very* concerned about you & ask that you reassure me concerning 1. your health 2. your untainted goodwill towards me.

And now very briefly about your letter: *you have convinced me completely*. I now know that what you write, if it were not to be a great deal more laborious and long-winded [albeit clearer to the likes of us], could not be said any better or more precisely, or more closely connected to the entire surroundings than you do. And that it therefore has a quite exceptional refinement of language & is of the highest standard. I admittedly never doubted this, but only reached irrefutable clarity in the matter through my extensive probing: on the one hand through debates with Schönberg & Webern etc. on the other hand through my letter to you & finally through frequent and numerous consultations with Morgenstern (& also Steuermann). And you will surely concede that it is a 'difficult case'; Morgenstern & Steuermann also state this, even though they *understand* every line & every word of your article (after reading it 3 to 4 times, I should add), and thus consider it very fine, but are nonetheless of the opinion that it is most certainly too difficult to understand for a journal & really only accessible to those who are accustomed to reading philosophers such as Kierkegaard, which explains, for example, Schönberg's rejection. Morgenstern is also of the opinion, and he intends to write to you himself concerning it (for he truly loves you & has the same longing for you as I do), that new words or word-formations unintelligible to novices (such as 'Personalität' instead of 'Persönlichkeit'!)[1] would in his view be better avoided.

But these are only petty concerns within my great appreciation for your style & your wealth of ideas & I have reached the firm conviction that in this field of the most profound insights into music (in all its previously unexplored aspects, whether of a philosophical, art-historical, theoretical, social, historical etc. etc. nature) it is your calling to achieve the *utmost* & that you shall furthermore fulfil this in the form of great philosophical works. Whether your musical work (I mean your composing), which I have such grand hopes for, will not lose out through it, is a worry that afflicts me whenever I think of you. For it is clear: one day you will, as you are someone who does nothing by halves (thank God!), have to choose either Kant *or* Beethoven. And only in this sense could any remark that I might have made to Rathaus [I do not by God remember speaking to him about you] be meant: as an expression of my concern that you will one day, despite your great talent, which would already destine you to become a composer of great quality, have devoted yourself once and for all to your philosophical work. – A pronouncement such as the one you cited me as saying in your last letter naturally never passed my lips. You will surely not even believe me capable of objecting to a composer on the grounds of his 'head playing tricks on him' (these are, I believe, the words that have been put in my mouth?) & you can safely leave this to Messrs. 'Réti[2]-Rat'*haus & those others who compose with their bowels. –

And now you must write to me very soon & at great length about yourself & also tell me what you think of the *idea*** of setting 'Pippa'. I have not got around to composing lately. Indescribable amounts of correspondence, & everything else to do with new fame, are stealing all my time. – On the 14th Wozzeck was done for the 5th time, with as excellent a turnout as all the performances. The next performance should be at the start of February. Schönberg has also been once. The next stages will be Breslau & Prague.[3] – But not before autumn, I think. Otherwise I am quite well. My nerves are also significantly calmer!

With warmest greetings to you (& your dear family) from your old
Alban Berg

Original: manuscript with sender stamp.

1 Translator's note: the exception has been made here of retaining the original terms, as the issue here is Adorno's choice of words. Both denote personality; but while the latter is the conventional word for it, the former is a more pointed, philosophically intended and by no means common way of expressing it.

2 The composer and music writer Rudolf Réti (1885–1957), who was the first to play Schönberg's Piano Pieces op. 11, founded the Internationale Gesellschaft für Neue Musik (International Society for Contemporary Music) in 1922.

3 The Prague premiere took place on 11 November 1926; *Wozzeck* was not performed in Breslau.

23   WIESENGRUND-ADORNO TO BERG
     FRANKFURT, 30.1.1926

Frankfurt, 30 January 26.

Dear, esteemed Herr Berg, I cannot tell you what joy I felt at your letter, which finally arrived today. For many reasons: for one thing, I feared I had offended you with my previous letter, for example in what I say against Schönberg. Then I feared you would be angry at me on account of the essay not yet having reached the Taktstock fellows (incidentally, an important letter to Heinsheimer has had no response to this day, and this for many weeks). Concerning the essay, the matter is as

* The combination comes from my wife, who sends her warmest greetings!
** it is no more than an idea at present. It comes from Morgenstern & I find it sympathetic. –

follows: I had set to work at once, but noticed after I was already deeply immersed in it that, in order to speak of the things I had casually mentioned to you in my letter before last with at least some finality, I would ipso facto have to cross over to a philosophical sphere far, far more inaccessible than the aesthetics of the first essay. I thus decided to take a different path. Then I fell ill. You know that I had a throat infection before Christmas, which I evidently did not allow to be fully cured. It now returned, and was recognized by the doctor as Angina Plaut-Vincenti, an especially persistent and recidivist form whose pathogenes resemble those of diphtheria and hollow out the tonsils. There was a very tedious and exhausting treatment that made any serious work impossible. (I wrote only the answer to that questionnaire,[1] in bed, as best I could; no answer from Cologne[2] either!) Now, only this week, I have been released from therapy and declared healthy in a general examination. I returned to the essay at once, and am writing it in the form of an open letter to you. I hope thus to paralyse certain difficulties.

To hear that my response to Schönberg's objections – which was intended to vindicate me before you and before myself – convinced you is the greatest joy that I could hope to gain from my writings on music. After all, whom do I write for – if not for you and people like Morgenstern and Steuermann! What I would like most is to limit what I write *about* music, for the time being at least, to the little that I can not only stand by, but which I also feel it is necessary in art-*political* terms to propagate: that is, you and Schönberg. And otherwise compose. Those of my other things that were not entirely in vain I shall then regard as surplus.

I had imagined the Rathaus case just as you relate it; once again, the truth is 'even more precise'.

Concerning Pippa. The matter is a very difficult one, and as I am deeply entangled in reflections upon opera theory in the context of the Wozzeck essay, I do not really feel I am in a position to advise you. My instinct, however, is that you should not set it. In its eerie and light character, admittedly, the play certainly seems well enough suited to music, and the manner in which naturalism and unreality are enmeshed could lead one to believe that it would be a task structurally related to 'Wozzeck', or even a continuation thereof. But this seems to me an illusion. Wozzeck's suitability for music grew from its history, which brought to light its hidden metapsychological (popularly 'expressionist') aspects. In the work's origin, these elements are inseparably tied to its object. Hauptmann's fairy-tale elements since 'Hannele', on the other hand, are sentimental corrections undertaken after the fact by a naturalism that no longer believes itself. Hauptmann poeticizes a rigid object-world. In Büchner's case, however, the demonic nature of reification through bourgeois society is precisely the poetic agent. But music can only encounter true, hidden and genuine fairy-tale elements, not illusory, manifest and poetically derived ones. This is why the Wozzeck libretto was such an ingenious creation and *radically* different from all 'musical' libretti, whose non-representationality is only the correlate of an ossified, in itself inarticulate representationality (Salome text!).[3] – This is connected to the theory of the operatic text that I touched on in my letter, which I sought in vain to translate into the essay. – I say this entirely informally, only as an intimation, and must read Pippa closely again. I shall then report back to you, if it interests you.

In other matters I have much to tell you, and hope I shall have an opportunity to do so very soon in Vienna (the songs are progressing). I think I have once again taken you as a model in new and important pieces without realizing it.

In haste – this only as a sign, not as a letter!

I wish you and dear Frau Helene all things beautiful and good,

your faithful Teddie W.

What about the quartet?!

Original: manuscript.

1 See letter no. 20 and note 12 there.

2 The context here could not be traced.

3 Oscar Wilde had written the stage play in French in 1892 for Sarah Bernhardt; Strauss composed his opera (premiere in 1905) using a German version by Hedwig Lachmann.

24 WIESENGRUND-ADORNO TO BERG
      FRANKFURT, 9.2.1926

fond regards on your birthday in devotion = teddie

Original: telegram.

25 BERG TO WIESENGRUND-ADORNO
      VIENNA, 14.2.1926

14 February 1926

Many thanks, my dear Wiesengrund, for your telegram. I was very pleased that you thought of me on this day [when I was also played

on the radio in Frankfurt (my quartet by Kolisch)[1] – did you hear it?].
Warmest greetings from your

Berg

Original: manuscript on the reverse of a portrait photograph of Berg.

1 The Wiener Streichquartett, Rudolf Kolisch and Fritz Rothschild (violins),
Marcel Dick (viola) and Joachim Stutshevsky (cello), played Berg's String
Quartet op. 3 and Schubert's String Quartet in D minor on Southwest
German Radio from 8.15 to 9.15 p.m. Rudolf Kolisch (1896–1978) studied
violin with Otakar Ševčic in Vienna and composition first with Franz
Schreker, then from 1919 until 1922 with Arnold Schönberg. The first Kolisch
Quartet, which was founded as the Wiener Streichquartett in 1922 (accord-
ing to other reports in 1921), played with its standard line-up of Kolisch, Felix
Khuner, Eugen Lehner and Benar Heifetz. In 1935, Kolisch and Adorno
planned to write the *Theorie der musikalischen Reproduktion* together, as
Adorno's letter to Ernst Krenek of 23 March 1935 reveals (see Theodor W.
Adorno and Ernst Krenek, *Briefwechsel*, ed. Wolfgang Rogge, Frankfurt am
Main, 1974, p. 72). After the outbreak of war in 1939, the quartet did not
return to Europe from a tour of the USA. In 1944, Kolisch became first violinist of the Pro Arte Quartet, which worked at the University of Wisconsin
as 'quartet in residence'. Kolisch's study 'Tempo and character in Beethoven's
music' was also written in America.

26   BERG TO WIESENGRUND-ADORNO
     VIENNA, 26.3.1926

ALBAN BERG VIENNA XIII/I
TRAUTTMANSDORFFGASSE 27 $26/_{III}26$
TELEPHONE: 84831.

My dear Wiesengrund, what is the matter with you? I received the congratulations you wired me almost 2 months ago & I thanked you on
a photograph card. And I do not recall otherwise owing you a letter.
Your long silence worries me & also offends me! Morgenstern keeps
asking me whether I have heard from you; we are communicating a
great deal, in fact almost exclusively with one another & you are
sorely missed as the 3rd or rather 4th in the clique. I have much to tell,
though nothing is happening. The day after tomorrow the 10th perf.
of Wozzeck in Berlin. Recently here the 'Bruchstücke',[1] under Jalowetz
with a female singer from the state opera, performed quite well. Under
the sign of a grand sensation. *Very good* reviews; even fr. Korngold[2]
(relatively speaking, of course), Stravinsky[3] was, despite a colossal
hullabaloo, disappointing. Summer is approaching & with it hope-

fully the possibility and ability to work, which has lain barren all this time. What are you planning? & above all what have you been doing in the last 2 months? –

In expectation of speediest news with greetings from your old
Berg

Also my wife, who is not particularly well at all!

When you have the chance, please send me back the Altenberg I lent you, my wife needs it. – Devoted kisses upon the hands of the ladies! –

How is your health!!

Original: manuscript with sender stamp.

1 The performance of the *Drei Bruchstücke aus der Oper 'Wozzeck'* had taken place in a Workers' Symphony Concert on 14 March under the direction of Heinrich Jalowetz; the singer was Wanda Achsel-Clemens. The conductor Heinrich Jalowetz (1882–1946), who had studied composition with Schönberg and musicology with Guido Adler in Vienna, was conductor at the Volksoper in Vienna, and from 1925 to 1933 principal musical director at the Cologne opera; he emigrated to the USA in 1938. Wanda Achsel-Clemens (1891–1977) sang at the Vienna State Opera until 1923, thereafter in Berlin.

2 Julius Korngold (1860–1945) was Eduard Hanslick's successor as music critic for the *Neue Freie Presse*.

3 On the programme of the concert – it was Stravinsky's first appearance in Vienna – were *The Firebird*, *Petrushka* and the Piano Concerto.

27 WIESENGRUND-ADORNO TO BERG
    FRANKFURT, 30.3.1926

Frankfurt, 30 March 1926.

Dear master and teacher,

I am replying to you at a moment when I can almost certainly hope to see you soon once more. Hermann Grab, who spent March in Spain with Zemlinsky and is now staying in Paris, has invited me to stay with him in Prague from April 1st–20th, and I intend to go, albeit somewhat later, around April 10th. Following this I plan to go to Vienna, where I hope to appear around the 20th. But I cannot go for so long without calming my conscience. For it is due to a guilty conscience that I have been silent, and my conscience became ever worse through my silence. Now comes your letter, for which I am more grateful than I can say, because it gives me an opportunity to speak out to you. You must know that there is no person to whom I am tied more deeply, decisively and gratefully than to you; and I could imagine nothing, absolutely nothing which from my side could cause us to part ways. But you do not know why, with this stable fundamental constitution, I have so long remained silent, when silence is otherwise certainly not my trademark and I always reject it so forcefully in theory. This is the nature of the matter: some time ago, you had requested a second essay on Wozzeck. At the time, I had set to work immediately, but due to the excessive difficulty of the essay – that is to say its subject – I had to decide upon a radical revision. The illness interrupted me; I then began the essay as an 'open letter to Alban Berg' – and ran aground once more. I then sought to construct a third version out of aphorisms; but this too was nothing acceptable. This aroused my defiance, and I determined to force the matter à tout prix. And was so ashamed of my failure that I decided not to write to you until a satisfactory manuscript had gone off to Pult und Taktstock.

That has not happened to this day. For although Wozzeck, with which I constantly occupy myself, is becoming ever dearer and more familiar to me, I am ever less capable of writing the essay. Since the autumn of last year – the extensive confrontation with Benjamin – my philosophy has been undergoing great developments whose first signs were already visible in the Anbruch essay.[1] After reflecting more emphatically, however, the incompleteness, the inadequacy of my previous categories transpired ever more powerfully. Also the musico-aesthetic ones: I had made it all too easy for myself with the concepts of personality and inwardness, had set up a homely private island with them, where I, albeit half-heartedly, presumed to be safe from the problems I had outlined objectively. Not that I would have abandoned them. But I am in the process of adding to them: from the metaphysical points of departure via epistemology through a positive philosophy of history and political theory. To tell you that politically it has brought me decisively closer to communism perhaps offers a drastic clarification of the development. For the music, however, I consider it necessary to establish, perhaps assigned correlatively to the concept of inwardness, perhaps even critically superordinated to it, a concept of 'extensivity'. Wozzeck has now helped me to find a material construction for it. The interpretation of the text led me to the problem of the recurrence of external reity[2] – which dissolved in language – in music (incidentally in Wozzeck as in Mahler: the way in which the choice of a drama *that already has its own history* corresponds exactly to the choice of the Wunderhorn poems[3] and to the objective intention, for example, that draws Kraus to Matthias Claudius). In this context I attempted, focusing on the text, and following on from a remark made in the first essay, an entirely new interpretation of the Wozzeck drama. And through the connection 'proletarian tragedy –

opera' arrived at a new theory of opera toto genere based on Wozzeck. (Fragments taken from it appeared in an essay entitled 'Opernprobleme'[4] that I sent to *Anbruch*, where it indeed arrived, but where no one has yet decided whether or not to accept it. Perhaps you can have a look at it: behind the critique of Intermezzo, which is extremely difficult, though *Anbruch* does not need to realize this, lies Wozzeck as its positive counterpart – as you will easily discover!). These few indications will perhaps show you the new perspectives that your work opened for me – but also make it clear to you that I, overwhelmed by my new insights, which have their metaphysical and sociological relations everywhere, feared to talk them to death prematurely. It will not be lost, and just as it crystallized around Wozzeck, it shall also be said about Wozzeck. – But the fact that I could not say it now was agonizing to me before you, and caused me some anxiety. I could perhaps have not written to you, and simply descended on you with my explanation and my notes in Vienna. But now it is better like this. And I hope you will sanction it.

The most important thing I can otherwise relate is: since recovering my health completely once more – only 3 weeks – I have been composing with the greatest vigour. That it seems decent to me; and that I hope to be able to show you a large *finished* piece[5] in April. I won't say what it is, out of superstition, for it could otherwise get stuck after all, as is the danger with me. But I have the clear feeling that I am only now reaping what you have sown.

Otherwise little news. In terms of music perhaps '10 Küsse' by Sekles,[6] which are not bad at all, and move towards small forms in a good way; artisanship, of course, without any contemporary relevance. And the catastrophic *4th* Symphony by Křenek.[7] For winds and percussion only. One cannot imagine what that sounds like.

It fills me with a certain feeling of triumph, to say nothing of the joy, that Wozzeck is having lasting success, although it is a shame that I did not happen to write it. But to think that this music is so strong that it compels the audience at the same time as snubbing it – this is a truly exemplary and real revolutionary sign that goes beyond the state of subjectivist isolation! And to think that it is *you* who are giving this sign!

Unfortunately I did *not* hear your quartet – by the time I learned that it was being played on the radio it was already finished! You can imagine my sadness.

What ails your wife? Still the fever, or an emotional matter? Please give her many warm regards from me. What is Morgenstern's address? You must also give him my regards.

I long to see you, and am happy that I shall come to you. Give me, for I am faithful to you, a sign before I go to Prague, a sign that you still favour me. – I am being sent your picture from all sides. The last one, which I received from you, stands upon my desk.

Lovingly yours,
Teddie W.

Original: manuscript.

1 This is Adorno's first essay on *Wozzeck*; see letter no. 12, note 6.

2 Translator's note: this neologism has been employed for the German *Dinghaftigkeit*. While a translation such as 'thingliness' or 'materiality' may seem more logical, these two would both ignore the fact that German, whose etymological convention is largely to draw on its own pool of word-origins, is not deviating from its idiomatic patterns of word-formation to arrive at *Dinghaftigkeit*. As English more often draws on Latin or Greek elements, as in 'reification' for *Verdinglichung*, I consider it more in keeping with the nature of English to coin this Latinate term, rather than forcing it into an imitation of the German that is blind to the original word's true context.

3 Adorno expands upon this in his book on Mahler:

> In the poems which Mahler's music soaks itself in, those of the Wunderhorn [horn of plenty], the Middle Ages and the German Renaissance were themselves already derivatives, as if written upon printed pamphlets that tell of brave knights, yet are already almost newspapers. Mahler's affinity to his texts lay not so much in the illusion of homeliness as in the presentiment of unchanged and wild times, which came upon him within orderly late bourgeois circumstances, perhaps motivated by the hardship of his own youth. For him, in his mistrust towards peace in the age of imperialism, war is the normal condition, and people are forced to be soldiers against their will. He pleads musically for peasant cunning against the rulers; for those who flee before marriage; for the outsiders, the prisoners, the starving children, the persecuted, and lost positions. It is only in Mahler's case that it would be appropriate to speak of socialist realism, if the word itself had not been so depraved by power; the Russian composers from the years around 1960 frequently sound like disfigured Mahler. Berg is the legitimate heir to this spirit; in the *Ländler* that rouses the poor folk in *Wozzeck* to awkward, unnatural dancing, we hear a clarinet rhythm from the Scherzo of the Fourth Symphony seeping in. (*GS* 13, p. 195f.)

4 'Opernprobleme' (Problems of Opera) was printed in the May issue of the *Musikblätter des Anbruch* (pp. 205–8); see *GS* 19, pp. 470–5. The essay 'glosses' the operas *Intermezzo* by Richard Strauss, *Otello* by Verdi and Wagner's *Ring des Nibelungen*.

5 Adorno probably has in mind the string quartet that he began under Berg's tutelage, and of which only two movements were composed; see letter no. 30, note 3.

6 The premiere of the opera '10 Küsse' (10 Kisses) in Frankfurt was conducted by Clemens Krauss; for Adorno's two reviews in *Die Musik* and *Musikblätter des Anbruch*, see *GS* 19, pp. 67f. and 73f.

7 *4th* underlined four times by Adorno. The performance of Křenek's op. 34 took place on 8 March 1926, in the tenth Monday concert of the Frankfurter Orchesterverein (Orchestral Society) under the direction of Ernst Wendel; for Adorno's concert review for *Die Musik*, see *GS* 19, p. 70f.

28 BERG TO WIESENGRUND-ADORNO
   VIENNA, 6.4.1926

ALBAN BERG VIENNA XIII/I
TRAUTTMANSDORFFGASSE 27
TELEPHONE: 84831.

Easter Monday[1] 1926 Dear Wiesengrund, your letter arrived just now, while my wife & I were sitting having a snack with Frau Hanna Fuchs*. She will be very happy if you look her up in Prague**. *But how much happier we are* that you are coming to Vienna. & here I must tell you the following!! On April 18th and 19th, Webern is to do Mahler VIII[2] in a glorious manner surely unheard of since the premiere. See to it that you are already *here* for it (*perhaps* also Grab, whom it should interest) If so, I must ask you to order a ticket post haste, as it is already almost sold out. Furthermore for your *current* address, so that I can reach you. – And now once again: we are *greatly* looking forward to your coming (incl. Morgenstern). Please do not delay it: for we, Helene & I, intend to go to Trahütten already at the start of May; I must *finally* work again, it's impossible in Vienna. So this time I would like to remain in the country from May until autumn. – All further matters then in 8–14 days! Until then Fond regards from your Berg & many thanks for your kind lengthy & interesting letter.
   $^{6\cdot}/_4 26.$ –

You must come soon. Warmest greetings to you dear Tedy and your loved ones!

   Helene Berg

Original: postcard; stamp: Vienna, 6.IV.26. Manuscript with sender stamp and an additional note by Helene Berg.

* who was here on account of illness
** Prague-Bubeneč, Zatovka 593 Tel 8792/VI

1 This was 5 April; Berg evidently finished the card only on Tuesday 6 April.

2 On the days mentioned, Webern conducted in the 200th Workers' Symphony Concert; on the programme, alongside Mahler's symphony, was the *Fanfare for Brass and Timpani* by Richard Strauss. Adorno attended the concert.

29 BERG TO WIESENGRUND-ADORNO
     VIENNA, 22.4.1926

I hope, my dear Wiesengrund, that you like the second setting of this song[1] better than the first; for I am sure I shall notice if it is not the case, and be unhappy; and you of all people, my dear fellow, would not want that.
22.4.1926
Your Alban Berg

Original: duplicate copy of the two versions of Berg's setting of Storm's poem *Schliesse mir die Augen beide*. Manuscript on the cover sheet of the papers.

1 This is based on the 'mother chord' discovered by Fritz Heinrich Klein, which is one of those twelve-tone chords also to contain all twelve intervals. On the first publication, see letter no. 9, note 4.

30 WIESENGRUND-ADORNO TO BERG
     FRANKFURT, 15.6.1926

Frankfurt a. M. – Oberrad
15 June 1926

My dear master and teacher,
    today I would merely like to ask you why my long letter[1] – which is now 4 weeks old! – has not yet had a single word of reply from you. Have I offended you? It could only have been the lines on Webern, but you know in any case that I do not support him blindly, and my critical words certainly do not go as far as the material critique which you direct at the lyrical miniatures through the very architecture of your works. At any rate, none of this is discussed in the essay,[2] it is entirely positive, or rather, as befits W., apologetic, and only the initiated might sense my quiet reservations in its tone.
    I do not know where you are, and am deeply saddened by this. Please give me a sign! I suspect you are at work in Trahütten, and hope for the best for you and for myself, the listener.

I have had a time of intensive and extensive work. Regarding the quartet,[3] the development section of the 1st movement, a very difficult contrapuntal piece, is finished. During its composition there was a mix-up with Anbruch. I had last agreed upon the Webern essay with Heinsheimer, and had largely prepared it, when the latest issue of this noble journal reached me, containing an announcement of a forthcoming essay of mine entitled 'Notizen über Zwölftontechnik',[4] which I had offered Heinsheimer at some earlier point. I thus presumed that I had to write this essay, and did so; it became a long one (7 Anbruch pages). Anbruch wrote back to me saying that the advance notice had been a mistake; he was awaiting the Webern; he could not print the twelve-tone essay, as he had already requested one from Herr Stein.[5] I thus had no choice but to complete the Webern essay (it became exactly half as long as the one on you), which will now appear in time for the festival in Zurich.[6] The twelve-tone essay is floating around in the world; perhaps it will now land in the Frankfurter Zeitung. These forced literary tasks, however – there was a further one on metronome markings[7] –, had rather taken me out of my compositional work, and because I, as your wife also wishes, would like to suppress all this writing on music for a considerable time, I thus took the opportunity of bidding farewell, so to speak, to the problems which have been assailing me for years, and which had taken on new relevance in the last essays, by exploring them to the utmost one last time and representing them programmatically. The ensuing treatise, which constitutes my current musical credo, and at the same time takes a renewed look at the question of music's legitimacy, reached its conclusion in the last few days. It is entitled 'Nachtmusik',[8] and is dedicated to you. I think that it is not a musical essay in the conventional sense, but rather an autonomous philosophical construction that can hopefully bear its dedication without offending the rule of modesty. The essay will be going off to Anbruch, which should print it despite its difficulty simply for the sake of the insights it offers, in the next few days. It is to bear the dedication publicly, and I would request your consent in the matter.

To find that Stein plundered my twelve-tone essay in his essay on the wind quintet[9] (the definition of the twelve-note technique as a mere determination of material comes from me) would, for the sake of the truth itself, be welcome; but the level of banality he has reduced it to I find embarrassing. If one is as unimaginative and unproductive a person as Stein, one should at least control one's works of reception.

I shall now return to the quartet and work on the *Habilitation* thesis;[10] incidentally, the matter of my *Habilitation* is not as simple as I had assumed. It seems that I shall not be able to get away for the whole summer, but rather confine myself to my work. And nonetheless

I hope to see you soon – without so far having a clear idea of how and when I might.

Many warm regards to your dear wife. And please: explain your silence, which is a burden upon me.

Devotedly yours,
Teddie W.

Original: manuscript.

1 It did not, as Berg's reply shows, ever reach its addressee.

2 On Adorno's first essay on Anton Webern, which appeared in the June/July issue of *Musikblätter des Anbruch*, see letter no. 19, note 15.

3 Adorno's *Zwei Stücke für Streichquartett* op. 2; see Adorno, *Compositions*, ed. Heinz-Klaus Metzger and Rainer Riehn, vol. 2: Chamber Music, Choral Works, Orchestral Works, Munich, 1980, pp. 6–28 (abbreviated in the following as: Adorno, *Compositions 2*). The second movement had already been completed in April 1925, while Adorno was still under Berg's tutelage; the completion of the first movement can be dated to 3 August 1926.

4 The May 1926 issue contained this announcement for the following issue. An essay with the title 'Notizen über Zwölftontechnik' (Notes on Twelve-Tone Technique) has not been discovered; it is presumably 'Warum Zwölftonmusik'? (Why Twelve-Tone Music?), an essay which remained unpublished during Adorno's lifetime, and of which a typescript copy has survived among Adorno's belongings. The dating supplied in the first edition (see *GS* 18, pp. 114–17) as 'c. 1935' would then have to be changed to '1926'.

5 See Erwin Stein, 'Einige Bemerkungen zu Schönberg's Zwölftonreihen' (Some Remarks on Schönberg's Twelve-Tone Rows), *Musikblätter des Anbruch*, 8 (1926), pp. 251–53.

6 On 23 June 1926, Webern conducted the premiere of his Five Orchestral Pieces op. 10 at the fourth world music days of the International Society for Contemporary Music (ISCM) in Zurich; on 19 June, Webern had directed the performance of Schönberg's Wind Quintet op. 16 in Zurich.

7 This essay was Adorno's response to the questionnaire on metronome markings in the March/April issue of *Pult und Taktstock*; see letter no. 20, note 12.

8 This work first appeared in the January 1929 issue of *Anbruch* in abridged form; Adorno included it in his 1964 collection *Moments musicaux* (see *GS* 17, pp. 52–9).

9 See Erwin Stein, 'Schönbergs Bläserquintett', *Pult und Taktstock*, 3 (1926), pp. 103–7. Adorno's clearly unjustified accusation of plagiarism is based on the sentence: 'For it [the row] is only material, and is no more defining for form and content than any material which the artist places in his service by taking its peculiarities into account is wont to be' (ibid., p. 106). Adorno's

description of his essay in this context supports the assumption that 'Warum Zwölftonmusik?' is identical with the 'Notizen über Zwölftontechnsik' announced (see above).

10 See letter no. 16, note 1.

31 BERG TO WIESENGRUND-ADORNO
TRAHÜTTEN, 23.6.1926

ALBAN BERG C/O NAHOWSKI
TRAHÜTTEN IN STEIERMARK
POST OFFICE: DEUTSCH-LANDSBERG
A./D. GRAZ-KÖFLACH RAILWAY   23.6.26

My dear Wiesengrund your letter of the 15th finally reassured me. It was the first sign of life from you since our parting in the foyer of the Burgtheater[1] & we were already most offended. Now it has become clear: I did *not* receive your first letter. We left Vienna on the 19.5. & did not immediately come up here. In the meantime it will have been put through the letterbox of my Vienna apartment's door*, and will now be in summer hibernation until I awaken it on July 25th, when we expect to return to Vienna.

At the same time, I received the Anbruch which contains your Webern essay & which I *particularly* liked & which I understood 99% of [which is how I was *able* to like it.] I hope it will also satisfy Webern & Schönberg, though I am inclined to fear that a few words & turns of phrase – particularly in the case of the latter – will once more cause offence [namely 'constructivism'] I was *very* pleased to find that you – through working on it, I think – have now warmed to it as only one can if one grows close to the music – & to this person, I should add. Your mishap with the 12 tone essay is most regrettable; but I cannot believe that Stein plagiarized you. At least, I read the manuscript of his *Pult & Taktstock* article on 12 tone music in the wind quintet months ago. (I have yet to read it in *Anbruch*.) I am sure that I first heard the 12 note technique classified as a determination of material by Schönberg, from whom Stein will have faithfully taken it, if he was not, as is quite possible with such things that are in the air, simply the 3rd to invent it himself. Such things are always discovered by several people at once. [I saw this once again in Stein's quintet analysis: in the way that many things there correspond to my own *quite independently garnered* 12 tone experiences. In my present quartet,[2] for example, I reached *very similar* results in the construction *without* ever having

* naturally against my precise postal instructions and forwarding addresses.

57

analysed the quintet. We shall discuss this some time.] – My work: The 2nd movement: an Andante (150 bars) is finished. (Not 12 tone music) the 3rd is being finished: 1 a sort of Scherzo (but truly *not* a jest!): in 12 tone technique; the trio free. The 4th & 5th movements (4th Adagio free; 5th Presto half free, half strictly 12 tone) I still hope to work on *here* & get rather further with, and certainly finish them in Vienna (where we will be again from July 25th). On Sept. 15th I can come up here once more & wish to end the quartet [with movement VI (Largo, also in very strict 12 tone technique)]. Unfortunately, I cannot remain here for the whole summer. Unfortunately, I must also proofread c. 500 pages *in between* (Wozzeck score and concert reduction!).[3] –

I look forward to your quartet. When shall it be ready for printing? – Sufficiently soon, I hope, for me *still* to be famous enough to promote it, which I am slowly but surely ceasing to be (famous, that is). *Besides Prague* no stage for Wozzeck in the coming season! –

Last night I finished the splendid 'Zauberberg'. This month's reading was a great joy to me. – Fontane's 'Irrungen & Wirrungen' a great disappointment! –

Morgenstern was staying at the Klenaus[4] until recently; now he is in Tyrol. –

Schönberg's chamber suite[5] finished. What does the Frankfurter Zeitung say about *Zurich*[6] (Schönberg, Webern?)

& now to end an expression of my *joyous surprise* at the *best news*: your essay 'Nachtmusik', dedicated to me. *1000 thanks*, my dear man! & now fond regards from us both & especially from your Berg

How did you like Landau's article[7] (in Anbruch) about Wozzeck; I liked it a great deal!

Please write again soon!

Original: manuscript with sender stamp.

1 Adorno – coming from Prague – stayed in Vienna from 18 April until 6 May; it is not known which performance he and Berg attended in the Burgtheater.

2 This is the *Lyric Suite*.

3 This is the piano reduction made by Fritz Heinrich Klein of the Chamber Concerto: *Kammerkonzert für Klavier und Geige mit dreizehn Bläsern: Ausgabe für zwei Klaviere und Geige* (Vienna and Leipzig, 1926).

4 That is, with the mother of his future wife, Ingeborg von Klenau.

5 This is the Suite for piano, E flat clarinet, clarinet, bass clarinet, violin, viola and cello op. 29.

6 See Karl Holl, 'Europa musiziert: das internationale Musikfest 1926', *Frankfurter Zeitung*, 26 June 1926, p. 1 (evening edition). In his letter of 12

July (no. 34), Adorno discusses this article (see in that letter's notes the excerpts from Holl's article).

7 See Alexander Landau, 'Die Musik und das soziale Problem', *Musikblätter des Anbruch*, 8 (1926), pp. 273–6.

32 WIESENGRUND-ADORNO TO BERG
FRANKFURT, 25.6.1926

deeply concerned request news = Wiesengrund

Original: This telegram – sent on 25 June – first went to Berg's Vienna address, and was forwarded to Trahütten on the 27th.

33 WIESENGRUND-ADORNO TO ALBAN
AND HELENE BERG
FRANKFURT, 28.6.1926

Frankfurt, 28 June 1926.

My dear master and teacher,

I cannot tell you my joy upon finally receiving your letter. I hope that the telegram I sent a few days previously did not overly shock you; but your silence had become so unsettling to me that I even resorted to that brutal measure in order finally to discover what is the matter with you. Now the thought of the letter slumbering in the letterbox is admittedly peaceful enough, but precisely this peacefulness can arouse anxiety in urgent situations. But a secure mode of correspondence with Austria indeed seems not to exist.

To hear that your quartet is growing is a source of joy to me for a hundred reasons, and I am already certain after the first movement,[1] and after the superb construction plan of increasing contrasts, that it will be *de toute première force*. Only you have such formal ideas today, and I am convinced that nothing has more gravity in music today than the formal-constructive imagination – more difficult indeed than that personality and inwardness of the 'individual element' itself (which it admittedly presupposes dialectically!) that I have been Kierkegaardianly banging on about for years. I mention some of this at the end of 'Nachtmusik'.[2] I would have liked to send you the essay first; it did not go off to U. E. before I had your consent to the dedication, for which I offer you my heartfelt thanks. But then there was no time left to send it first to Trahütten, as, in order still to

59

be considered for the September issue, it still had to reach Vienna before the holidays, so before July. But now it is there, waiting to be read by you.

It is particularly gratifying to me that my Webern met with your approval; all the more because the essay is so disfigured by crossings-out[3] that I was most concerned about its effect. In a few places, it is indeed objectively incomprehensible; through Heinsheimer's fault. Perhaps you could cast a glance at the manuscript some time. It is quite true that I increasingly warmed to the works during my study of them, as also while writing. Some of them, for example the song 'Welt der Gestalten' from op. 4, or the second movement from op. 5, or the 5th bagatelle from op. 9, truly contain some of the purest, most beautiful lyricism that there is. All the same, I was not about to forget in my essay that Webern is pursuing a lost cause, not only privately, but also historically; that he lacks the explosive power of construction, and the essay is coloured by this realization. Yet it is precisely his work's forlornness that lends it its radiance.

I am now working on the quartet once more;[4] on the reprise of the 1st movement and on the last, which shall be difficult, as its rhythmic characters are the deciding factor and I must keep it jazz-free. I have put a provisional end to my writing on music with 10 aphorisms.[5] At the same time, however, I have to work hard at the *Habilitation* thesis. It is no joy to me, as I am constantly having to keep it beneath my own standard. What is more, my life is currently very active, which we shall have occasion to discuss. It is composing that is really the defining spiritual reality for me.

How are you now in the country? And how is your wife? The theory of a connection between your fame and the – currently – singular production of Wozzeck shows that you are as yet incorrigible in your coquettish masochism; for you know as well as I do that it has nothing to do with your real success, only with the factual *difficulty* of Wozzeck and the *economic situation*, which prevents German opera houses from having the necessary number of rehearsals; and that at present only a few German opera houses are capable of putting on Wozzeck. Only really Dresden, Breslau, Frankfurt; Munich and Hamburg are excluded a priori, Klemperer obviously does not have the necessary resources in Wiesbaden, and it goes without saying that Herr Szenkar[6] in Cologne is out of the question for Wozzeck. It has been taken on by Breslau; it caused sufficient displeasure that Krauss[7] – he of the pudding-basin haircut – did not take it on here (even to Paul Hirsch,[8] a very influential man here, with whom I recently spoke!); I hope that Krauss is not kept here, and will do what I can to prevent it. That leaves Dresden as a riddle, admittedly. I certainly suspect Busch of being a classic-lover, and the sequence Faust – Protagonist[9] is hardly coincidental. But it is inexplicable nonetheless.

It is hard for me to speak fairly of Landau's essay. For it addresses the subject of my painful 2nd Wozzeck essay, and of course in insufficient depth. But it is already a great deal that he saw it at all, and he at least realizes something. The essay certainly has decent intentions, and is valuable as a pointer. – Incidentally, what did you think of my opera essay[10] in the issue before last with the Intermezzo analysis? And did you read the self-consciously literary, but *very gifted* essay there on Stravinsky by Else Koliner?[11]

It is strange that the Fontane does not speak to you, although Irrungen Wirrungen is by far not the best, but rather Effi Briest and Stechlin! But it seems that in order to appreciate this Christian manner, one must be 100 or, like myself, 50% Jew. Otherwise it's tedious.

Read Ilya Ehrenburg:[12] Julio Jurenito and T.D.E. It is not great, but amusing and destructive in a good way, and there is some truth to it.

Dear Frau Helene, I implore you in the name of the Kaiser Matriser[13] to steal early songs from your husband and give them to me!

When shall we finally deikitz[14] again?!

Devotedly yours,

Teddie W.,

who longs to see you.

Original: manuscript.

1 Adorno had presumably become acquainted with the first movement of the *Lyric Suite* during his last stay in Vienna.

2 The essay ends: 'The dissolution of the illusory interior reinstated the true exterior of music. It should, in its historical timeliness, prove more fitting and more profound to speak of musical materialism than of an ahistorical material determinacy in music' (*GS* 17, p. 59).

3 The manuscript of the essay has been lost.

4 Adorno's String Quartet op. 2 has only two movements, and there are no sketches for a further one among his belongings; Adorno also speaks of a – planned – third movement in letters 37, 42 and 45.

5 These are the 'Motive', which were published in April 1927 in *Musikblätter des Anbruch*; see *GS* 16, p. 259f. and *GS* 18, p. 13f.

6 The Budapest-born conductor Eugen Szenkar (1891–1977) worked at the opera house in Cologne, after spells in Frankfurt (as musical director 1920–23) and Berlin.

7 Clemens Krauss.

8 The businessman and music bibliophile Paul Hirsch (1881–1951) emigrated to England in 1936.

9 Fritz Busch (1890–1951), who was chief musical director at the Staatsoper Dresden, had conducted the premiere of the opera *Doktor Faust* by Ferruccio Busoni on 21 June 1925, and in the next season – on 27 March 1926 – the premiere of Kurt Weill's opera *Der Protagonist*.

10 This is the essay 'Opernprobleme'; see letter no. 27, note 4.

11 See Else Kolliner, 'Bemerkungen zu Strawinskys "Renard"', on the occasion of the performance at the Berlin State Opera, in *Musikblätter des Anbruch*, 8 (1926), pp. 214–16.

12 Ehrenburg's novels *Die ungewöhnlichen Abenteuer des Julio Jurenito und seiner Jünger* (Berlin, 1923) and *Trust D.E. Die Geschichte der Zerstörung Europas* (Berlin, 1925).

13 Adorno's nickname for Helene Berg; concerning its origin, Adorno writes in his memories of Berg of 1955 – 'Im Gedächtnis an Alban Berg' (*GS* 18, pp. 487–512): 'Amongst ourselves, we interacted in a coquettish manner; she called me Tēdie with a long e, and I called her Kaiser Matriser, after the expression used by one of the commanders at Schloss Schönbrunn, who referred to Maria Theresia by this name' (ibid., p. 507).

14 Concerning this expression, Adorno wrote in a letter more than two decades later: 'The logic of Kraus himself has an element of rationalism – to use the Viennese Yiddish expression: Gedeikitztes – that is paralysed precisely by the force which the linguistic fabric has in relation to the mere subjective intention in his work, but where I can never quite shake off the recollection of meaningful birthday poems by distinguished businessman.' Soma Morgenstern gives the following explanation in a footnote to Berg's letter to him of 22 November 1926: 'Alban loved the word, which would presumably have been Viennese Yiddish, as I only ever heard it in Vienna. It roughly means: to chat profoundly' (Morgenstern, *Berg und seine Idole*, p. 162).

34 WIESENGRUND-ADORNO TO BERG
    FRANKFURT, 12.7.1926

Frankfurt, 12 July 26.

My dear master and teacher,
having gone once again for 14 days without news from you, I would like only to ask you today if you received the lengthy letter – the answer to yours – I sent to *Trahütten*. The post is starting to become a source of horror to me, and is certainly doing its bit to convert me to Strindberg.
Otherwise I have little to report today: have you read

Hofmannsthal's 'Turm'? It is a peculiar coincidence: the piece is based on Calderon – whom you had hoped for a text by – and incorporates the Kaspar Hauser motif[1] that I suggested to you. It deviates radically from the tradition of German classical tragedy as otherwise only Wozzeck does, and seems – in a particular way – open to music. The parts that I read in the Neue Deutsche Beiträge[2] made a great impression on me, and Benjamin sees fit to be most generous with his praise.[3] Cuts would be necessary. But you must have a look at it. Consideration for Kraus might not be so important in this truly quite exceptional case.

Scherchen, who would like to perform your concerto,[4] is starting a charitable initiative for Webern[5] in which I intend to participate, and no doubt also other friends. He would be spared all embarrassment, and I wanted to ask you if such a measure would be welcome. Perh. one could organize some form of monthly support. – Anbruch has asked me for a few 'conductors' portraits'.[6] I shall write on Furtwängler, Scherchen and Webern. I have incidentally heard *nothing* from him in response to my essay about him – much to my astonishment.

Anbruch sent the essay 'Nachtmusik' back to me today, finding it too difficult and not relevant to our times (!). I shall send it to you as soon as I know whether or not my previous letter reached you. And if it too has been lost, then I do not wish to entrust the essay, of which I have only 1 copy, to the Graz–Köflach railway, and shall wait until you are in Vienna.

My quartet, which I work at constantly, is progressing. I think I shall be finished with the first movement very soon.

How is your quartet faring? If you are deeply engrossed in it, then please do not write a letter, which would rob you of your time, but merely a card of enlightenment to your devoted

Teddie W.,

who sends you and Frau Helene all his fondest, warm regards.

Holl wrote a lot of nonsense about the wind quintet, and something more agreeable on the Webern pieces;[7] but ultimately has no sense for what is timely. I didn't speak to him, as he is on holiday. Scherchen was greatly impressed by the quintet, and also by Webern's way of conducting. Apparently, the pieces were truly a great success. During the quintet, people became restless.

Original: manuscript.

1 Adorno probably made this suggestion to Berg during his visit to Vienna earlier that year.

2 In this journal edited by Hofmannsthal, the first two acts of the tragedy *Der Turm* (The Tower) (vol. 1, issue 2, pp. 18–91), and acts III to V (vol. 2, issue 2, pp. 9–90) were printed in 1923.

3 On 9 April 1926, Benjamin had published a review in the *Literarische Welt* (see Walter Benjamin, *Gesammelte Schriften*, vol. 3, ed. Hella Tiedemann-Bartels, 3rd edn, Frankfurt am Main, 1989, pp. 29–33). Beyond this, Benjamin probably also made conversational remarks to Adorno about the work.

4 Hermann Scherchen conducted the Berlin premiere of the *Kammerkonzert für Klavier und Geige mit dreizehn Bläsern* on 19 March 1927, as well as the immediately subsequent performances in Zurich (23 March) and Winterthur (25 March).

5 Unknown.

6 See Adorno, 'Drei Dirigenten', *Musikblätter des Anbruch*, 8 (1926), pp. 315–19; *GS* 19, pp. 453–9.

7 The passages from Holl's article in the *Frankfurter Zeitung* (see letter no. 31, note 6) about Schönberg's Wind Quintet op. 26 and Webern's Five Orchestral Pieces op. 10 are as follows:

> Rarely has a new piece by the Viennese master been as disappointing as this op. 26, celebrated by his followers as a breakthrough into the realm of musical merriment, yet in reality an arch-problematic piece. It can already claim historical significance as an entirely valid, internally correct document of his theory of 'composing with twelve tones related only to one another', but for the time being it remains indifferent in its immediate effect. [. . .] Only once more was there occasion to perk up one's eyes and ears. The five pieces for (chamber) orchestra by Anton Webern are, even if one chooses to consider them chamber music, certainly not to be dismissed with a hiss or a smile. Webern is, along with Berg, one of those students of Schönberg who, while under his spell, have been most able to retain their own personality. The five miniatures contain the sounding 'seals' of a lyricism that is already very abstract in its direction, yet still retains its sensuality. Eccentric, but not entirely solitary.

35 ALBAN AND HELENE BERG TO WIESENGRUND-ADORNO TRAHÜTTEN, 14.7.1926

ALBAN BERG c/o NAHOWSKI
TRAHÜTTEN IN STEIERMARK   14.7.
POST OFFICE: DEUTSCH-LANDSBERG
A./D. GRAZ-KÖFLACH RAILWAY

Only very briefly my dear Wiesengrund. Thanks for telegram & letter of 28.6. The latter very interesting. Am very keen to read Nachtmusik. Is it to appear in Anbruch? Is the quartet finished in the meantime? I shall hopefully finish mine in the autumn, though the interruption (in Vienna from I.VIII) is unlikely to do it any good, but I have done some work *in advance* precisely with this in mind, which I never do otherwise. On I.VIII, Schneevoigt is doing the 'Bruchstücke' in Scheveningen with that very talented van Geuns lady.[1] In February Kleiber in Petersburg. But perhaps the whole opera can be done there after all, with Coates[2] cond. at the academ. theatre. I am not hearing anything about *German* opera houses. We Viennese have been spared Krauss, *thank God*. But what *else* is there? Schneiderhahn,[3] of Fackel fame, is the head of the men's choral society. (On the trip to America: 'where's my flannel?') So he's a clown beyond compare. But he wants to bring *Turnau*[4] to Vienna as director, which would be *not* undesirable. –

What did you hear about Zurich? I heard: that the 'New Classicism'[5] *triumphed* over Schönberg once and for all there. An utterly short-lived partita by Casella[6] that had the *greatest* success. Once again, everyone succeeds at Schönberg's expense! For how long? I would reckon 1–1½ years! Incidentally, Webern had a colossal success (especially in the French part of the I.S.*f.k.m.a*).[7] A success that I had prophesied: for no one can resist the delights issuing from *his* orchestra. It is the most *un-heard-of* sound in New Music! You have no idea! –

Schönberg has been in Vienna since July, in August he will retire to the country. Is well, but still not entirely at ease. Still working on the 'Jakobsleiter'[8] (discretion!) –

Fare thee well & write soon to your

Alban Berg

Dear Teddy, If you had beseeched me in the name of Kaiser F.J., we could more readily discuss a song-theft – but the Matriser: 'Precisely not!' I hope we shall meet soon!
Fond regards to you & your two d. mothers!

Yours,

Helene Berg

Original: manuscript with sender stamp and an additional note by Helene Berg.

1 The Finnish conductor and cellist Georg Schnéevoigt (1872–1947), who conducted in Düsseldorf between 1924 and 1926, and Co van Geuns also gave the Viennese performance on 14 October 1926.

2 The St Petersburg-born conductor and composer Albert Coates (1882–1953) worked at the St Petersburg opera from 1911 to 1918; the Russian premiere of *Wozzeck* took place on 13 June 1927 in Leningrad, as St Petersburg was still called at the time.

3 Franz Schneiderhahn (1863–1938) was president of the state theatres; see also *Die Fackel*, issues 735–742, October 1926, p. 41.

4 The director Josef Turnau (1888–1954) was opera manager in Breslau at the time, then later occupied the same position in Frankfurt.

5 Allusion to the third of Schönberg's Three Satires for Mixed Choir op. 28, entitled 'The New Classicism'.

6 The Partita for Piano and Orchestra by Alfredo Casella (1883–1947) had been premiered on 22 June 1926 in Zurich.

7 Berg often referred to the ISCM as the 'I.G.f.l.m.i.A', standing for 'Internationale Gesellschaft für leck mich im Arsch' (International Society for kiss my arse).

8 The composition of the oratorio for soloists, mixed choir and orchestra *Die Jakobsleiter*, whose text already existed in print in 1917, remained a fragment. Winfried Zillig (1905–1963), a student of Schönberg, reconstructed a full score of the fragment from the short score and sketches in 1955.

36   BERG TO WIESENGRUND-ADORNO
     TRAHÜTTEN, 23.7.1926

ALBAN BERG c/o NAHOWSKI
TRAHÜTTEN IN STEIERMARK
POST OFFICE: DEUTSCH-LANDSBERG
A./D. GRAZ-KÖFLACH RAILWAY   23./7.

Dear Wiesengrund from the 30th I shall be back in *Vienna*. I expect you have received my letter of the 14th. It crossed your letter. Answer only in brief: *What* is the name of the play by Hofmannsthal 'Türen'? Charitable initiative for Webern to be carried out at all costs, if possible. Excellent idea. Monthly support for a certain time also strikes me as best. Please do all you can to fulfil this wonderful plan. 'Nachtmusik' please to me in Vienna! Greatly looking forward to it. Conductor essays good idea! What do you say to Bekessy?[1] The N. Fr. Presse is acting as if *it* had fought against him for 1 year & not Kraus. These leader articles are orgies.

Yesterday Alma Mahler & Franz Werfel visited us for 18 hours, coming from Semmering by car. It was a ray of light!

Warmest regards yours Alban B

Original: postcard; stamp: Deutsch-Landsberg, 24.VII.26. Manuscript with sender stamp.

1 The Budapest-born journalist and newspaper editor Imre Békessy, whom Karl Kraus 'chased' out of Vienna; see *Die Fackel*, issues 732–734 (August 1926), pp. 1–56 ('Die Stunde des Todes' [The Hour of Death]).

Frankfurt a. M., 3 August.

Dear master and teacher,

just this moment I concluded the 1st movement of my quartet, a –
by my standards – quite fully grown piece of 190 bars. You are familiar with the start, which you liked, and as I do not believe that the
piece has grown any worse, I hope that it will satisfy you to some
degree. You will receive the score as soon as I have copied it out; it will
be another 14 days before I can do that in peace, however. I am otherwise also composing very eagerly; the 3rd movement,[1] a sort of
rondo with many musical shapes, piano pieces in the strictest twelve-
tone technique,[2] but short (the 1st is finished), and songs, one of which
I have likewise finished,[3] while the others have already progressed very
far. As you can see, the other work, of which there is certainly no
shortage, is not – as you sometimes fear – keeping me from what is
most important.

The play by Hofmannsthal is entitled 'Der Turm'. *Turm*.[4] The essay
'Nachtmusik' has still not been printed; perhaps 'Musik' will publish
it. Today, in its stead, please accept 10 musical aphorisms that will
perhaps entertain you.

On August 15th I am taking a holiday; namely going to Egern-
Rottach by Lake Tegern for 14 days; after that perhaps to Aussee. It
is possible, albeit by no means certain, that I shall come to Vienna for
a few days at the end of September, to report on the sociologists' congress[5] for the Frankfurter Zeitung. Will you still be in Vienna then?

My private life is not particularly well; for many reasons. I long to
see you, and would like to speak to you about all these matters. – My
commitment to the *Habilitation* is also weighing on my shoulders as
a constant pressure. And I am truly utterly overworked.

How are you both? How do you feel in a Vienna finally cleansed of
old Budapest?[6] Do you sometimes dine at the Weide?[7] Do you think
of me? I am so very, very much in need of it!

Soma sent me an essay for the F.Z. that my friend Kracauer found
very gifted;[8] I hope the story shall be published, at least fragmentarily.
Sadly, it is a little too broad.

One further request: on my last stay in Vienna, I left my two George
songs[9] behind, and I strongly suspect that it was at Kolisch's. Would you
mind calling him about this? I would not like to write to him especially
for this reason – it would seem so self-important. Perhaps you could also
tell him again that he can reckon with my quartet for the autumn.

Has the Chamber Concerto come out? And Schönberg's Suite? Is the Jakobsleiter finished?

Dear Frau Helene, if the Matriser is no good, then Ferenz-Joseph will just have to do, though I would have preferred to spare him, as he is really not spared anything. But please, obtain the early songs for me.

Send a few lines soon   to your devoted
                               Teddie W.

Original: manuscript.

1 Neither a third movement nor sketches for one have been found among Adorno's belongings.

2 There are no *finished* piano pieces among Adorno's belongings.

3 The song 'Steh ich in finstrer Mitternacht (aus dem Krieg 1914–18)', composed in 1926, which Adorno later included in his Six Bagatelles for Voice and Piano op. 6 (see *Compositions 1*, p. 68f.).

4 Adorno repeats the word in Latin letters.

5 Adorno did not travel to Vienna for this occasion.

6 Allusion to Imre Békessy.

7 The name of the restaurant to which Berg, as Adorno later recalls, had taken him: 'I was able to learn from him [Berg] what Austrian sensual culture could mean; I shall never forget his sense for good food and wine, the likes of which one normally finds in Paris. It is to him that I owe my acquaintance with the then excellent, literally and metaphorically utterly black and yellow restaurant Weide in Speising, with the famous crab pasties [. . .]' (GS 13, p. 343f.).

8 Adorno had undertaken, with the help of Kracauer, to have Morgenstern's short story 'Personenwaage' (Scales) published in the *Frankfurter Zeitung*, where it indeed appeared on 13 February 1927.

9 These are the third and fourth songs of Adorno's op. 1: 'Wir werden noch einmal zum lande fliegen' – whose manuscript bears the note: 'Vienna, 25 April 1925' – and 'Es lacht in dem steigenden jahr', with the note: 'Vienna, 4 May 1925'.

38   BERG TO WIESENGRUND-ADORNO
       VIENNA, c. 13.8.1926

Dear Wiesengrund, in Vienna since the 2nd & at work (quartet) which however I hope to complete in September in *Trahütten* again. My thanks for the letter of 3.8. with the nice aphorisms.[1] Stravinsky superb![2] Reger[3] is arguable. I do not understand 'Fremdwörter in der Operette'.[4] – I daresay it would be a fine thing if you came to Vienna, we shall presumably be here until mid-Sept., then 2, 3 weeks in Trahütten & from early Oct. in Vienna once more, where on Oct. 13th Schneevoigt is doing the Bruchstücke, which he performed 14 days ago in Scheveningen. Prague premiere[5] probably *before* Christmas. Petersburg one[6] January, February. Melos published a brilliant and *accurate* article on Wozzeck by Schäfke[7] (?) (accurate both on my treatment of the *text* and on the music). A very nice one also in Signale f.d. musikal Welt by Herbert Connor (?). – Otherwise nothing new from me. Mood: 'serious, but hopeful'! – Schönberg in Ragusa, composing variat. for full orchestra.[8] – Kolisch is coming to Vienna soon, shall ask him about your songs. – I saw Soma Morgenstern for a few hours. He is – and rightly so – cross that you have not written to him, not even about the article. Warmest regards yours Berg

In July Alma Mahler & Franz Werfel visited us for 1 day in Trahütten, as you can see here.[9]

Original: photograph postcard: Alban and Helene Berg with Alma Mahler and Franz Werfel in the latter's car. Manuscript.

On the dating: Written fourteen days after the premiere of *Drei Bruchstücke aus der Oper 'Wozzeck'* on 1 August in Scheveningen.

1 These are 'Motive'; see letter no. 33, note 5.

2 Adorno's aphorism is as follows: 'One need not fear any revolution from Stravinsky. He takes care of the dynamite attack and the life insurance himself, in the same breath and with the same policy; he visits today's bomb craters tomorrow with sightseers in the state carriage of the *ancien régime*, and the blue bird soon builds its peaceful nest in them' (*GS* 16, p. 259).

3 See letter 39, note 1.

4 See *GS* 16, p. 260.

5 The Prague performance of *Wozzeck* took place that year on 11 November.

6 The Leningrad premiere took place only on 13 June 1927.

7 See Rudolf Schäfke, 'Alban Bergs "Wozzeck"', *Melos*, 5 (1926), p. 1131ff.

8 Schönberg worked on his Variations for Orchestra op. 31 until 1928.

9 Written on the picture side.

19 August 26.

Staudach-Rottach 109
Haus Schwab
(Upper Bavaria)

Dear master and teacher,

by the same token that I was happy to receive the picture and the
greetings on your card – which was forwarded to me here yesterday
–, I was also inflamed by the apparently injured tone of your message.
What do you hold against me? The Soma matter is quite different than
you think; I pursued it immediately and energetically, and only
abstained from writing to him because I wanted to wait until I could
tell him the news with certainty – and also in the hope of arranging a
stay with him – a hope that I still cling to now. In any case, I shall write
to him today; the letter to him will be sent with this same delivery to
your address, as I do not know his.

But you must hold something else against me? Perhaps you found
the Reger irreverent?[1] But you would have told me that; I certainly did
not write it lightly! Or did the tone of my last few letters offend you?
Well, it may not have been a fitting one, but this is purely the fault of
my condition, which, as I told you in the last letter, is very poor, and
affected by severe depressions. The combined effects of the increasingly far-reaching conflict with my friend[2] and erotic entanglements
without hope or escape have brought me to this point. I can only keep
my head above water at all by forcing myself to work (I have lately
been practising the piano like a madman once again, along with everything else!), and in all private utterances I am no doubt a shadow of
my true self. Be patient with me! And above all: write to me openly
what charges are being made against me! The thought of losing you,
even the mere thought of our estrangement, is completely unbearable
to me!

I am here together with a lady friend[3] under very difficult circumstances; in fact, it is really through you that I know her; met her at the
house of my friends the Oppenheims,[4] where Grab took me. She is an
actress; her husband, from whom she is divorced, a friend of mine.
Our relationship is most peculiar, a mixture of intimacy and foreignness as incomprehensible to me as it is to her. And offers me once more
a terrible demonstration of the impracticability of human relationships that have grand intentions. In mute nature, which is also native
to people, even women, lies something unassailable which we are
hopelessly repelled by, even if it seemed broken in a thousand places!
If only one did not always have to be repelled!

Otherwise I am living here in, as one says, a state of recovery. I lie in a boat on the lake all day, and needless to say I have been heavily sunburnt as a result. I am sleeping a great deal, doing philosophical work. – There is a Herr Slezak[5] here, with a villa that stands behind coloured-glass balls. I met his son today. He is someone whom you could have invented in a nightmare.

I have one great request of you. Anbruch had asked me for three 'conductors' portraits'. I wrote to them, mentioning Furtwängler, Scherchen (who is incidentally very interested in my works!) and Webern. The manuscript was supposed to be in Vienna a week ago! Would you take a look at it when you next go to see Hertzka? Especially concerning Webern, I am *most urgently* in need of your opinion! For there are a few things in it which, if he misunderstands them, could perhaps offend him, which would be terrible for me. And his silence on my essay, which (despite having been horribly disfigured) was fit to please you, has made me quite unsure of myself! So please look at it with a view to this! And a further request: use *your* authority (the gentlemen care little what I write!) to ensure that I am sent the proofs for correction! I *must* make a few changes. There are, for example, a few sentences in the part on Webern, where I describe his conducting style, that all begin with a journalistically capitalized 'And'. That is unacceptable; each sentence should begin with 'He'.

Forgive me for burdening you with such stuff.

A few more words on the twelve-tone technique (my essay will most likely appear in the F.Z.; I shall also analyse the quintet with Holl).[6] I have now done a good deal of work with it myself, and from the inside the matter does in fact look quite different. In particular because it is only thus that one can understand the *relief* offered by the technique: namely that the possibility of *continuation* is always guaranteed by the content of the row. It would be impossible to recognize this solely through analysis, which can never adequately grasp the act of composition, but only the 'composed'. Admittedly, I have meanwhile come to view this relief as the danger in dodecaphony. The process of originary listening is broken off too soon; there is no guarantee that the relation to the material that represents a 'definite multiplicity' genuinely involves *that same* possibility of continuation demanded by the ear at this point in its own particular form! I refuse to accept that it should be forbidden, bad or 'wilful' to write something like the end of the 5th orchestral piece.[7] As a *regulative* for keeping away tonally cadential residues, the twelve-tone technique is necessary in its lucid rationality, and appeared at its own rightful time. But it cannot and should not dictate a positive compositional canon. This is what I currently believe: that there is only a 'negative' dodecaphony, being the utmost rational borderline case of the dissolution of tonality (even when tonal elements appear within dodecaphony; for then they, as a construction, are *coincidental in their tonality*, being simply dictated by the row!). Positive dodecaphony as a guarantee of music's capacity for continuation as objectivity does *not* exist.

All this is but a suggestion and a question for you; not for the public at large, which must first discover the purifying force of dodecaphony; and certainly not for Schönberg. In my quartet I admittedly resort, in order to avoid leading-note cadences, to using rows, which I deploy using such devices as rhythmic variation, inversion, retrograde and ret. inv.; but I permit myself the acoustic liberty of choice – interruption of the row; freely following the harmonic tendency – and reserve this right at all times, and tie the movement's large-scale dimensions purely to the *formal architecture*, which is certainly related to the row's manifestations, but not identical. In the piano pieces,[8] I invented something new for myself: *vertical rows*, i.e. ones which are not, as with Schönberg, the result of folding a melodic row – one with a clear, single character (or rather four) – on top of itself, but which appear *chordally* in the sense of Wozzeck's death scene, are *only* used chordally, and, rather than being combined to form sounds, are *dissected* melodically; here one has the possibility of any given permutation and ordering, not only the 4 Schönbergian modifications. Of course, the precondition for this is that the row, in order to take on a binding function, should contain only a limited number of the 12 possible pitches – probably not more than precisely your 6.[9] I hope to demonstrate this to you at much greater length soon. I am writing the songs[10] very freely, and am quite content to do so.

What is the state of your quartet? How much is finished? And what of your other plans? – The divorced wife of the painter Ottomar Starke[11] spoke to me about opera texts that he (Starke) writes; a grotesque one has just become available, and is very modern. I am extremely distrustful of the wife, who is false and a salon communist. But maybe the husband, who is supposedly gifted as a painter, could be some good after all. Should I inquire further in the matter?

Has Schönberg *really* finished the chamber suite?[12] And how far has he got with the Jakobsleiter? And how about the variations? Does he want to switch to the symphony? How strange, how incomprehensible this manner of production is once again! Have the choral pieces come out, the suite in printing?

I hope finally to hold the 'Nachtmusik' essay in my hands in the next few days. As soon as I do, you shall receive it.

It has now become very uncertain whether I shall come to Vienna in September. You shall soon receive word from me.

Did you see my Scherchen music festival review[13] in Musik?

The authors of the two new commentaries on Wozzeck are

unknown to me. Could they send the essays to me here? I shall stay until the end of next week.

Forgive the long epistle!

Please accept my very fondest regards to you and your wife
from your devoted

Wiesengrund.

Original: manuscript.

1 'Reger's sequences are comparable to contemporary interior design. Unable to divide the broad façade clearly, and equally unable to obtain a reality for its grandiose appearance, one has carefully withdrawn into the interior, and there imitates the edifice's lost order on the smaller scale: not without first drawing the blinds. One finds it rather homely by the light of privacy, in front of the artificial fireplace of the soul; the rooms complement one another, their sequence is secure from door to door. But it is just a little too spacious for the few inhabitants: when the light fails, they lose their way in the dark' (GS 18, p. 13).

2 Siegfried Kracauer.

3 Presumably Ellen Dreyfuss-Herz; see also letter no. 54.

4 Paul Oppenheim (1885–1977), who held a managerial position in the chemical industry until 1933, and his wife Gabrielle. Paul Oppenheim later worked in the USA as a scientific theorist.

5 The tenor Leo Slezak (1873–1946), who lived in Rottach Egern, had worked at the Vienna Court and State Operas from 1901 to 1926.

6 According to Adorno's own words, the detailed analysis of the Wind Quintet op. 26 by Schönberg disappeared within his preface to the essay collection Moments musicaux (see GS 17, p. 11); nothing is known of any contribution to the analysis by Holl.

7 From Schönberg's op. 16.

8 Probably those mentioned in letter no. 37, which were there still conceived as being 'in the strictest twelve-tone technique'.

9 See Wozzeck's death scene (act III, scene 4), in which the hexachord B flat–C sharp–E–G sharp–E flat–F fulfils the central function; see also letters 13 and 15.

10 Adorno's Vier Gedichte von Stefan George für eine Singstimme und Klavier op. 1.

11 The set-designer and writer Ottomar Starke (1886–?); at Adorno's request, he sent Berg a manuscript entitled Der Geizhals (The Miser) on 24 August 1926.

12 Schönberg had finished op. 29 on 1 May.

13 See GS 19, pp. 79–81.

ALBAN BERG VIENNA XIII/I
TRAUTTMANSDORFFGASSE 27
TELEPHONE: 84831.
21.8.26

My dear Wiesengrund, these few words just to deliver you from uncertainty or error: Aside from that little, entirely *objective* irritation about the Soma business*, I have neither held nor do I hold *anything at all* against you & I cannot imagine *what* gave you such an idea. The brevity of my letters (and likewise this card) has been caused by nothing other than having too little time: composing, proofreading, business, [x]¹ etc. etc. Every day is too short for me!!!! *Your* depression & its causes weigh very heavily on my mind, and it would be a great joy to me if I could help you. But *nature* will be better equipped to do so than your *friend!* – Next week I hope to be successful in sorting out the matter of your article with U. E. As far as the 12–tone technique is concerned: The most conspicuous thing about it, I would say, is the fact that it does not exclude tonality (intentional tonality – not simply chance tonality, which would be very fishy) at all. This makes me consider much of what you put so elegantly rather questionable. All the more as I am currently on the final (6th) quartet movement, which shall once again be *very strict*. [N.B. 4 movements are completely finished, the 3rd (the Allegro) half-finished.] I received *Starke's* libretto, and found it quite excellent! *But sadly not for me!* I recommended him most warmly to Zemlinsky. – Do you know a Frankfurt painter Benno Elkan. I received a Chinese 'Tristan' from him (through U. E.).² This, on the other hand, would *greatly* appeal to me, but the libretto contains (in addition to a *low* standard of language) many mistakes. I can answer all your questions relating to Schönberg with a *yes*. That means: choral pieces about to appear. I know nothing of symphonic plans!

Fare thee *well* & recover your *health!*

Warmest regards Yours B

Fond regards! Yours Helene Berg

Original: postcard; stamp: Vienna, 21.VIII.26. Manuscript with sender stamp and an additional note by Helene Berg.

1 Here a word could not be deciphered.

2 The sculptor, painter and writer Benno Elkan (1877–1960), whose libretto draft was entitled *Samurai*.

* Soma shall receive his letter tomorrow. He is in Vienna.

ALBAN BERG VIENNA XIII/I
TRAUTTMANSDORFFGASSE 27 $^6/_9$26
TELEPHONE: 84831.

I have long been meaning, dear Wiesengrund, to write to you at length
& thank you. But always waited until I had half a day completely free
to *study* your article*. Which has not happened to this day. I naturally
read it immediately, & then once more, & I sense how beautiful & fine
it is –. But I am so engrossed in my quartet that I simply cannot allow
myself the pleasure of such 'studies' at present. At any rate, it is clearly
a *most particularly fine piece* & the dedication is a great source of joy
to me. My *warmest* thanks for it.

   In c. 8 days we shall take another trip to Trahütten. I intend to
compose the last movement there, the first 5 are as good as finished
but did, on the other hand, turn out to be very difficult. Oct 7th & following in Vienna again, as on the 13th the Bruchstücke are being done
with Schneevoigt & van der Geuns. Then in Oct I intend to produce
a fair copy of the quartet.

   Please keep me informed as to your whereabouts. As long as you
hear nothing to the contrary from me, please write to me in *Vienna*. I
spoke to Kolisch concerning your 'George songs'. He knew of *nothing
here*; but will *search*. Perhaps you can nudge him in writing & give him
points of reference, such as when & where he received them from you.

Fond regards from your

B

As soon as I am certain of your whereabouts, I shall send the aforementioned Melos article

Original: manuscript.

Frankfurt, 7 September 26.

   Dear master and teacher, my thanks for your card, which reassured
me completely. I have still had no news from Soma,[1] and therefore,
after extending my stay in Rottach to 4 weeks, returned here and set

---

* which is once again so difficult that I cannot read it with a work-worn head.

to work: quartet finale,[2] which I am finding difficult to compose and is progressing only slowly at present, but which I *definitely* expect to finish before the winter. The difficulties are of a particular nature; for the rondo has tendencies towards dance that demand to be carried through, and yet it should at all costs avoid becoming some artfully stylized foxtrot or Stravinskian romp. It should thus be rhythmically conceived at the vertical level, and at the same time *genuinely* polyphonic, which demands the utmost control. A shame you are not here. I am checking through the first movement, and suppose that I can make the fair copy now; I hope it satisfies you. The second is a piece consisting of variations that I worked on while I was with you.

Otherwise, I am studying 'Wozzeck' in its technical aspects, and do not cease to be amazed.

It is especially pleasing to me that you are making such good progress. Where have you got to now? How long are the movements? You should call the piece a quartet after all, not a suite. For the massively expansive spread of its disposition already exceeds its suite character. A dance piece simply has nothing in common with the absolute gravity of your music. What is more, one should keep one's distance, externally too, from the new – fascist – classicism.

If you are answering all my questions concerning Schönberg in the affirmative – does this also mean that the Jakobsleiter is *finished?* This would of course be an event of incalculable importance!

You must *on no account* have anything to do with Benno Elkan! He is the biggest art fraud I know, an even worse type than Willi Grosz[3] and incapable of producing anything worthwhile. From what you say, I can imagine his Tristan only too well.

I sent you 'Nachtmusik' 8 days ago from Rottach, and I hope you received it. I am naturally *extremely* desirous of your opinion. Please also show it to Soma and Steuermann, and extend my fond greetings to them. – As 'Musik' requested the manuscript (after 'Anbruch' rejected it), I would be most grateful to you if you could send it there once you have read it. Address: 'Musik' editorial office, Berlin W 9, Linkstrasse*[4] 16.

The 'Frankfurter Kammermusikgemeinde',[5] whose lady director is a former friend of mine, has placed songs of mine on its programme without my prior knowledge. I suppose the only suitable ones would be the two George songs that Kolisch has.

I am now well recovered, it was necessary and I am now in great need of my strength. My private life has improved, though it is still all rather complicated, not least because I must release myself from a relationship that has run its course, which is difficult for me. But I have

* Linkstrasse

enough work to live off. Fond regards to you and Frau Helene your faithful Teddie W.

Original: manuscript.

1 Soma Morgenstern replied to Adorno's critical remarks on the story *Personenwaage* on 9 September 1926.

2 See letter no 37, note 1.

3 The Viennese composer Wilhelm Grosz (1894–1939) published *Baby in der Bar: ein Tanzspiel von Béla Balasz* as his op. 23 in 1927.

4 Adorno repeated the street name in printed Roman letters at the bottom of the page.

5 See letter no. 12, note 3.

43   BERG TO WIESENGRUND-ADORNO
     TRAHÜTTEN, 17.9.1926

ALBAN BERG c/o NAHOWSKI
TRAHÜTTEN IN STEIERMARK   17./₉26
POST OFFICE: DEUTSCH-LANDSBERG
A./D. GRAZ-KÖFLACH RAILWAY

Here since a few days ago, my dear Wiesengrund, unfortunately asthmatic, so unfit for work. But I *must* overcome it! Thank you f. y. letter of the 7th. Meanwhile you must have received my letter regarding your article? I sent it to 'Musik' by registered mail on the 13th & look forward to reading it *in print* & thus also becoming *thoroughly* acquainted with it. Soma wrote to you in Rottach; we have spent every day together. Even at football! Give me further news of your work. Mine has to be finished here in 2, 3 weeks. If only I could breathe! Did you receive Melos? The quartet most certainly *is* a suite, even a lyric suite. What do you think of the Tybuk [*sic*] as a libretto.[1] I am considering, but must ask the *very utmost* discretion of you. – If you wish to have an experience that is beyond compare, have a look at the pno. reductions of the Lästerschule. I would *advise* you to take flight from Frankfurt for the premiere![2] Jakobsleiter *not* finished. We are happy to hear that you have recovered so well, & send our very warmest greetings.
                     Yours Berg
Klemperer is putting on the Bruchstücke in Wiesbaden.[3]

Original: picture postcard of Trahütten, without any postage stamp or stamped date; on the upper left hand side an arrow, with '*Our little house in Trahütten.*' written in Berg's handwriting. Manuscript with sender stamp.

1 See An-Ski [i.e. Salomon Rappaport], *Der Dybuk: Dram. Legende in 4 Akten*, trans. from the Yiddish by A. Nadel; only authorized translation [edition of the Jüdisches Künstler-Theater], Berlin [1921].

2 The premiere of Klenau's opera *Die Lästerschule* took place in Frankfurt am Main on 26 December 1926.

3 It is not known whether Otto Klemperer, who was chief musical director in Wiesbaden, actually performed the *Bruchstücke*.

44 WIESENGRUND-ADORNO TO BERG
FRANKFURT, 24.10.1926

Frankfurt-Oberrad.
24 October 26.

Dear master and teacher, here is at last some news from me. I have had a very peculiar time of late, one during which I was unable to come to my senses, and which was also a difficult time for me. Also externally difficult; because suddenly, from one day to the next, I found myself either having to force the issue of my *Habilitation* or abandon it. In this matter too you were right, as you always are with grim predictions; a hundred obstacles appeared that I had not reckoned with; rivals also appeared, among them – which complicated matters particularly – a friend of mine.[1] I had to address the matter very energetically; conclude my preparatory work, draw up a large abstract; and if the abstract is accepted, which will transpire within the next few days, I shall finish the thesis in 6–8 weeks. All this would not be so troublesome if the *Habilitation* were certain; but it is by no means certain, even if the thesis is accepted. And meanwhile, it is costing me all my powers. I had to lay aside the quartet finale, which had already progressed very far, for 4 weeks. But once my work on the *Habilitation* thesis[2] – which is not a fully fledged philosophical achievement, but purely a means to an end – is under way, I can finish the quartet. I will force the matter or abandon it. Either I shall fulfil my intention, and then have all my time for my work – or I shall let it be once and for all, and endeavour to find my place in musical life, if such a thing still exists, which, at least in our understanding of the notion, I am coming to doubt. And my dégout at the *Habilitation* had even driven me so far as to apply for Pisling's[3] former post at the 8 o'clock evening paper in Berlin – without being dignified with any response. I had given you as a reference – did anyone ask you about it?

78

And do you think there might be an opening for me in Vienna – for example with the International, or with a decent newspaper? I would still be happy to avoid the academic teaching profession, and I can think of nowhere I would rather be than with you. Forgive me for accosting you with requests in this letter, which is once again terribly late. But my silence and my requests have the same reason, namely an extremely muddled situation that does not allow me to speak, but only permits, now at last, a cry for help! I need hardly tell you that I cling to you with my entire person and all my artistic conviction. You will sense that these are weighty, dark matters that I have to deal with; matters whose human origin I do not suppose anyone but you could understand!

I had hoped to travel to Prague for Wozzeck.[4] But at present, I cannot leave here. If the premiere were to be much further delayed, I would certainly do so, and perhaps subsequently go with you to Vienna for a few weeks. I can certainly not go for much longer without seeing you. So please write to me of your plans, in particular for the second half of December and January.

I truly hope Leningrad goes well.[5] Should any introductions to Wozzeck be required, then I would passionately like to write them, and beg you to inform me in good time. And I give you my firm promise that I shall write *truly simply* and *drastically*; I can certainly manage that for proletarians, it is only with the middle classes that I do not succeed, as I am simply never allowed to tell them directly what I mean.

Are you and your dear wife *in good health?* Did Trahütten do you good? I presume that the bad weather has caused you to return to Vienna; if not, the letter will hopefully follow you!

Your quartet will be finished by now. I cannot tell you how eager I am for it. For there is otherwise truly no good music. Apart from the new piano pieces by Eisler,[6] which I like a great deal (which would incidentally be inconceivable without Wozzeck!), I have lately seen only bad, appropriated and false stuff. Although I am sent reams of music. The new classicism has completely petrified the old composers, and made the young ones cowardly, lazy and irresponsible. – I now despair of reaching the heart of the external musical situation, that is, the chance of something serious, just as much as you do.

In fact, I am generally no longer lagging behind you in terms of defeatism.

I will write to you soon concerning the Melos essay. What I liked most about it was the wrapping paper; a fragment from your Chamber Concerto,[7] which I have kept. Can you not wrap more journals, e.g. Anbruch? – The essay is solidly and even affectionately written, but with an ultimately subaltern philologists' devotion, and has the dangerous intention of drawing a reactionary ideology out of Wozzeck (the harmonic and the linear being simultaneous; the primacy of the connection to the old formal tradition; obviously wicked lies). But at least the piece maintains a certain standard, and is better than all the hack jobs that have otherwise been done on Wozzeck. But he clearly comes from the Berlin music history class of Professor Abert.[8]

Did you read my essays ('Conductors' and 'Metronome Markings'[9])?

I shall write to Soma in the next few days.

Warm regards to you and to dear Frau Helene from your faithful Teddie,

who longs to
see you both.

Original: manuscript.

1 This is Leo Löwenthal (1900–1993), who, after studies in literature, history, philosophy and sociology, began as a teacher; he became a full-time employee of the Frankfurt Institut für Sozialforschung (Institute for Social Research). Löwenthal did not pursue his plan for a *Habilitation* any further after November 1927.

2 Adorno was working on his first *Habilitation* thesis, 'Der Begriff des Unbewußten in der transzendentalen Seelenlehre' (see *GS* 1, pp. 79–322), at the time; see also letters 72 and 76 and the accompanying notes.

3 The music critic Siegmund Pisling (1869–1926) was correspondent for the *Berliner National-Zeitung* until his death.

4 The premiere of *Wozzeck* at the Prague National Theatre, under the musical direction of Otokar Ostrčil, took place on 11 November 1926.

5 The performance at the Leningrad State Opera followed only on 13 June 1927.

6 It is not known whether Adorno was familiar with Hanns Eisler's *Piano Pieces* op. 8, probably composed in 1925. But he certainly reviewed Eisler's op. 3 in July 1927 for *Die Musik* (see *GS* 18, p. 522f.).

7 'The fragment from the original score of the Chamber Concerto' – as Adorno noted down on it – has survived among his belongings.

8 The musicologist Hermann Abert (1871–1927).

9 See letter no. 20, note 12.

ALBAN BERG VIENNA XIII/I
TRAUTTMANSDORFFGASSE 27   Vienna <u>29.10</u>
TELEPHONE: 84831.   26

Many thanks,
   dear Wiesengrund, for your kind letter. Let me quickly reply to the
most important points.
   I am *deeply* affected by the matter of your *Habilitation*, as likewise by
your various plans. I would like to discuss this *at length* with you. This
would be very difficult in writing. – I have not yet heard anything about
the 8 o'clock evening paper. But I can imagine how many hundreds of
people want to take Pisling's old position. I heard that e.g. from Bittner,[1]
who wants to move to Berlin à tout prix. To be honest, he is right; I
should do so too. For there is *nothing* more to be had *here*; it is now even
worse than last year. That is why it is so difficult to give you advice.
   Perhaps you can come to Prague after all, where the premiere is on
Nov. 11th. If not there, then around the turn of the year, at which time
I definitely hope to see you in Vienna. – Leningrad will only be at the
start of next year. Should any articles be necessary, I shall of course
give your name. – For my part, I was in Trahütten until October 5th,
where I feverishly completed the quartet; feverishly in every sense,
mentally and physically. For I became very ill towards the end, and am
only now recovering slowly. – What you say about my music and subsequently about the new classicism is most pleasing to me. You *must*
get hold of Schönberg's new choral pieces![2] (U. E.) They say it all! –
Forgive me for not writing to you myself, but I am in a great hurry, as
I must still complete the fair copy of the quartet and in c. 8 days also
expect to travel to Prague with my wife.
   We both send you our warmest greetings, and I hope still to hear
from you before my departure.
                         Affectionately yours,
                            Alban Berg
Postscript: Soma has been in Berlin since 14 days ago; addr. W 50
Augsburgerstr. 44[III]

Original: manuscript written by a third party from dictation, with Berg's own
signature.

1 The Viennese composer and jurist Julius Bittner (1874–1939), who had
been made an external member of the Akademie der Künste (Academy of the
Arts) in Berlin in 1925, did not succeed in moving to Berlin.

2 Berg is thinking of the piece 'The New Classicism', to Schönberg's own text, from the Three Satires for Mixed Choir op. 28.

---

46 WIESENGRUND-ADORNO TO BERG
    FRANKFURT, 11.11.1926

thinking of you I accompany you and your work with the most affectionate wishes = your faithful wiesengrund

Original: telegram.

---

47 WIESENGRUND-ADORNO TO BERG
    FRANKFURT, 12.11.1926
    JOINT CARD

Frankfurt. 12 Nov. 26.

Dear Herr Berg, although Casella, Milhaud and d'Albert[1] have thrown us together here, we feel unified under a radically different sign, and send you our heartfelt greetings.
Your faithful Wiesengrund.

We would love to know some details about Wozzeck in Prague! Our travels[2] have so far been most successful. Yours Rudolf Kolisch

I am in Vienna on Sunday. Very excited about everything.
With devotion
Steinberg[3]

Emmy Ferand[4]   Valeria Kratina[5]

Original: postcard; stamp: Frankfurt (am Main), 13.11.26. Manuscript with additional notes by Rudolf Kolisch, Emmy Ferand, Hans Wilhelm Steinberg and Valeria Kratina.

1 Alfredo Casella played the solo part in the German premiere of his Partita for Piano and Orchestra under Clemens Krauss (for Adorno's review, see *GS* 19, p. 87). The programme for that concert also included Casella's *La Giara*; in addition, Adorno reviewed the performance of Darius Milhaud's *Le bœuf sur le toit* (see *GS* 19, p. 86) for *Die Musik*. The premiere of Eugen d'Albert's opera *Der Golem*, in a production by Lothar Wallenstein and under the musical direction of Clemens Krauss, took place on 14 November in Frankfurt (for Adorno's review, see *GS* 19, p. 85f.).

82

2 A concert tour with the Kolisch Quartet.

3 The conductor Hans Wilhelm (later William) Steinberg (1899–1978), who became Alexander Zemlinsky's successor at the Deutsches Landestheater in Prague, was musical director at the Frankfurt opera from 1929 to 1933. Steinberg emigrated first to Palestine, then to the USA.

4 This is presumably the wife of the musicologist Ernst (Thomas) Ferand, who was director of the Helleraus-Laxenburg Schule near Vienna from 1925 to 1938.

5 The dancer Valeria Kratina (1892–1983) had been director since 1925 of the Laxenburger Tanzgruppe Kratina, who performed the piece by Milhaud in Frankfurt.

48   WIESENGRUND-ADORNO TO BERG
     FRANKFURT, 19.11.1926

Frankfurt, 19 November 26.

Dear master and teacher,
I have just read in the Frankfurter Zeitung[1] that Strindberg has been proved right once again, that you were once again spared nothing, and I see you before me now, declaring with defeatist pride that you had expected as much all along. This time, in the face of the truly astrological coincidence, I find myself unable to disagree with you. I can do nothing other than assure you, as ever, that I consider the life of 'Wozzeck' absolutely unassailable, that the work cannot be crushed by the merely existent, whose raw mythical force is its enemy; that it will perhaps only become truly manifest after the downfall of that fiendish society which snubs it today. Wozzeck, like no other aesthetic construction of our times, has a part in the truth, and everything that exists will sooner crumble before the truth than wield any power to eradicate it. A dead deputy mayor[2] can do as little to change this as a living critic can.
What seems more important to me than all this, which after all does not even touch Wozzeck, is what happened to you, who are not as resistant as your work. You have experienced enough horrors finally to learn to despise the persistent malice of the human race. But you have experienced too many horrors not to be filled ever more deeply with bitterness, to draw ever sharper boundaries to all things extensive. I certainly know how hard it is to reach you in your aloneness, and do not presume to do so. But perhaps it is of some value to you to know that there are a few people who cling to you with all their heart, with all their gratitude and all their faith. I can count myself

among these, and although it need hardly be said I wish to tell you once again today that I feel bound to you throughout all that fate brings, that my existence is inseparable from yours, and that, to me, your existence is in fact the measure of my own.

I could hope for nothing more than to be allowed the privilege of your company, and then to walk with you among the hills in Schönbrunn. This will, I hope, occur soon. Until then, I tenderly wish you all the best, and wish 'Wozzeck' triumph.

Extend many greetings from me to Frau Helene, Herr and Frau von Fuchs and Hermann Grab, who shall no doubt pay you a visit. Send me word: of how you are, how the performance was, how the situation lies.

Yours with faithful love,
Teddie W.

Original: manuscript.

On the dating: Adorno seems to have written *November 11th*; as, however, the scandal around *Wozzeck* began only with the performance on November 16th, which had to be broken off after Act II, and Adorno refers to the article in the *Frankfurter Zeitung* of November 19th, the letter can be traced to that date.

1 The *Frankfurter Zeitung* of 19 November 1926 (second morning issue, p. 3) stated: 'The state administrative committee has decided to forbid any further performances of Alban Berg's opera "Wozzeck" on the stage of the Czech National Theatre. The ban was issued following the scandalous scenes that took place during the work's repeat performance at the National Theatre on Tuesday.'

2 The mayor's deputy had died of a stroke during the performance on 16 November.

49 BERG TO WIESENGRUND-ADORNO
      VIENNA, 22.11.1926

ALBAN BERG VIENNA XIII/I
TRAUTTMANSDORFFGASSE 27 $^{22}/_{11}26$
TELEPHONE: 84831.

Thank you, my dear Wiesengrund, for the telegr. & the *kind* express letter. You have probably heard about the exciting days in Prague through the newspapers. But there was also much, very much in the way of fine things there: rehearsing with those so deeply musical Czechs (I was there 5 days before the premiere) The magnificent *voices across the board:* for the opera is for *singing*, like *any* other. Only now would you have had the chance to know the music completely. Ostrčil[1] perhaps not exceptional, but colossally diligent, correct, willing, enthusiastic; – orchestra superb (learned it outstandingly in *30* rehearsals) So that the premiere truly became a feast (for my ears too). Tremendous success: much greater than in Berlin. Already after Act I (where the love scene, finally sung with dazzling voices, went off like a bomb) In all I was called out some 30–40 times. All opposition to it *disappeared*; no one knew anything about the stroke-struck mayor (apart from those in his *immediate* vicinity) & people only found out through the newspapers the following day. For people abroad (including Austr.), this concurrence: (Wozzeck, mayor †) was of course a real treat!

The 2nd perf. was also a great success f. t. singers & went without incident before a full house. This was too much for the Czech Nationalist and clerical lobbies & they staged the scandal at the 3rd perf. (at which Alma Mahler & Werfel were present & sat with us in the box). So it was *purely political!* (To them I am the Berlin Jew Alban (Aaron?) Berg. Ostrčil bribed by the Russian Bolsheviks, the whole thing arranged by the 'Elders of Zion' etc.)

But it is certainly not the end of the matter. None of the other Czech parties, which all Czech composers belong to, will tolerate the *cancellation* of Wozzeck striven for, but *not yet achieved*,[2] by the Czech Nationalists (virtually Nazis); so there is still a chance that everything will turn out favourably.

Prague was also quite enjoyable in other respects. And I was together with Grab, whom I rather like.

I was very, very pleased by your truly friendly words & hope very much that you shall come to Vienna!

Otherwise nothing new. Or at least nothing so interesting that I would mention it in this hasty letter.

Write again soon to your
    old   Alban Berg
Fond regards from my wife!

Original: manuscript.

1 The Czech composer and conductor Otakar Ostrčil (1879–1935).

2 The Bohemian State Committee had, in fact, ruled after 16 November that further performances of the opera would be forbidden. Numerous Czech musicians, writers and artists protested against this intention, albeit without success.

Frankfurt a. M. 22 Nov. 1926.

Dear master and teacher, having received no reply to either my telegram, letter or card, I am only indirectly informed through Heinz Ziegler,[1] whose parents saw you in Prague. I can imagine that you are not in the mood for writing letters, and wish only to request from you a card to tell me how you are. Soon we shall see each other. Much to my surprise, Kolisch, whom I met here, has put my quartet variations[2] on the I.S.C.M. programme, and intends to perform them together with the 1st movement, which has long been finished. The scores went off yesterday to Vienna for copying; there was no time to send them to you first, as the fair copy of the score was only completed in the last few days. Greissle[3] (!) is to copy the parts. Perhaps you can take a look at the 1st piece before Kolisch receives the material and – hopefully – give your approval. *If you do not, I shall withdraw the piece!*

I arrive in Vienna at the start of December to work with the Kolischs. There will be much work to do, but I look forward to learning, regardless of whether or not the piece is performed.

Kolisch intimated to me that there was a possibility of Bach[4] vetoing the performance of my things in order to clear the way for a diligent Salmhofer.[5] If there should genuinely be difficulties, I would ask you to intervene.

With Heinsheimer, whom I met here at the indescribable Golem premiere, and who brought my folk songs[6] to Vienna, I have arranged for a substantial essay on your Chamber Concerto.[7] This time it shall *truly* be easy to read; despite all my reservations, I can no longer ignore the realization that the state of that music which matters, i.e. yours and Schönberg's, is so critical in our society that an apologist must above all act at the art-political level, and that means: comprehensibly.

Please see to it that U. E. undertake what they had promised me anyway: that I would receive the score *and* the piano reduction of the Chamber Concerto.

In a certain sense, I am relieved that the Prague scandal was fascistic, not musical. It is then less likely to harm Wozzeck in Germany and Austria than to aid it. Yet it is not as symptomatic of the musical situation as I was led to fear.

I enclose the essay on twelve-tone technique,[8] which, together with the one about you and 'Nachtmusik', represents my present theoretical stance. The F.Z. turned it down as too musically specialized, but now it looks to appear in Anbruch after all. I am very curious what you will think of it.

My *Habilitation* business is so far looking favourable; that is, the professor in question[9] has accepted the detailed abstract of my thesis. – The eight o'clock evening paper plagiarized me! –

My very fondest regards to you and Frau Helene. Write a card soon to your faithful

Teddie W.

Original: manuscript.

1 The Prague writer Heinz Ziegler (1903–1944) was a friend from Hermann Grab's youth.

2 This is the second of the Two Pieces for String Quartet op. 2.

3 Felix Greissle (1894–1982), a student of Schönberg, whose daughter he was married to, worked as lector for Universal Edition; he emigrated to the USA in 1938.

4 The music writer David Josef Bach (1874–1947), a friend from Schönberg's youth, had started the Workers' Symphony Concerts, and was director of the social democrat art office at that time; he emigrated to England in 1938.

5 The Austrian conductor and composer Franz Salmhofer (1900–1975).

6 Adorno's *Sept chansons populaires françaises arrangées pour une voix et piano* (see *Compositions 1*, pp. 92–100) were premiered at Southwest German Radio in Frankfurt on 20 June 1929 by Margot Hinnenberg-Lefèbre and the composer; they were not published by Universal Edition.

7 The plan seems not to have been carried out. For his Berg monograph, Adorno wrote his 'Epilegomena zum Kammerkonzert' on the Chamber Concerto (see *GS* 13, pp. 434–51), and there is a radio lecture on the work from 1954 (see *GS* 18, pp. 630–40). There is a longer passage in Adorno's essay 'Die stabilisierte Musik' from summer 1927 that deals with the concerto (see *GS* 19, pp. 100–12).

8 See letter no. 30, note 4.

9 This is Hans Cornelius.

51 WIESENGRUND-ADORNO TO BERG
   FRANKFURT, 24.11.1926

Frankfurt, 24 Nov. 1926.

Dear master and teacher, our letters appear to have crossed once again. Mine, with the twelve-tone essay, went out yesterday evening, and this morning I received yours, which has entirely reassured me. I am happy to have been delivered post festum from my Strindberg position, which I had taken up – this time mistakenly – for your sake, and to be allowed to congratulate you on the Prague Wozzeck in spite of the 木 mayor. I shall also see to it immediately that the F.Z. amends the announcement of Wozzeck's cancellation[1] that it had printed. I am only sad not to have heard Wozzeck *sung*; I have always *thought* it.

My coming to Vienna shall now be a fait accompli in 10 days, assuming there are no further surprises. I cannot tell you how I long to see you. And the chance to study my quartet pieces[2] and hear them performed properly is of course quite something for me. Fond regards to you and your wife

from your old Teddie W.

I have just spoken to Holl on the telephone, and he told me that he received a telegram from Steinhard[3] yesterday that 'Wozzeck' has been approved, but only for private performances,[4] which strikes me as a little improbable. The F.Z. will print an article of its own on the matter,[5] but is of course prepared to include an authentic account of the current situation in Prague. Perhaps U. E. could send them one.

Original: manuscript.

1 Adorno is presumably referring to the announcement in the *Frankfurter Zeitung* of 19 November 1926 (see letter no. 48, note 1).

2 Berg wrote to Morgenstern on 3 January 1927 'that his [Adorno's] quartet, a truly splendid piece of work, was a great success here & that he can be sure of its being taken up by Universal Edition very soon' (Morgenstern, *Berg und seine Idole*, p. 171).

3 Erich Steinhard (1896–1944), from Prague, had been editor-in-chief of the journal *Auftakt* since 1921.

4 The rumour that 'the performance of "Wozzeck" has meanwhile been approved for private workers' and society concerts' (according to the editorial remarks in the *Frankfurter Zeitung* following the report cited in the next note) was not confirmed.

5 This article appeared on 27 November on p. 2 of the first morning issue:

A new 'Wozzeck' case. Prague, November 20th.

Alban Berg's opera 'Wozzeck', as is well known, was the object of loud protests and malicious attacks in the press on the occasion of its premiere in Berlin just one year ago. Now that same work, which is reckoned – also here – to be very significant, has been subjected, after a truly dazzling first performance at the Czech National Theatre, to similarly spiteful and embarrassing treatment. The Bohemian State Administrative Committee ruled after the third performance that it should definitively be removed from the season's programme on account of the disturbances (or as it is rather differently put: 'owing to the leading lady's illness').

It should first of all be emphasized that the premiere and the follow-up performance surpassed all expectations in their success, as the Prague audience did justice to their reputation as one of those in Europe most attuned to the times. If a certain resistance could be sensed during the first two performances of 'Wozzeck', it applied – so it seems to me – more to the certainly well-meant applause of those equipped with a little too much endurance, as well as dynamically extraordinary powers. It was a tragic coincidence that the deputy mayor of Prague, a well-known man also in literary circles, suffered a stroke on account of the surges of applause and the stirrings of resistance in his box, and died. But the theatre management should not be blamed for placing the third performance – which came to a premature end – on the burial day of this victim, a performance which, in the presence of Alma Maria Mahler, the work's dedicatee, became a debacle of a kind that has surely taken place only rarely in the history of theatre. 'Wozzeck' was broken off after the second act, the theatre had to be cleared by the police, and the heated debates continued in front of the building. The resistance was organized; the mere news that the mayor of Prague was protesting against the opera with six box-subscribers was sufficient to animate the sirens and whistles of various youths that evening during the work's gentle interludes, and thus to cause the curtain to fall.

The majority of serious Czech newspapers condemned the tumultuous events, and also did justice to the qualities of 'Wozzeck' in an objective, even enthusiastic manner. Admittedly the conservative newspapers, primarily for 'anti-communist' reasons (Berg has little to do with such tendencies!), saw in the performance a triumph of Bolshevism: 'a new aspect of the efforts to bolshevize behind the innocent mask of art'. The conductor was even turned into 'a Bolshevist exponent of Leningrad'. For art-historical reasons (one could recall Wagner's dictionary of invective) we shall cite one of these 'judgements':

'It was Berg's intention to cast a bomb of depravity on stage and to spread anarchy in order to mask his own creative impotence; if you were to hear the orchestra, you would suppose yourself in a menagerie at the beasts' feeding time; unbearable intervals, such that the listener has the impression of sitting before alcoholics who, in their delirium, are emitting screams of desperation, in fact everything in this opera reeks powerfully of liquor . . .; Alban Berg, the "Berlin Jew" . . . (it is well known that Berg is Viennese and stems from a line of upper-class Bavarian Catholics).'

52 WIESENGRUND-ADORNO TO BERG
FRANKFURT, 28.11.1926

Frankfurt, 28 Nov. 1926.

Dear master and teacher, I beg you *urgently* and *immediately* to attend to my quartet, to look at it and, in case there is some resistance

89

(of which I know nothing, but which I certainly expect, as I am currently being pursued by disasters), to defend it. By the time you receive these lines, the quartet should have been copied and should be at U. E., and Kolisch should have returned from his concert tour.

The performance is, in human terms, literally an *existential* matter for me. If I cannot come to you this week and talk, make music and study the piece with you, I do not know how I am to go on living for the next weeks, as there is otherwise little reason to do so. Even the fact of the public performance of a piece of mine, which I would not normally care about if I were hearing it for myself, has taken on an entirely distorted and disproportionate significance for me.

I am so devastated by events that no help or support could be too drastic for me.

What I had implied to you in the summer has now occurred, in a terrible and utterly senseless manner. The woman[1] for whom I had given everything has left me for another – in a way that only Kafka would be equal to.

Assuming that the quartet business does not take a catastrophic turn, I shall be in Vienna on Sunday, perhaps already Saturday, and will presumably stay at my usual guesthouse again.[2] Telephone 22–1–32, I believe.

Write a few words before then

to your faithful Teddie W.

Original: manuscript.

1 This – as is clear from letter no. 54 – is Ellen Dreyfuss-Herz.

2 In 1925, Adorno had stayed at the guesthouse Luisenheim, situated in the 9th district at Eisengasse (now Exnergasse) 2.

53   MARIA WIESENGRUND-ADORNO TO BERG
     FRANKFURT, 27.12.1926

Frankfurt M.-Oberrad 27.12.26

Dear esteemed Herr Berg, your most kind and affectionate card[1] was such a great source of joy to myself and to us all as I can hardly express! I only wish to thank you with all my heart for your love and concern for Teddie. Today we received a long, happy letter from him. –

By all accounts the 'Wiener-Streichquartett' played wonderfully. Naturally, we too hope to hear the quartet[2] soon. –

But now: when will you and your dear wife come to visit us? We would be so very happy to receive you, and would do our best to make it as pleasant as possible for you.

I hope we shall meet again very soon indeed!

With many warm regards from my sister my husband and myself to your dear wife and to you

Yours,

Maria Wiesengrund-Adorno

Original: manuscript.

1 Berg's card to Adorno's parents has not survived among their belongings.

2 Berg wrote to Schönberg on 13 December 1926 concerning Adorno's quartet:

> The performance of Wiesengrund's incredibly difficult quartet was a *coup de main* for the Kolisch Quartet, who learned it in 1 week and performed it quite clearly. I find Wiesengrund's work very good and I believe it would also meet with your approval, should you ever hear it. In any event, in its seriousness, its brevity, and above all in the absolute purity of its entire style it is worthy of being grouped with the Schönberg school (and nowhere else!). (*The Berg–Schoenberg Correspondence*, p. 355)

54 WIESENGRUND-ADORNO TO BERG
FRANKFURT, 15.1.1927

Frankfurt M.-Oberrad.
15 January 1927.

Dear master and teacher, please accept my most heartfelt congratulations upon the success of the quartet,[1] which, so I hear, was by all accounts quite unheard of, and many thanks for your message.[2] The work's inner success was beyond doubt after a perusal of the score; but it is particularly gratifying and affirmative that it has now been followed so self-evidently by external success, that people are engaging with your lonely music. I need hardly tell you how much it pains me that I had to miss the premiere of the quartet – this of all quartets –; it is but a small comfort that I heard 4 movements and studied 2 with you. But it was not possible with the best will in the world to leave Frankfurt at present. I must stick at it here for the sake of my thesis: in the hope of buying myself, through a few months of subaltern concentration, sufficient freedom finally to be able to apply myself entirely to what matters. I am all the more constrained to keep up this concentration for having still been affected, after my return from Vienna, with the influenza I had managed to suppress (and not

91

sublimate!) there, which made itself rather painfully felt in swellings of the glands and considerable chest pains. Meanwhile I have taken the time to recover in peace, and I am now physically quite well and fit for work.

Please tell me more about the performance. Did you work much with Kolisch? How did Stutshevsky[3] fit in? What did the sustained chords in the Presto sound like, in fact the Presto in general? And the Allegro misterioso, which I have not yet heard? And how did you have them play the end of the Largo? I am certain that the greatest surprise of all was the completely new quartet sound, which retrieves those experiences which had initially been transferred from chamber music effects to the orchestra, this dark, crackling Wozzeck orchestra, and thus orchestrally enriched, for the chamber style! Please write to me at length of these matters, if you can find the time! Every detail of it is of the greatest importance to me!

Now I hope you are immersed in the Baudelaire,[4] and am curious in the extreme.

Today, if I am correctly informed, Wozzeck is on once more in Berlin for the first time; in the Kroll-Oper.[5] My friend Carl Dreyfuss,[6] who travelled to Berlin yesterday, hopes to be able to hear it. As he is presumably coming to Vienna around the middle or end of next week (on account of his lady friend, the dancer Ilona Karolevna,[7] who is currently appearing with Ronacher), he will thus, assuming you wish to see him, be able to tell you at length about it. It would incidentally mean a great deal to me if you could make his acquaintance and tell me your opinion about him. He is, to give you some information, the former husband of my lady friend Ellen Dreyfuss-Herz, namely the same one who left me. I should add that he is a philosopher by training, a major industrialist by profession and out of necessity, and a man of letters by inclination.

I had arranged with Heinsheimer for a substantial essay on the Chamber Concerto, and he wanted to send me the piano reduction, but has so far failed to do so. Would you see to it? This time the essay will truly be easy to follow, i.e. it will restrict itself to an explication of intra-musical aspects and of the formal idea, without taking my interpretation any further than the most immediate material evidence allows. I shall also write without the least terminological encumbrance.

– My external situation has rather changed, to the extent that my foremost rival[8] for the *Habilitation* has been disqualified through the resistance of the professor in charge, which has greatly increased my chances. The question is now only whether the influence of a different professor[9] not directly involved in the *Habilitation*, who hates me for private reasons, extends far enough to block the *Habilitation* indirectly. Aside from this, there should not be any other substantial obstacles.

I intend to prevent the performance of my songs in the 'Frankfurter Kammermusikgemeinde', where they had been placed on the programme without my involvement or even consent, as my conditions (a set of at least 7 songs and an accompanist of my recommendation, preferably Steuermann) were not fully accepted. It is less due to the conditions than because the entire setting does not appeal to me.

The state of my private life is unchanged; i.e. bad. It is very difficult for me to be unable to come to Vienna all the time; your company and the music-making in our circle were the only things that could balance me. Here everything is more of a muddle than ever.

How is Frau Helene? From the programme, I see with joy (namely from her signature!) that she celebrated with you, and is hence no longer entirely lost to the world![10] Perhaps she will also join the celebrations after my next quartet, in so far as there is anything to celebrate!

Has your toe recovered completely?

– I am composing songs, as far as my dull work allows, and working on the quartet finale. It is of course progressing slowly.

Fond, warmest regards to you both
from your ever devoted
Teddie W.

Original: manuscript.

1 The premiere of the *Lyric Suite* by the Kolisch Quartet had taken place on 8 January 1927 in the Kleiner Musikvereinssaal (small music society hall) in Vienna.

2 This message, which appears to have been written on the programme booklet from the premiere of the *Lyric Suite* with the Bergs' signatures (see further down in the letter), has not survived among Adorno's belongings.

3 The cellist Joachim Stutshevsky (1891–1982) had been a member of the Wiener Streichquartett since its formation; he left the quartet in February 1927. Adorno may have confused him with Felix Khuner (1906–1991), who had joined the quartet as second violinist in mid-1926.

4 The meaning of Adorno's question is unclear; Adorno is still inquiring about 'Baudelaire songs' as late as May 1928 (see letter no. 76), citing Soma Morgenstern as his source. Possibly Berg had told Morgenstern that the final movement of the *Lyric Suite* was based on Baudelaire's poem 'De profundis clamavi' from *Les Fleurs du mal*, and that, according to one of the first plans, this movement was even intended as a song. Berg did not, however, compose any 'Baudelaire songs' at this time (see, however, letter no. 56), and the concert aria *Der Wein* came into being only during the first half of 1929.

5 The new production of *Wozzeck* with the cast of the 1925 premiere took place on 15 January 1927 in the Krolloper (Kroll Opera House), as the Staatsoper's own building was closed for renovations.

6 Carl Dreyfuss (1898–1969), who wrote his name 'Dreyfus' after the Second World War, had occasionally worked for the Institut für Sozialforschung before 1933; in 1933 he published the work *Beruf und Ideologie des Angestellten* (Profession and Ideology of the White-Collar Worker), in which he was able to draw on his experience as a leading industrial manager; Dreyfus emigrated to Argentina in 1938. Adorno collaborated with him on the 'Lesestücke' that appeared in the journal *Akzente* in 1963 under the pseudonym Castor Zwieback (see *GS* 20.2, pp. 587–97).

7 Unknown.

8 This is Leo Löwenthal.

9 Unknown.

10 An allusion (in the original German) to Mahler's setting of Friedrich Rückert's poem *Ich bin der Welt abhanden gekommen* (I have become lost to the world).

55 BERG TO WIESENGRUND-ADORNO
BERLIN, 18.1.1927

Dear Wiesengrund, this time (15.I.) it went without scandal. On the contrary: a colossal success 30 curtain-calls (Soma counted them!) almost certainly to be repeated. Thursday a lecture by Schönberg,[1] Friday his Pelleas[2] under Kleiber, Sunday return to Vienna, where I hope to find your reply awaiting me. A shame you are not here! All the very best from us all.
Your Berg
3.7. my concerto in Frankfurt a/M.
Very warmest regards Helene

Original: postcard: Berlin by night, Kurfürstendamm at the Fasanenstraße (Kempinski); stamp: Berlin/Charlottenburg, 18.1.27. Manuscript with an additional note by Helene Berg at the top of the picture.

1 On 20 January 1927, Schönberg gave a lecture in the Prussian Academy of Arts entitled 'Problems of Harmony' (see Arnold Schönberg, *Gesammelte Schriften I: Stil und Gedanke: Aufsätze zur Musik*, ed. Ivan Vojtěch, Frankfurt am Main, 1976, pp. 219–234).

2 The symphonic poem *Pelleas und Melisande* op. 5, after the drama of the same name by Maurice Maeterlinck.

ALBAN BERG VIENNA XIII/I
TRAUTTMANSDORFFGASSE 27   25./$_1$27
TELEPHONE: 84831.

Thank you, dear Wiesengrund, for your lengthy letter. Unfortunately,
however, I am not in the middle of Baudelaire, but was rather stuck in
Berlin until a day ago (not without its own poetry!) Awaiting me upon
my return was an overwhelming abundance of work (correspondence,
U. E. etc. etc.). For this reason only short & in telegram style!
    Chronologically: in daily rehearsals, which were truly pleasing in col-
laboration with *all 4*, the quartet prospered ever more under Kolisch,
receiving a quite surprisingly consummate performance on the 8th.
Equally surprising was the enthusiastic response from the musicians,
the audience and the press (which even makes me start to have serious
doubts about myself) A shame that you were not there. What *you* heard
of it was as good as *nothing* in its incompleteness. I was shocked to
death by my own work. But later it grew ever more beautiful & then all
the more *in context!* The 3rd movement even surprised me in the
novelty of its sound. It is a veritable *da capo* piece. And the realization
of the sustained chords was *very* close to how I imagined them. –
    Responding to a telegr invitation from Berlin, we went to the (only!)
orchestral rehearsal and the new production of Wozzeck in Berlin. A
repeat performance 3 days later, then a lecture by Schönberg on problems of harmony in the Akademie der Künste, & Schönberg's Pelleas
under Kleiber extended our stay to 8 days, which were by all accounts
very agreeable, albeit a little tiring. Unfortunately, we did not see as
much of Soma (who lived in our *immediate* vicinity)[1] (& Inge) as we had
hoped, as we were together with the Schönbergs (and Schrekers) *a great
deal*, & Soma also suffered a bout of influenza. But he should come to
Vienna for a while very soon. Incidentally: he is no longer the Soma we
knew; the struggle for existence has left its mark. But Berlin is glorious!
A metropolis! Impossible even to *compare* it in any respect to Vienna. –
    Perspectives for the near future: premiere of my concerto[2] in *New
York Stokovsky* with Gieseking and Szigeti. *Freiburg* Lindemann with
Miss C. Kraus &? *Zurich* & Winterthur – Scherchen with Walter Frei
and Steffy Geier – finally $^{3.}/_7$ in *Frankfurt* with Scherchen Steuermann
& Kolisch. I expect I shall certainly travel to Zurich.
    Petersburg is just around the corner.[3] Will I go?? I'd certainly like
to! –
    My quartet is to be printed any day now.
    But when am I to *compose?*

You at least must do so, so that you can inform me of your fine quartet's completion as soon as possible.

And do tell me at length about everything else concerning you yours with fondest regards

Alban Berg

And the Lästerschule????[4]

Original: manuscript.

1 Soma Morgenstern stayed in the guesthouse Duncan in the Augsburgerstrasse (see Morgenstern, *Berg und seine Idole*, p. 175, n. 2).

2 The first American performance of the *Kammerkonzert für Klavier und Geige mit dreizehn Bläsern* was, according to a report in the *Frankfurter Zeitung* of 18 May 1927, conducted not by Leopold Stokovsky, but rather by Artur Rudinsky; the soloists were Oscar Ziegler and Joseph Achron (1886–1943). The Berlin premiere followed on 19 May under Scherchen, with Walter Frey (b. 1898) and Stefi Geyer (1888–1956); the Zurich performance with the same artists, which Berg attended, took place on 25 March. In Winterthur, on the invitation of the patron Werner Reinhart (1884–1951), rehearsals for the world premiere and the Swiss premiere were held (see Peter Sulzer, *Zehn Komponisten um Werner Reinhart: ein Ausschnitt aus dem Wirkungskreis des Musikkollegiums Winterthur 1920–1950*, Winterthur, 1979 [309th New Year's bulletin of the Winterthur city library], p. 148). A Freiburg performance has not been traced; C. Kraus is presumably the pianist Else C. Kraus (b. 1899), a pupil of Artur Schnabel, who was particularly dedicated to performing the piano works of Schönberg (see also her recording, for which Adorno wrote the sleeve notes, *GS* 18, pp. 422–6).

3 Berg travelled to the Leningrad premiere of *Wozzeck* on 13 June (cf. letter no. 63).

4 Berg is asking about Adorno's review of the premiere of Klenau's opera *Die Lästerschule* in Frankfurt; it was printed in the April issue of the journal *Die Musik* (see *GS* 19, p. 90f.).

57   BERG TO WIESENGRUND-ADORNO
      VIENNA, 12.2.1927

ALBAN BERG VIENNA XIII/I
TRAUTTMANSDORFFGASSE 27
TELEPHONE: 84831.

My dear doctor, I am really *very* pleased that you remembered my birthday & sent me such a lovely present for it.[1] Your telephone greeting yesterday (via Gall)[2] also gave me a most pleasant surprise & made me exclaim: '*I* too have a telephone!' Which may have been caused above all by the fact that I have heard nothing from you for so long (not even in 'Musik'!). I daresay you received my letter of the 25./I. So please write at length about how you are. I am almost beginning to worry about you! Mid-March we are travelling to Switzerland (on the invitation of Reinhart), where Scherchen is doing my 'Concerto' on the $^{25.}/_{III}$ On the $^{29.}/_{III}$ Webern is doing it *here*[3] with Steuermann & Kolisch, after which follow Freiburg & New York. The 'Quartet' will be premiered, so to speak, in Donaueschingen.[4] Kleiber had great success with the 'Bruchstücke' in Leningrad.[5] The complete opera will follow there soon. I am not finding *any* time to compose! Fondest regards from us both

Your Berg

LÄSTERSCHULE????

Original: postcard; stamp: Vienna, 12.II.27. Manuscript.

1 Adorno's present on the occasion of Berg's forty-second birthday on 9 February has not been traced.

2 On this telephone conversation and on Erna Gál, see letter no. 59 and note 2 there.

3 The Vienna premiere of the Chamber Concerto took place on 31 March.

4 The *Lyric Suite* was originally to be played by the Amar Quartet during the Donaueschinger Musiktage, which had been taking place in Baden-Baden under the name Deutsche Kammermusik Baden-Baden since 1927; in fact, however, it was performed by the Kolisch Quartet, to whom Berg had granted exclusivity rights.

5 The performance of the *Bruchstücke* from *Wozzeck* on 5 February had finally paved the way for the opera, whose premiere – planned for early May – took place on 13 June; see Ernst Hilmar, *Wozzeck von Alban Berg: Entstehung – erste Erfolge – Repressionen (1914–1935)*, Vienna, 1975, p. 56.

58 ALBAN BERG TO WIESENGRUND-ADORNO
   VIENNA, c. EARLY MARCH 1927
   JOINT POSTCARD

Dear Wiesengrund, I read your opera review in 'Musik' in vain*

Fondly yours Berg

* for I am slightly drunk & confuse the verbs. NB. On the 25th the 'Chamber Concerto' is in Zurich (we are going there) on the 29th in Vienna: please do write!

Dear Teddy, I still await a report on the Lästerschule!
Fondly   Helene

Dear Teddy, I have been awaiting your letter for months!! From the 16.III. I am back in Berlin. Fondly Soma

Original: picture postcard: Schönbrunn; evidently sent in an envelope, as not stamped. Manuscript with additional notes by Helene Berg and Soma Morgenstern.

On the dating: The card was most likely written in the first half of March, as Berg makes no mention of the month when giving the date of the Zurich premiere, and Morgenstern wanted to be back in Berlin 'from the 16.III'.

59 WIESENGRUND-ADORNO TO BERG
    FRANKFURT, 16.3.1927

Frankfurt, 16 March 1927.

Dear master and teacher, I would long since have written to you if I had only been able. But I have been in bed for many weeks – have had a decidedly painful operation;[1] and now, during my convalescence, a feverish influenza has also taken hold of me, and so I must lie in the dark at all times – getting up is out of the question. I am at least up to writing a few lines today, whose purpose is to tell you that I am not disloyal, but simply dead. Above all, I want to clarify a misunderstanding that was especially painful to me. That telephone conversation with Erna Gál did not arise through a call from me, but rather from her – and which took me so much by surprise that my only response to the announcement 'Vienna here' and the sound of a female voice was to shout into the receiver 'Frau Helene, Frau Helene'. I only discovered much later why Miss Gál had called me; you will no doubt have heard what has happened to the poor woman since then.[2]

Now a request. You may know from Stein that I have agreed to deliver the essays on op 16, 24, 26, 27, 28 for the Schönberg issue of Pult und Taktstock[3] – which will now be somewhat delayed, as I am not yet allowed to work. Stein wrote to me that you are dealing with Pelleas and the Chamber Symphony,[4] and I would be very happy if my analyses of the late works could follow on directly from yours – firstly, because this is fitting if I am allowed to write with you about A. S.; secondly, because then the continuity of Schönberg's work would also

98

come to the fore in its representation. But for this I would need to *know* your essays. Could I have them – for a very short time only, they would be returned *immediately* – ? Or are there perhaps duplicates? I would be very, very grateful, and as my essays cannot be in Vienna by the 20th in any case, U. E. could no doubt also do without the manuscripts for 3 days.

In hospital, I have been examining the choral pieces and the satires in great detail, and have beaten time through most of them – and I am disappointed by both, especially the satires. Only the Chinese songs[5] are truly fine, above all the first, the second being rather too lacking in accompanimental characters; I am certainly aware that this is intentional, and I should think it would excite Schönberg, of all people, to fashion an extended piece for once without the tonal resource of contrast – but the structure of his music seems not to tolerate this – especially if, as here, it cannot even parry with *harmonic* contrasts. The first two choral pieces fail on account of the hair-raising, truly inartistic texts (has Soma seen them?); and the entire first song is, in its composition, of a blankness that is radically denatured, but to such a degree as to have consumed the very last of its substance. And the satires! Would the preface,[6] extended and printed in Anbruch, not truly have sufficed? Does all this have to be chewed over compositionally, must the 19th century be prolonged into all eternity, and must art be made out of art – After the Teutonic Palestrina, is there really any need for a Yiddish one? And what sort of humour is this, who laughs about this, for whom has all this been written anyway? If Schönberg (rightly!) recognizes that today's objectivism is worthless and reactionary, then he should make better music than the other, and restrict his polemic to the literary kind, if at all, but not confuse achievement with opinion and produce a childish aberration! If he's doing it out of resentment – well, then *he* should find another way to deal with it! The entire business is shameful.

The fact that Schönberg's current crisis stems not from the twelve-note technique, but rather from himself, is shown by your quartet. It is utterly impossible to compare your and Schönberg's recent works: yours are alive, while his have themselves become historical. Unless his demon still breaks free once more, unless the Suite[7] offers something truly new, he will become historical even to us. I do not say this lightly, you know better than anyone how much his music means to me, but I cannot ignore this insight.

What seems tragic to me is that his last works have all been absolutely right in their conception – but neither has he overcome their challenges at the aural level, nor do they overcome the listener! If *nothing* were to remain but this music, one would have to despair!

– I had hoped to surprise you with the little Klenau review in 'Musik'. Unfortunately this is no longer possible, but perhaps the pale manuscript can give you some notion of it too.

I have so infinitely much to tell you, and had intended to accost you in Zurich; but now I must still remain lying down. But I hope nonetheless to see you again very soon!

And thank you for the love and the faith that moved you to write that sweet card despite my silence.

Devotedly yours   Teddie W.

Forgive the handwriting; I am lying down, so I can do no better. Extend my greetings to Soma! And please also to Kolisch, and tell him of my illness, for I owe him a letter.

Original: manuscript.

1 No further details are known.

2 Rudolf Kolisch had told Adorno on 16 February 1927 that the pianist Erna Gál, sister of the composer and music writer Hans Gál, had attempted suicide on 13 February.

3 The special issue 'Arnold Schönberg und seine Orchesterwerke' contained only one essay by Adorno, on the Five Orchestral Pieces op. 16; see GS 18, pp. 335–44.

4 Berg did not contribute to that issue; Erwin Felber wrote on *Pelleas und Melisande*, and Ernst Kunwald on the First Chamber Symphony.

5 See Arnold Schönberg, Four Pieces for Mixed Choir op. 27; Schönberg took the texts to songs 3 and 4 – 'Mond und Menschen' and 'Der Wunsch des Liebhabers' – from Hans Bethge's translation *Die chinesische Flöte*, and the first two songs are based on texts of his own. Adorno wrote on both sets of choral pieces for *Anbruch* in 1928; see GS 18, pp. 354–7.

6 In the preface to his Three Satires for Mixed Choir op. 28, Schönberg explains to whom the individual pieces refer.

7 Schönberg had already finished composing the Suite for Piano, E flat clarinet, clarinet, bass clarinet, violin, viola and cello op. 29 in May 1926.

60 BERG TO WIESENGRUND-ADORNO
      ZURICH, 26.3.1927

Yesterday the *Chamber Concerto* in the delightful building overleaf under Scherchen (Walter Frey, Stefy Geier) A few days previously prem. in Berlin. Both probably inadequately prepared but presented very atmospherically. Warm 'succès d'estime'. On the 31.III. in Vienna under Webern (Steuerm. Kolisch). Thank you for your very kind letter, to which I shall respond from Vienna. I hope you are *well!* What operation was performed?

Fond regards from your Berg
& Helene[1]

Original: picture postcard: Zurich: Tonhalle; stamp: Zurich, 26.III.27. Manuscript.

1 In Berg's handwriting.

61   WIESENGRUND-ADORNO TO BERG
     FRANKFURT, 16.4.1927

Frankfurt, 16 April 1927.

Dear master and teacher, today in haste a request: you will probably receive a telephone call within the next few days from a lady by the name of Liselotte Reifenberg, who will probably also call on you at some point. She is the sister of the well-known art critic Benno Reifenberg, who, as you may know, is in charge of the review section of the Frankfurter Zeitung. She and her brother are close friends of Heinrich Simon,[1] and naturally also know the Klenaus. Liselotte Reifenberg[2] studies singing, wants to join the opera; and as she does not fit into the required mould for singers, she has asked me to recommend her to you and Steuermann so that she can receive your advice. Please take a look at the girl, and, if you have a favourable impression of her, advise her and perhaps recommend some suitable teachers or répétiteurs. I have only met her very briefly; she is no joyful sight, but seems serious, very astute and is reportedly musical. I do not know, of course, if you and your dear wife will develop any close contact with her, though I would certainly be very happy for the girl if you did, as she seems to be rather isolated in Vienna.

Many thanks for the card from Zurich – I heard accounts of Berlin from ear-witnesses who had a very strong impression of it. I was naturally particularly sorry to have to miss the Vienna performance, which was no doubt magnificent. But travelling was still out of the question; even now I am confined to Frankfurt, as I have still not fully recovered; but my condition has improved sufficiently that I can hope to go to the country after the holidays and finish my thesis.[3] As soon as I have done so, I shall come to Vienna.

Are you and Frau Helene coming to Frankfurt for the I.S.C.M. festival?[4] Sutter[5] told me that you are naturally invited, but did not yet know if you would come. It would of course be splendid and I would see to your accommodation – assuming you are not tied to Milton Seligmann.[6]

How is your health? And how is your wife? What is the state of Baudelaire, and of the symphony?[7] What became of your Schönberg essays? Did you see my long article on the orchestral pieces?

The address of Liselotte Reifenberg: III, Ungerstrasse 13, c/o Jungmann.

My sincere thanks in advance. I hope to see you soon at last; there is so much to tell that I would not know where to begin with it all in a letter.

Fond regards to you and Frau Helene
from your faithful
Teddie W.

Original: manuscript.

1 Heinrich Simon (1880–1941) was editor of the *Frankfurter Zeitung* until 1934. Paul von Klenau was married to Simon's daughter Annemarie until 1926.

2 Elise Charlotte (Liselotte) Reifenberg (1906–1973) studied singing; in 1939 she emigrated via Cuba to the USA, and for a time worked at the Metropolitan Opera in New York, then later – until 1969 – at the New York City Center for Fine Arts. Her stage name was Maria van Delden. (Source: letter from Dr. Jan G. Reifenberg.) No more could be ascertained about her stay in Vienna.

3 Adorno withdrew to Kronberg im Taunus to finish his first *Habilitation* thesis, 'Der Begriff des Unbewußten in der transzendentalen Seelenlehre'.

4 The programme of this music festival included Berg's Chamber Concerto; see Adorno, 'Die stabilisierte Musik: zum fünften Fest der I.G.N.M. in Frankfurt am Main' (*GS* 19, pp. 100–12).

5 Otto Ernst Sutter was director of the Frankfurt Trade Fair at the time (see Paul Hindemith, *Briefe*, ed. Dieter Rexroth, Frankfurt am Main, 1982, pp. 130–2).

6 Berg had already stayed at the house of this affluent Frankfurt jurist as early as 1921.

7 See letter no. 8, note 2.

ALBAN BERG VIENNA XIII/I
TRAUTTMANSDORFFGASSE 27 $^{2.}/_{5.}27$
TELEPHONE: 84831.

Do not think, dear Wiesengrund, that I am unaffected by the various
matters related in your last letters – *in particular your illness*. Not a
day passes on which I do not frequently think *most intensely* of you.
But it is for this very reason that I have not written for so long: a brief
'note', such as my extensive correspondence involves daily, is too short
for me, too trivial for you & I do not have time – *though I would
dearly love to* – for a big one, one in which I could truly get everything
off my chest once and for all.

But now tell me at last what was wrong with your health?! What
operation did you have? It must have been a serious matter if it has
taken so long & caused so much pain. We are still *concerned* about it.
Will it be possible for you to come to Vienna? But when? I fear I will
be unable to see much of you; for in the 2nd half of May I expect to
be in Petersburg & after my return (presumably early June) I am
straight off to Trahütten to work, and will remain there until *July*
30th. In August presumably recovering in Vienna, or Karlsbad or
wherever & in the autumn perhaps another few weeks in Trahütten
working some more. (I shall hardly be offered a professorial post,
really, all the more so because I recently (on the occasion of the elections) contributed my signature to a social democrat manifesto[1] (of the
40 intellectuals (Freud, Webern, Werfel etc. are also on it)) & the state
is Christian-Germanic.) So that I can hopefully continue to work
during the autumn, in so far as I have any, or in so far as I *can* still
compose, which I am inclined to doubt.

From this monthly agenda you can also see, however, that I shall *not*
come to Frankfurt. I am really not needed there at the performance of
my 'Concerto'. Steuerm. & Kolisch know everything. As Scherchen will
have more rehearsals than in Berlin & Zurich, he shall do his best with
more success, so that I am truly *superfluous*. And after the incredible performance by Webern[2] (13 rehearsals with the V^{na} Philharmonic), I am
anything but eager to hear it *differently*. On this count I went through
enough in Berlin & Zurich. At any rate, I thank you and your loved ones
most fondly for the invitation; it certainly would have given me great
pleasure to follow you and celebrate the 'succès d'estime' in your
parents' house over a few glasses of Rhine wine from your father's cellar.

Should your graphological talent attribute nervousness to this
writing of mine, then this is doubly true: in part I am writing while

riding on the tram, in part I am truly very nervous: twice per day I am visiting a sanatorium in Döbling where my wife has had an operation.[3] It is *frightful* to go through that; there are hours which consist of 60 eternities . . .

I only have the *peace of mind* to write to you, my dear Wiesengrund, because there is a truly well-founded prospect of recovery.

I greatly enjoyed your Schönberg article for Pult & T. & I very much hope that Schönberg will look kindly upon it – and thus upon its author.

I have so much to tell you that I do not [know][4] where to begin. Nor do I know what things I have actually *written* to you about already, and what things I have related to you only *in my thoughts*. For example, Soma was in Vienna, we spent much time together, but he, who had been utterly worn down in Berlin by these existential worries that suddenly came down upon him, was back to his old self in his beloved Hietzing. And: Mrs Mahler happened to make his acquaintance at our house & they got on uncommonly well. Each could sense the great quality of the other. When Werfel joined us – by chance – the following day [it was in the apartment of Mrs Mahler], a pointed literary discussion ensued; also one about 'Paulus'[5] in which Werfel was really rather cornered. But Soma was 'on form' like never before! – For the time being, however, this contact has not been continued. –

I have now heard nothing from Soma in months & I am worried. –

In Berlin I was together with Schönberg, who was most agreeable this time.

Today (after a long, inexplicable pause) Wozzeck is on there again: today the 4th time this season.

Switzerland is absolutely provincial. The population: Christians & Swiss to boot, that really is *too much!* But the gallery of that one Reinhart fellow[6] in Winterthur really is something *fabulous*. The Wave by Courbet, the Grand Inquisitor by Greco & another 100 or so of only the *very finest* works of art & all this in such a setting –

Enough for today. I am really too nervous to relate such matters coherently. Therefore only these fragments in old friendship fr. your Berg.

Original: manuscript with sender stamp.

1 The call for votes – 'A declaration by intellectual Vienna. A testimony to the great social and cultural achievement of the Viennese community' (cited from a photocopy of the printed announcement in the Sigmund-Freud-Institut, Frankfurt am Main, which Herbert Bareuther made available to the editor) – for the Viennese municipal elections of April 1927 bears thirty-nine signatures, including those named in the letter; it is not known why Berg's name is missing from this manifesto.

2 The performance had taken place on 31 March.

3 According to a message from Berg to Morgenstern, Helene Berg had an operation on a cyst on her neck (see Morgenstern, *Berg und seine Idole*, p. 180).

4 Editor's conjecture.

5 Franz Werfel's play *Paulus unter den Juden* from 1926, which was playing in Vienna at the time.

6 The art collector and patron Oskar Reinhart (1885–1965), brother of Werner Reinhart.

63 BERG TO WIESENGRUND-ADORNO
    LENINGRAD, 15.6.1927

15.6.27

Fondest greetings from Leningrad, where I & Wozzeck (the latter in a very expressionistic constructive directorial production)[1] have had a most especially good time, from your Berg, who is, however, a little cross that you did not ignore his long letter of c. $^{3.}/_{5}$.
   From 22.6. in Trahütten Post: Deutschlandsberg via Graz Steiermark

Original: picture postcard: Leningrad, state opera (formerly Marientheater); stamp: Leningrad, 15.VI.27. Manuscript; on the picture side in Berg's handwriting: *Das Opernhaus.*

1 The director of the Leningrad performance was Sergei Radlov; the conductor was Vladimir Dranishikov; the sets were designed by Moisei Levin.

64 WIESENGRUND-ADORNO AND
    EDUARD STEUERMANN TO BERG
    FRANKFURT, 3.7.1927
    JOINT CARD

Dear friend, now it is over, the performance[1] was very good (I shall still write to you at length about it) and a true popular success. In many things I admired the conductor, – though I no less often invoked your spirit and Webern's. What a shame you were not here! Warmest regards to you and your wife. Yours,

                    E. S.

   Kolisch

Dear master and teacher, allow me, before I report to you at length –
I heard the work and all the rehearsals – allow me to thank you with
all my heart for the great, the one and only true thing that you have
given to me and to us all! Yours with faithful love Wiesengrund.

Warm regards   Stina Sundell[2]
                Josie Rosanska[3]
                Felix Khuner[4]
Such a pleasure to hear your work, warm regards Else C. Kraus.[5]

Original: postcard: Town Hall, Unity Monument; stamp: Frankfurt, 3.7.27.
Manuscript with additional notes by Rudolf Kolisch, Stina Sundell, Josefa
Rosanska, Felix Khuner and Else C. Kraus.

1 Under Scherchen's direction, Steuermann and Kolisch performed Berg's
Chamber Concerto on 2 July at the ISCM festival in Frankfurt; for Adorno's
review within his article on the Frankfurter Fest der Internationalen
Gesellschaft für Neue Musik, 'Die stabilisierte Musik', see *GS* 19, pp.
103–5.

2 This pianist, born in Sweden in 1902, studied with Berg from 1926 to 1927
and with Eduard Steuermann from 1927 to 1928.

3 The pianist Josefa Rosanska, Kolisch's first wife.

4 The violinist Felix Khuner (1906–1991) was a member of the Kolisch
Quartet at the time.

5 The pianist Else C. Kraus (see letter no. 56, note 2).

65   WIESENGRUND-ADORNO AND
     RUDOLF KOLISCH TO BERG
     CRONBERG-KÖNIGSTEIN, 22.7.1927

                                          Cronberg-Königstein
                                               22 July 1927.

Dear master and teacher, the two of us here, loyal even in our disloyalty, send you our greetings, and are with you in our thoughts. I have
now managed to hear your quartet (not in Baden-Baden, but in
Frankfurt) in the *wonderful*[1] performance by the Kolischs,[2] and taken
with me the most profound impression of it: the 3rd movement, which
I heard for the first time, was an exceptional surprise. I shall still be
confined here by my work[3] for some 14 days. Today I ask only that
you accept this card from your old Teddie W.,

                          who longs to see you!

Dear, esteemed friend, I hope you will not think badly of me for taking so long with my report. I have only the most pleasing things to report, but I have not found the time, as we are working very hard here. We have found an ideal residence in Seligmann's castle in Königstein. I hope you and your wife are well! The warmest of regards, yours Kolisch

Original: postcard; stamp: Höchst (Main) / Königstein (Taunus) / Bahnpost, 23.7.27. Manuscript.

1 There is a crescendo marking under this word.

2 The *Lyric Suite* had been played by the Kolisch Quartet to the greatest of acclaim during the Frankfurter Internationales Musikfest, which took place from 30 June to 4 July 1927, and in Baden-Baden on 15 July. In addition, Berg's quartet was the only work to be chosen (with request notes) for repeat performance on the morning after the final concert of the Frankfurter Musikfest, as Kolisch told Berg on 24 July. Beyond this, there seem also to have been private performances of the quartet.

3 Adorno's first *Habilitation* thesis.

66   RUDOLF KOLISCH AND
     WIESENGRUND-ADORNO TO BERG
     KÖNIGSTEIN, 23.7.1927

Königstein i. T.
23.7.27.

Esteemed friend,
    the explanation for my long silence: since being called to Frankfurt unexpectedly soon by telegram, I have had no time to gather myself for a letter.
    I immediately had to jump into the turmoil of rehearsals, concerts, receptions, luncheons, dinners, visits, discussions, excursions etc., from which – completely exhausted – I escaped here, where we are able once more to work in peace under ideal conditions, freed from all concerns by the exceptional hospitality of the Seligman family.
    Owing to the delay in my report, I shall probably not be the first to tell you of the incredible success of your quartet in B-Baden. (I suppose my telegram did not arrive?)
    Whatever you may have heard is insufficient to give you a notion of the intensity of this success, which means all the more in the context of the American-mechanical orientation of the whole festival, geared towards a triumph by Hindemith, which was certainly unlikely to aid the reception of your music. (Now Teddy is coming, and will once more thwart the resolution I had made with such incredible energy to write this letter!)

Dear master and teacher, my guilty conscience grows in proportion to the days we are apart, and now the letter that Rudi has half-way managed to write is finally driving me completely to despair. And now – even that has come to a halt. Within the next few days you shall receive my long essay about Frankfurt, id est the Chamber Concerto[1] – as an advance payment, so to speak. Tomorrow I shall hopefully hear your quartet twice more.[2]

Do not entirely condemn your Teddie.

Dear Frau Helene, how are *you*? I have grown quite fat and heavy, and you would not scold me on account of my spirituality.

Original: manuscript.

1 In Adorno's essay 'Die stabilisierte Musik: zum fünften Fest der I.G.N.M.', Berg's Chamber Concerto forms the central focus; on the history of the essay's publication, see letter no. 68 and note 4 there.

2 Kolisch reported to Berg from Kronberg on 24 July that the quartet had played the *Lyric Suite* to 'various pilgrims from Frankfurt, among them Jemnitz' that day.

67 BERG TO WIESENGRUND-ADORNO
    VIENNA, 4.9.1927

4.9.27 My dear Wiesengrund, I read your article on the music festival & thank you *with all my heart for those words in it devoted to me*. I can safely say that what you have written there is the finest that has so far been written about me. I – & my wife also – are very happy with it & are reconciled, even though you had not given us any news for months. But the rest of the article is also *magnificent*. It makes one feel as if one had been there in person.

What else do you have to tell? Do you no longer come to Vienna at all these days? It seems that I shall come to Germany more often again Dec. Amsterdam (Bruchstücke)[1] January Zurich (jury)[2]

I shall also have numerous performances once more this season. Even Wozzeck in Kiev, Kharkov & Odessa.[3]

But *where* will it be that we see each other?

Morgenstern has been planning to come to Vienna *for the last month*. But he seems to be quite immovably stuck in Keilhof.[4]

Since Aug. 1st I have been in Vienna. Composed *nothing!* Heavy gastroptosis, on the way to recovery.

But now write soon to your warmly greeting
                                    Alban Berg

Original: manuscript.

1 The work was announced within the Concertgebouw Orchestra's concert series with Co van Geuns as the soloist (see *Pult und Taktstock*, 4 [1927], p. 135); the date of the performance is not known.

2 The jury meeting for the sixth ISCM festival in Siena, in which Berg participated, took place at the end of March 1928 in Zurich (see also Alban Berg, *Briefe an seine Frau*, Munich and Vienna, 1965, p. 561f.).

3 These cities had shown interest in the opera following the success of the Leningrad performance (see Ernst Hilmar, *Wozzeck von Alban Berg*, p. 56).

4 Morgenstern was staying on the Klenaus' estate in Beuerberg, Upper Bavaria.

68 WIESENGRUND-ADORNO TO BERG
    FRANKFURT, 6.9.1927

Frankfurt, 6 September 27.

Dear master and teacher, your letter – my greatest source of joy in a long time – has taken a great burden off my shoulders. For, things being as they are, the guilt I felt on account of my silence weighed so heavily upon me that it in fact prevented me from writing, and it is only now that I know you are not cross with me that I dare do so once more. And yet, I am less to blame for my silence than you may think. I spent the entire summer – already since May – in Cronberg im Taunus, working on my (hopefully) *Habilitation* thesis; I was only in Frankfurt for the festival, and otherwise not even a human being, only a moderately well functioning thought-machine, and incapable of even the slightest communicative utterance. Though I should explain that I did not withdraw to my isolation purely on account of the work, but in fact rather fled – from a quite unbearable mess that my existence here had become entangled in, and which has actually cleared somewhat in the months since.

Since a few days ago I have now finished my thesis, which has become a bulky volume, once and for all, and sent it to the responsible professor.[1] I can now breathe once more; but I am completely overworked, and my health and nerves are in very poor shape, the more so for not even having recovered from my operation; so that I intend to take 8 weeks of holidays, now, during the university holidays, when I can do nothing for my cause in any case. I shall thus travel to Italy via Switzerland on the day after tomorrow, stay in Fiesole, near Florence, for 14 days, then in Sicily for 14 days, and intend, if I obtain the visa, to spend October in North Africa, in Tunis and Algiers.[2] I shall return in November; my *Habilitation* duties will, if at all, only

109

arise in December; I shall finally be able to compose at length and without pressure once more, though I suppose I shall remain confined to Frankfurt until my business has been decided. Meanwhile, I think I shall be able to conclude my new songs,[3] and hope for a performance in the cycle by Steuermann and Kolisch, will *most definitely* come to Vienna in the course of the season.

It is really too obvious to require any mention that when you travel to Amsterdam, you must stop off in Frankfurt (which is on the way) for a few days, and, with all due respect to the Seligmanns, as *our* guest. But I shall still write it here now, in order to leave you no possibility of doing otherwise.

It is a source of profound joy to me that my essay and the words concerning you in it meet with your approval – all the more for my having had to abridge the essay for 'Musik',[4] allegedly because of its length, but in truth for political and art-political reasons, to such an extent that barely the skeleton remained; you would otherwise, I should add, have received the manuscript from me long ago. I also had to disfigure the section on the Chamber Concerto quite terribly. I am therefore especially pleased that you found it readable nonetheless.

The Kolischs – as I wrote to you – played me your quartet three more times, so that I have now heard it five times. Of all your works it is the dearest to me, perhaps even objectively the greatest. I cannot hide from you that the 3rd Quartet by Schönberg, which I also heard a few times, is in all seriousness no match for it, for all its technical comfort and all the greatness of its distanced objectivity. Its humanity has become mute, while your quartet, which is God knows no less constructed and not 'romantic', preserves its personal relation in blind confidence. This is the deciding fact. After listening frequently to the Schönberg quartet and studying the Suite op. 29 *very closely*,[5] I can no longer ignore the realization that, for Schönberg, the twelve-tone technique did become a recipe *after all*, and functions *mechanically* (above all in the rhythm, which grows monotonous through its incessant complementarities, but also in the arbitrary melodic formation; e.g. the crab-like continuation of the main theme[6] in the 2nd movement of the chamber suite). Essentially we all know it, only no one yet dares say so. This is not to belittle the significance of the Suite, its grand formal intentions, but it has unlearned the freedom of constraint, that property I sought to classify in your concerto. I cannot imagine how the last of Schönberg's pieces are to have a *history*: already now they are as transparent as glass, without secrets – there it is.

Quite independently of me, incidentally, and entirely spontaneously, Jemnitz[7] voiced during a rehearsal the same sentiment regarding the relationship between Schönberg's current music and yours. – I heard from Anita Seligmann (Walter Herbert's sister)[8] that Soma intends to come to Frankfurt *for good* with Inge Klenau in the autumn. I had wanted to ask him in the next few days whether he is still enough of an adventurer to accompany me to Africa in October – but I daresay Daddy[9] will hardly allow this, on account of the foreign harems.

It is *very* sad that you did not have time to compose (not *at all* for the entire summer?!), let alone because of a stomach complaint, and I am sorry with all my heart. I hope you will soon be entirely back in shape. I hope your dear wife has completely recovered and is well.

Please accept my very warmest greetings to both of you, and do not, once again, repay evil with evil, silence with silence   to your faithful

Teddie W.

Mail will be forwarded to me; my addresses are still unclear.

Original: manuscript.

1 This is Hans Cornelius.

2 In September, Adorno went to Florence, Fiesole and San Remo with Gretel Karplus (1902–1993), later his wife; the journey to Sicily, Tunis and Algiers never took place.

3 Adorno presumably means the *Four Songs for Middle-Register Voice and Piano* op. 3 (see *Compositions 1*, pp. 24–47), which he dedicated to Berg after completing the composition (the last song is dated 14.7.1928 in the autograph).

4 Adorno's essay 'Die stabilisierte Musik', which only appeared in *Musik* in September 1927 with the aforementioned distortions, was first published in its complete form in 1984.

5 Adorno published an essay on both the Third Quartet and the Suite in *Musik* in May 1928 (see *GS 18*, pp. 358–62).

6 Translator's note: the word *Krebs* connotes both the crab and, in the context of twelve-note technique, the retrograde of the series. Adorno's use of *krebsig*, while not necessarily a pun, thus automatically implies both meanings.

7 The composer and conductor Alexander Jemnitz (1890–1963). See also Adorno's letters to Jemnitz, which have been edited – together with Berg's and Schönberg's letters to Jemnitz – by Vera Lampert, in *Studia Musicologica Academiae Scientiarum Hungaricae*, 15 (1973), pp. 355–73 (Adorno's letters here pp. 364–73).

8 Anita Seligmann, who studied philosophy and had discussed a PhD on Robert Walser with Adorno before the Nazis' rise to power, and her brother, the conductor and student of Schönberg Walter Herbert Seligmann, who was known as Walter Herbert, were children of Milton Seligmann. Walter

111

Herbert, who had studied violin and viola with Rebner, was married to Rudolf Kolisch's sister Maria. Both emigrated to the USA.

9 Paul von Klenau.

69 BERG TO WIESENGRUND-ADORNO
    VIENNA, 29.9.1927
    JOINT CARD

Do you remember,[1] dear doctor, how the 4 of us sat here? *Where* might you be now? We extend you our affectionate greetings
Yours Berg

I hear that you intend to invite (not ask!) me to come to Italy: Please do not say no
Yours Soma

Dear Teddy, we long to see you!   Helene

Original: picture postcard: Vienna XIX Schlosshotel Kobenzl; stamp: 29.IX.2[7]. Manuscript with additional notes by Helene Berg and Soma Morgenstern.

1 Adorno was at the Kobenzl on 30 May 1925 with the Bergs and Soma Morgenstern.

70 BERG TO WIESENGRUND-ADORNO
    VIENNA, 30.11.1927

ALBAN BERG VIENNA XIII/I
TRAUTTMANSDORFFGASSE 27   30./11.27
TELEPHONE: 84831.

Dear doctor, I have decided to begin work on an opera early next summer. For this I have 2 plans, of which *one* will *most definitely* be carried out. So the question is now only *which*. For this purpose I am asking you too for advice: It is: either 'Und Pippa tanzt' or Lulu (the latter through compressing 'Erdgeist' & 'Büchse der Pandora' into a 3-act (6–7 scene) libretto)

What do you make of this?[1] As I will compose one (or perh. both) at all costs it is necessary to decide *which* of the two (or perh. which *first*).

In expectation thereof with many greetings to you, my dear Wiesengrund, your

Rushed!   old Berg

Do I owe you a letter? I think your last message was a card from Rome! (??)[2]

I request the utmost discretion![3]

Original: manuscript with sender stamp. Facsimile reproduction of the letter in Theodor W. Adorno, *Berg: der Meister des kleinsten Übergangs*, Vienna, 1968 (*Österreichische Komponisten des XX. Jahrhunderts*, vol. 15), p. 34f.; 2nd edn, Frankfurt am Main 1995, p. 58f.

1 At the time, Berg had already been occupied for weeks assembling the Lulu libretto, but had – as he wrote to Morgenstern on 27 November – become 'utterly indecisive' through the new production of Hauptmann's *Und Pippa tanzt* at the Burgtheater (Morgenstern, *Berg und seine Idole*, p. 194f.). In the same letter, Berg had discussed the advantages and disadvantages of the two opera plans, asking Morgenstern and, three days later, also Adorno for advice. Morgenstern supported the idea of using Hauptmann's play:

> I am in favour of Pippa for practical reasons. [. . .] I am no musician, dear Alban, but I have the feeling that you will not at all be retreating from your position in setting Pippa. Pippa is a playful, fairytale world. This world addresses all spheres of art, if it does not indeed surpass (as a genre) all others. And we have, in any case, often spoken [about] everything that speaks for and against Pippa. I believe I can even recall that at the beginning, when I first suggested the text to you, you had no reservations. And I only recommended Pippa because you were after something 'playful'. I think Wiesengrund was against it [see letter no. 23]. Wiesengrund naturally understands music better than I do, but I am certain that Wiesengrund would also have had reservations about Wozzeck before Wozzeck, as he simply wants to be covered on all fronts. Wiesengrund will presumably also have reservations about Lulu, which I shall also understand, as you yourself know. (Ibid., p. 201)

Adorno, for his part, evidently answered a few days after receiving Berg's letter, as Berg writes to Morgenstern on 8 December 1927 (ibid., p. 203). This letter seems to have been lost; it is located neither in the Berg collection at the Österreichische Nationalbibliothek nor in the Theodor W. Adorno Archiv, although Morgenstern, in his note on a passage in Berg's letter of 8 December – 'Wiesengrund's letter has just arrived, and far from making me unsure, has only reinforced my aforesaid intention to compose Lulu later. I shall send you this letter of W's, as I am certain that you will find it very interesting' – writes: 'Alban sent me the letter by Wiesengrund mentioned here, to show me that I was right in my assumption that Wiesengrund would be firmly against Lulu as a libretto. After realizing, however, that his opinion had made no impression on Alban, he asked Alban to send the letter back to him. Therefore Alban sent me this letter to Berlin for perusal' (ibid., p. 203, note a). There are no further witnesses to this request by Adorno. Berg's characterization of Adorno's letter does not, ultimately, give cause to suppose that he had actually argued against setting the Wedekind plays. It reads: 'Wiesengrund's letter [. . .] far from making me unsure, has only reinforced my aforesaid intention to compose Lulu later.' To suppose that this 'reinforcement of intention' can only refer to a rejection of Adorno's opinion is – to say the least – an act of mystificatory half-blindness or a deception of memory; Berg's formulation certainly does not support a questioning of Adorno's own account that he 'encouraged him with all my arguments to pursue the Wedekind opera' (*GS* 13, p. 357).

2 A card sent by Adorno from Italy – he was not in Rome – does not appear to have survived.

3 Added at the top of the second page of the letter.

71   BERG TO WIESENGRUND-ADORNO
      PORTOFINO, 30.1.1928

30.I.28.   We have been here – on the invitation of Alma Mahler & Franz Werfel – c. 8 days & – marvel, marvel & savour without end! Tonight I shall make the acquaintance of Gerhard Hauptmann![1] Warmest greetings dear doctor from
                                        Alban Berg & Helene

Original: picture postcard: Strada Portofino – Castello di Paraggi; stamp: smudged. – Manuscript with a signature from Helene Berg.

1 *Gerhard* [not Gerhart] *Hauptmann*: thus in Berg's handwriting.

72   WIESENGRUND-ADORNO TO BERG
      NEUWEILNAU, 6.4.1928

                                        Neuweilnau, 6.IV.28.

Dear master and teacher, finally, after shameful and tormenting delay,[1] free to do the only thing that is fitting: composing, I call upon you as my guardian, to rule as you see fit, and greet you with all my heart. Hopefully you are spending the holidays as pleasantly and calmly as I am here; and hopefully both in good health. An extensive letter to follow!
      Fond regards from your devoted
                                        Wiesengrund.

Original: picture postcard: Neuweilnau im Taunus; stamp: Neuweilnau, 6.4.28. Manuscript.

1 Also an allusion to Adorno's first *Habilitation* attempt. He had handed in his thesis 'Der Begriff des Unbewussten in der transzendentalen Seelenlehre' to the philosophical faculty on 14 November; his teacher, Hans Cornelius, rejected it as a *Habilitation* thesis in a letter to the committee members of 8 January 1928, whereupon Adorno withdrew his application – which he had, as a precaution, made only as an 'inquiry' – on 11 January.

73   MARIA WIESENGRUND-ADORNO TO BERG
FRANKFURT, 24.4.1928

Frankfurt-Oberrad M.
24.4.28

Dear Herr Berg,

Teddie asks me to write to you, and to say that he had wanted to write to you these last few days. Unfortunately, he has not yet been able to. For he was involved in a serious car accident on Saturday the 21st, and is lying in hospital, whence the ambulance brought him, with concussion, a deep head-wound, and heavy bruising. A bus drove into his taxi! –

Today, he is now feeling somewhat better, the doctors have declared him out of danger, and I am hurrying to carry out his request and to send you and your dear wife his regards. –

I hope you are both well! As soon as Teddy is able and allowed to write, he shall write to you.

Many warm regards to you and your dear wife from my sister, my husband and myself

Yours,
Maria Wiesengrund-Adorno

Original: manuscript.

74   BERG TO WIESENGRUND-ADORNO
VIENNA, 26.4.1928

Alban Berg, Vienna, XIII.
Trauttmansdorffgasse 27

26.4.28

My dear, poor friend, your mother's hand on the envelope immediately made me fear the worst. And upon seeing that the letter was indeed also from her, I was quite certain that something had happened to you. What a frightful business! How dearly I would like to be with you now, and reassure myself each day that you are feeling better. How dearly I would like to learn more than what your dear mother was so kind as to tell me. *How* heavy is the concussion? *Where* is the head-wound? The face injured? Where are the bruises? And how the healing of the various injuries is progressing.

How peculiar it is: you, who always lived outside of your body, are now forced to sense in every one of its fibres that you have one!

Thank goodness that Morgenstern* is there and is soon coming to Vienna. He can then tell me at length about all this.

We have not heard from each other (aside from your Easter card)[2] for a long time and I was very much looking forward to the letter you had promised – and now I receive *such* news!

For my part, I do not really have any news. I am still wavering between Pippa and Lulu. In the end I'll probably decide on Leonce und Lena.[3] *In any case*, I shall begin composing one of these operas in May or June (when I shall already be out in the country).

Some time ago, on Klenau's suggestion, I orchestrated the 'Sieben frühe Lieder' (1907), which he premiered on the radio.[4] They will be published – and I know you have always wished for this – some time from now.[5] They are the following: *Nacht* b. Karl Hauptmann, *Nachtigall* by Storm, *Schilflied* b. Lenau, *Traumgrekrönt* by Rilke, *Im Zimmer* b. Schlaf, *Liebesode* b. Hartleben, and *Schöne Sommertage* b. Hohenberg,[6] a school friend. As a sample, I enclose, in place of a bouquet for the sickbed, the manuscript of one of these.[7] The remarks in pencil are Schönberg's.

Now I wish you a speedy and complete recovery, and as painless a time as possible. If Soma does not come soon, I would ask your kind lady mother to give me further news of your condition very soon. Extend many thanks to her for her letter, and my warmest greetings to her and her sister, and also your father. Fond regards and best wishes, yours

Berg

Original: typescript with Berg's signature.

1 These date from 17 April 1928; see Morgenstern, *Berg und seine Idole*, p. 209.

2 See no. 72.

3 Georg Büchner's comedy from 1836.

* please greet Soma from me and thank him for his lines,[1] and tell him that on May 7th Karl Kraus is reading for the 1st time: Die Unüberwindlichen (Bekessy and Schober) (a play)

4 The premiere at the Wiener Rundfunk, in which Wanda Achsel-Clemens (1891–1977) sang and Paul von Klenau conducted, had taken place on 18 March.

5 On 3 November 1928.

6 Paul Hohenberg (1885–1956), with whom Berg had gone to school, later became an engineer; see also Joan Allen Smith, 'The Berg–Hohenberg Correspondence', *Alban Berg Studien*, ed. Franz Grasberger and Rudolf Stephan, vol. 2: *Alban Berg Symposium 1980*, conference report, ed. Rudolf Klein, Vienna, 1981, pp. 189–97.

7 The manuscript of the song 'Traumgekrönt' (see letter no. 76) is not among Adorno's belongings.

75   MARIA WIESENGRUND-ADORNO TO BERG
     FRANKFURT, 28.4.1928

Fft.-M-Oberrad 28.4.28

Dear Herr Berg, many thanks in Teddie's name and from us all for your most kind letter and your warm condolences. You cannot imagine Teddie's joy at receiving the song and your very kind letter. He sends you and your dear wife a thousand warm greetings!

It is a miracle that Teddie came out of it with his life, and *so* lightly. The concussion, that is to say the unconsciousness, lasted for a long time, and was then followed by heavy vomiting. He has a deep wound on his forehead that is healing well. The whole left side of his head is a rainbow of colours. –

The x-ray revealed three fractures of the pelvis! Yesterday and today he was allowed to lie in his armchair in the sun on the veranda. He was also allowed to make his first attempts at walking. The doctors are most satisfied, and we all hope that he will not retain any injuries except the scar on his forehead. In 8–10 days he should be allowed to come home. –

He asks me to tell you that he had just completed a lengthy song[1] on that unhappy day. He can hardly wait to be able to return to work. But it would be better for him to remain in hospital for a few more days and rest. He is not yet allowed to receive visitors, as much as he would already have liked to see Herr Dr Morgenstern.

Once again many thanks and many warm regards to you and your dear wife from my sister, my husband and your

Maria Wiesengrund-Adorno

Original: manuscript.

1 The completion of the setting of Theodor Däubler's poem 'Verloren' – the first of the *Four Songs for Middle-Register Voice and Piano* op. 3 – is dated 21.4.1928 in the manuscript.

76 WIESENGRUND-ADORNO TO ALBAN AND HELENE BERG
FRANKFURT, 14.5.1928

Frankfurt, 14 May 1928.

Dear master and teacher,

now the abominable intermezzo has more or less been terminated; I am at home once more, my head wound has healed, I can walk freely and without a walking-stick once more (albeit with a certain limp), I no longer have headaches and am more or less fit for work again; my hearing also remained completely intact. Of all the things that have happened to me these last three weeks, it was *your letter and the manuscript* that were the greatest source of joy to me. The song is magnificent; the first bars, with the opening on the Neapolitan sixth and the unbelievably bright effect of the tonic upon its first appearance, are among the most beautiful moments that could still have been wrested from our expiring tonality; and how clearly it is already Berg in its restraint and shy warmth, in spite of its seemingly Schönbergian technique and economy. I am happy that you are now publishing the early songs after all, and am quite sure that they will last as equals of Schönberg's op. 6; though it saddens me a little that only Daddy Klenau convinced you to do so, whereas I imagine that I myself already recognized some three years ago the incomparable beauty of the songs[1] more clearly than Klenau would ever be able to; but in those days I was still small and slight, and you would not believe me. – It is also very clear to me now, after seeing the texture of the Rilke song (start of the second verse!), why you orchestrated the songs; for the constructive polyphony at work throughout cannot content itself with the piano! Though I would consider it most favourable for the *distribution* of the songs if there were also a parallel edition with piano; but U. E. will no doubt take care of this.

To tell you a few things concerning myself: the *Habilitation* business indeed took the course you had prophesied. The same professor who had encouraged me to pursue the *Habilitation* let me down shamefully at the last moment, even though the entire faculty was in favour of my *Habilitation*; there was admittedly no actual rejection; but as the professor has fallen seriously ill and is about to retire, a *Habilitation* under his tutelage is certainly out of the question. It is

118

now the question whether I shall turn to Max Scheler, who has just been called to Frankfurt, whom you will certainly have heard of through Franz Blei or through essays by Hermann Bahr, and who is certainly an unusual man; there are a number of factors in favour of the idea, as I have many of the deciding people on my side, but it is by no means certain, as Scheler will be bringing a number of *Habilitation* students from Cologne. Whether my current, hardly Schelerian thesis (an epistemology of psychoanalysis) will be suitable is still completely uncertain; and it would certainly pain me greatly if that book, which I wrote largely as a means to an end, were to fall entirely short of this end, and I had to write something else; although with Scheler I would not have to make as many concessions. For the time being I am, to be quite frank, giving very little thought to all this, and if the entire *Habilitation* – a social matter, essential to me neither for its content nor out of economic necessity – were to miss its mark, I could not care less, and would au fond even be content. For my mind is now entirely on music, that is to say composing, and even if I were to carry out the *Habilitation*, my academic commitments would remain a secondary occupation. I have thus begun to compose energetically once more, and I think it is proceeding well. On the very day of the accident, I had just concluded the first in a cycle of four lengthy songs, and it seems to me that it is of some worth; I cannot tell you how eagerly I await your verdict; but you shall only receive the songs once the cycle is finished, as they are connected – not thematically, but according to formal weighting, as with the four movements of a classical quartet. I am confronted ever more clearly with the problem of developing a new technical approach that is carried out with complete motivic-thematic rigour, but at the same time transfers the connections present at the constructive level behind the scenes, so to speak, and appears entirely free on the external surface (thus in contrast to the technique of a piece such as the Chamber Symphony,[2] where it is visible at all times how one thing develops out of another). I remain convinced that the freedom of imaginative construction, as created for poetic purposes in 'Erwartung',[3] will be decisively fruitful for absolute music, more fruitful than any reconstruction of past forms; and I increasingly see in the twelve-tone technique the means for transferring the organization of material behind the façade, i.e. behind the sounding surface of the music, leaving that domain to imaginative freedom. Should you have seen my note on Schönberg's op. 29 and 30 in the latest issue of Musik,[4] you could find a more detailed exposition of some of this, precisely concerning the twelve-tone technique; and while writing about the Chamber Concerto, I was already getting at the problem of reinstating musical freedom, in the sharpest opposition to the new classicism; but I feel that I can realize these ideas better in

119

composition than through all theoretical analysis; compared to a single decent bar, all this talk about music is entirely meaningless. I have therefore told you about my latest opinions more for seeking your advice as a composer than for presuming any great autonomous value to my theories.

In Berlin, where I spent a considerable amount of time, perhaps with a view to taking over a critic's post (though nothing has come of it, even though Kastner in particular did his best to aid me),[5] I witnessed the premiere of Stravinsky's Oedipus. It was indescribably abhorrent, despite the magnificent performance under Klemperer; did you see my review in the Stuttgart 'Neue Musikzeitung'?[6] If not, I shall have it sent to you.

I am now, on the invitation of the Frankfurter Tonkünstlerbund, to hold seminars here offering an introduction to modern works and the problems of New Music. I have begun with early songs by Schönberg, and I shall then closely examine your sonata, which I have also analysed in great detail, with not only the greatest pleasure, but also gain; for one can really learn in nuce everything that is at all important from this piece. After that I shall take the Chamber Symphony. The seminars are very well attended (25 people, all musicians) and the participants contribute well.

I am naturally following the growth of your opera plans with the greatest excitement; Leonce und Lena strikes me as exceptionally suitable; it has been set only by Julius Weisman,[7] i.e. not at all. But Lulu would of course also be very good and if you do decide on Pippa, this decision will be enough to redeem Hauptmann.

What has become of the Baudelaire songs?[8] Soma told me that some of them have been written; I would naturally be most eager to see them, and would certainly consider it a good thing if you were to adhere to your plan.

Dear Frau Helene, many thanks for your card.[9] I had actually hoped to be able to come to Vienna very soon, even at Whitsun, but I am not yet sufficiently mobile to risk a long voyage, and will have to content myself with spending Whitsun in Königstein, which could best be compared to Mödling; except that there is no Schönberg or Webern there, only the Seligmann family. But I do hope to come to Vienna soon and then bring a decent amount of music with me, for which you shall forgive me some of my sins.

In the programme of the I.S.C.M.,[10] dear master and teacher, I was overjoyed to recognize your hand as a jury member – it is the first decent programme, in its totality, in the society's whole existence. I hope to travel to Siena for 'Musik'. Will you be there?[11] I would be most grateful if you could inform me soon, as my efforts for 'Musik' will depend on it; i.e. only if you are to come will I apply for it again.

A final request. Frau Dr Oppenheim,[12] whom I surely told you about, will be in Vienna over Whitsun. She is my closest (innocent!) lady friend, and a quite extraordinary woman whom you are both sure to like. She will call you, and I would be most pleased if you could arrange something with her and perhaps introduce her to one or two substantial people (Frau Mahler, whom she has long been wanting to meet); only, of course, if it should be possible without any compulsion or inconvenience for you. But it would be very important to me to learn of your impression of Frau O. Or is it immodest of me to occupy your time with this? If so, then tell me; I shall then tell Frau O. that you are not in Vienna. You should know that I would not have suggested this upon my own initiative, but rather upon the suggestion of Frau O, who naturally knows a great deal about you through me and would like to make your acquaintance!

Please give my regards to Soma, and ask him where the joint card he promised has got to. – Once again a thousand thanks for the indescribable joy that you, dear master and teacher, have given me. – Fond regards to both of you

your faithful Teddie W.

Original: typescript with handwritten ending and signature.

1 See also letters 33 and 37.

2 Schönberg's op. 9.

3 Schönberg's monodrama op. 17.

4 See GS 18, pp. 358–62.

5 No information could be gained concerning Adorno's attempts to take over any such post during his Berlin stay in early 1928. Rudolf Kastner was music critic for the *Berliner Morgenpost*.

6 'Berliner Memorial'; see GS 19, pp. 259–66.

7 The opera by Julius Weisman (1879–1950) had been premiered in Freiburg in 1925.

8 See letter no. 54, note 4.

9 Not preserved among Adorno's belongings.

10 Berg, as the Austrian delegate at the preparatory executive meeting in Zurich, had succeeded in having Webern's String Trio op. 20 and Alexander Zemlinsky's Third String Quartet placed on the programme of the ISCM festival in Siena from 10 to 15 September 1928.

11 Berg did not travel to Siena.

12 See letter no. 39, note 4.

ALBAN BERG c/o NAHOWSKI
TRAHÜTTEN IN STEIERMARK $^{15.}/_{7.}28$
POST OFFICE: DEUTSCH-LANDSBERG
A./~~D.~~ GRAZ-~~KÖFLACH RAILWAY~~

I have long owed you a letter, dear Wiesengrund. This Viennese life! –
As fruitless as it is – it takes up so much time! I have now been here
for 1 month & was very ill again (asthma) & needed a long time to
get myself back together again physically & mentally. But now I have
been working again for the last 8, 14 days, & am thus also managing
to work off some of the extreme pessimism of recent times. From
August 1st I shall be at the *'Berghof am Ossiachersee', post office:
Sattendorf near Villach*

                           Carinthia
and I intend to stay there well into the autumn & work. I hope I'll
succeed. To tell you a little more of myself: Expected performances:
$^{6.}/_{11.}$ the '7 Early Songs' with Heger & Miss Lehmann (?) in Vienna
then the same in Munich.[1] Furtwängler is likely to play the 3 movements f. strings from the lyr. suite in Vienna (Philharm.), Berlin &
Hamburg.[2] Darmstadt is once again *most* interested in Wozzeck.[3] Also
– Oldenburg![4] But that is all! Berlin & Leningrad will play it again.

It was wonderful in Paris,[5] all the more terrible in Zurich, a frightful city with even more frightful people.

But now to *you:* I have your last – exactly 2–month-old letter
before me. Daddy Klenau's suggestion was simply to perform the old
songs *on the radio*. Occupying myself with them then made me decide
(*presumably* in recollection of your *earlier*[?] suggestion:) to *publish*
them. What finally made me do so, however, was Frau chamber singer
Wanda-Achsel-Klemens exclaiming with the utmost enthusiasm:
'Well, I'll be blowed!' at one of the songs. Orchestrating them, I
should add, was most enjoyable. For now, only the piano edition will
be *published*. –

What is now – with Max Scheler dead – to become of your
Habilitation? And what is the state of this matter anyway, which I
[wish] for your sake could still be brought to a favourable conclusion[?] (despite your lack of interest).

Your *compositions* naturally concern me more. Is the song cycle finished? When am I to see it? Only then shall I be able to understand
clearly and respond to your theorizing in your letter. Being myself
stuck in a composing problem. This being: to write an opera from one
12 tone row!

I am very pleased to hear about your seminars in Frankfurt $^a/_M$! Something like that would even be suitable for *me*!

I have *not* written any Baudelaire songs.

Are you travelling to Siena? The only worthwhile items on the programme are Webern* & Zemlinsky (who was a tough nut to convince the others of) The other 12 works are *just about* ones that are 12 a dozen. I myself will not be in Siena.

I assume you received the joint card written with Frau Oppenheim?!⁶ We spoke only briefly, but quite pleasantly.

But! I have greatly enjoyed your various articles in 'Musik', 'Anbruch' & Pult + Taktstock.⁷ Especially the last one on Schönberg & the aphorisms in 'Anbruch'**! I am also convinced that Schönberg would like them very much. I was often together with *him*, incidentally, in June. He is splendid as always – & in pretty good shape.

& now to end! To you, who have hopefully *fully recovered* [for which our congratulations once more] the very warmest regards from your old

Berg

Also from my wife!

Warm and devoted regards to your dear 'mothers'!

Original: manuscript with sender stamp; loss of text through a tear in the centre of the second sheet. All square brackets inserted by the editor.

1 The soloist in the concert premiere of the Seven Early Songs conducted by Robert Heger on 6 November 1928 in Vienna was not Lotte Lehmann, but rather Claire Born; nothing is known concerning the follow-up performance in Munich.

2 The premiere of the arrangement of movements II, III, and IV for string orchestra was conducted by Jascha Horenstein on 31 January 1929 in Berlin.

3 The premiere at the Hessisches Landestheater Darmstadt did not take place until 28 February 1931; Karl Böhm was musical director.

4 The premiere was on 5 March 1929.

5 At the end of March 1928, Berg had played the piano accompaniment for Růžena Herlinger in a performance of the Seven Early Songs; the concert, which took place in the salon of Mme Jeanne Dubost, also included the *Lyric Suite* (see *Alban Berg: Leben und Werk in Daten und Bildern*, ed. Erich Alban Berg, Frankfurt am Main 1976, p. 200). Before this, the Paris premiere of the Chamber Concerto had taken place on 3 February in the Salle Pleyel, under the direction of Walther Straram; for Max Deutsch's report on this in a letter,

---

* Incidentally, what do you make of the Webern trio?

** In particular the *3rd* p 200 (serenitas)⁸

see *Alban Berg 1885–1935*, catalogue for the exhibition at the Österreichische Nationalbibliothek from 23 May to 20 October 1985, ed. Günther Brosche, Vienna, 1985, no. 370.

6 This has not survived among Adorno's belongings.

7 The May issue of *Musik* (pp. 605–7) contained the article 'Schönberg: Suite für Klavier, drei Bläser und drei Streicher, op. 29, und Drittes Streichquartett, op. 30'. The *Musikblätter des Anbruch* had published Adorno's sequence of aphorisms 'Motive II' in the issue for June/July 1928 (pp. 199–202) (see *GS* 16, pp. 260–5 and *GS* 18, p. 14f.; English translation in T. W. Adorno, *Quasi Una Fantasia: Essays on Modern Music*, trans. Rodney Livingstone, London, Verso, 1998). The essay 'Schönbergs Bläserquintett' appeared in the June/July issue of *Pult und Taktstock* (pp. 45–9); see *GS* 17, pp. 140–4.

8 The third aphorism reads:

> They are now speaking so much of serenitas, who comes marching along arm in arm with the new functionalism. If only one knew why we are suddenly all supposed to be cheerful. Is this why one has forsaken ailing Tristan, to turn his painfully twisted mouth into the grimace of 'keep smiling'? And even if expression in music has become dubious: why then must this expressionlessness, whose intention is still unclear, immediately stoop to the cheer of bright emptiness? Should it not be more difficult, indeed more meaningful, to realize the expressionless? Has serenitas not ultimately been hastily invented merely to convince people that emptiness is the Holy of Holies in their community? Is serenitas not in fact supposed to prevent that society from asking too many questions? There is an authentic serenade at the moment: by Schönberg. It is not particularly cheerful. (*GS* 16, p. 261f.; English translation [not used here]: T. W. Adorno, *Quasi Una Fantasia*)

78 WIESENGRUND-ADORNO TO BERG
FRANKFURT, 16.7.1928

Frankfurt a. M.-Oberrad
Seeheimer Strasse 19.
July 16th 1928.

Dear master and teacher,

I have heard nothing from you since my very lengthy letter shortly before Whitsun, and am somewhat concerned as to your well-being, or as to whether you hold something against me. Certainly your signature at the bottom of the joint card with Gabi Oppenheim and Gabi's accounts do not support this – but perhaps afterwards you did find the entire request inappropriate after all, and resented me for it. As I have not heard anything from Soma either since he left Frankfurt,

I am truly uneasy and would be infinitely grateful for some word from you. For the time being, I am helping myself with the best and most promising consolation: that you are composing, and are therefore in no state for any, absolutely any correspondence. I would thus be entirely satisfied with a card of clarification.

Today I am writing to you to tell you of the successful completion of my song cycle. It consists of four songs after various poets, two poems by Däubler, one by Trakl, one by Georg Heym; all fairly large and inward in character, and in addition also connected motivically; the whole a manner of requiem, in a way that no one will understand better than you yourself. So it is no occasional song production, but rather a heavily loaded and conscious attempt directed at song form as such.

On account of these songs I would now like to ask you – always thinking of that postcard – a number of things. First of all: would you make me very happy by accepting the dedication of the four songs? I have been planning a dedication such as this for years, but until now there was nothing I found sufficiently good, and above all nothing sufficiently expressive. But this time I hope I might dare, and that with the dedication I can display to you and to the public, which these songs are after all intended for, a small part of the great and profound gratitude I feel towards you.

Then: should I send you these songs now, i.e. as soon as there is an easily legible copy, or are you composing? In that case, I would naturally understand *completely* if you were unable to occupy yourself with any other music, and would spare you mine, and only send you the songs once you are back in Vienna. But I would ask that you tell me this quite frankly, as your own production of course takes priority *objectively* over all others and I could never justify the slightest disruption of this production.

Finally: I am considering having the songs duplicated for the time being – that is, until I have reached an agreement with U. E. I now recall that your student Klein owns a copying device, and wanted to ask you if you would advise it, whether it is very expensive and how I can reach him. I believe his address is Linz a. Donau, Volksfeststrasse, but cannot remember exactly, and certainly do not wish to undertake anything without asking you first.

This much for today. I am completely well, I am very much able to work and the conclusion of the songs by no means suggests the conclusion of my composing for this summer; I am working at the same time on the completion of another set of songs,[1] on the quartet finale, which I am now entirely rewriting after all – and at the same time have many far-reaching plans. I do not think that I will abandon composing again.

I hope you and dear Frau Helene are quite well, in the peace of Trahütten without asthma and at work, which I am of course extremely eager to see.

Are you cross with me for accidentally referring to the B flat major in the Rilke song as the tonic,[2] whereas it is naturally the subdominant of F major? But the passage is no less beautiful for it!

Fond, warm regards

Your devoted Teddie W.

In August, I hope to send you the analysis of your sonata[3] which I presented in my course, and which I shall have a lady student of mine put together. – I am now beginning the Chamber Symphony on the basis of your analysis.[4]

Original: typescript with signature and handwritten postscript.

1 Adorno's op. 1, *Vier Gedichte von Stefan George für Singstimme und Klavier* (see *Compositions 1*, pp. 8–23).

2 In letter no. 76, Adorno does not refer expressly to the key, but speaks of 'the unbelievably bright effect of the tonic upon its first appearance'. Adorno is presumably thinking of bars 9 and 10, where 'F major' is indicated in the printed version; the song – with two flats in the key signature – moves between B flat major and G minor.

3 The manuscript has been lost; see, however, the analysis of the Piano Sonata in Adorno's book on Berg from 1968 (*GS* 13, pp. 374–82; English translation: T. W. Adorno: *Alban Berg: Master of the Smallest Link*, trans. Julian Brand and Christopher Hailey, Cambridge, Cambridge University Press, 1991), which first appeared in the 1937 Berg monograph edited by Willi Reich.

4 See *Arnold Schönberg, Kammersymphonie, op. 9: Thematische Analyse*, Vienna, n.d.

79　BERG TO WIESENGRUND-ADORNO
　　TRAHÜTTEN, 20.7.1928

ALBAN BERG C/O NAHOWSKI
TRAHÜTTEN IN STEIERMARK
POST OFFICE: DEUTSCH-LANDSBERG
A./D. GRAZ-KÖFLACH RAILWAY

$^{20}/_{7}28$

Your dedication, my dear friend, was a source of great joy to me. I thank you for it with all my heart, and can tell you how *much* I am already looking forward to it. Naturally I wish to see the songs as soon as possible & insist upon it!

Our letters – obviously – crossed. Therefore only these few lines today. I am expecting to hear from Klein in the next few days & will then ask him about your copies. I think he has given that up.

I am otherwise also thinking of you a great deal: while reading – with the greatest delight – the 2nd volume of Proust (Within a Budding Grove).[1] Incidentally, I also derived great enjoyment from reading Kracauer's 'Ginster' fragment recently.[2] Please tell him!

My thanks again, my dear fellow & warmest regards
    Yours Berg

Fond regards!
    Helene

Original: manuscript with an additional note by Helene Berg.

1 See Marcel Proust, *Im Schatten der jungen Mädchen*, trans. Walter Benjamin and Franz Hessel, Berlin, Verlag Die Schmiede, [1927]; now in Walter Benjamin, *Gesammelte Schriften: Unter Mitwirkung von Theodor W. Adorno und Gerschom Scholem*, ed. Rolf Tiedemann and Hermann Schweppenhäuser, Supplement II, ed. Hella Tiedemann-Bartels, Frankfurt am Main, 1987.

2 Before the novel *Ginster: Von ihm selbst geschrieben* (Ginster: Written by Himself) was published anonymously in late 1928, Kracauer's novel had been printed in seventeen episodes in the *Frankfurter Zeitung* in April 1928 under the title of *Ginster: Fragmente aus einem Roman*.

80 WIESENGRUND-ADORNO TO BERG
    FRANKFURT, 17.8.1928

Frankfurt a. M.-Oberrad.
Seeheimer Strasse 19.
17 August 1928.

Dear master and teacher,

here I finally enclose a copy of my 4 songs, which are your songs. The copy is certainly not particularly pleasing to the eye and in the banal copyist's notes my music seems quite degraded. But if the music has any value, it must also be apparent in this guise and this copy is at any rate clearer and more legible than my handwritten one, although I am not a little proud of the progress in note-writing that I have made since that Viennese afternoon in the Imperial.[1] There should not be too many mistakes remaining; but if there are any, you will no doubt quickly espy them.

I have discussed the performance of the songs[2] with Steuermann, who has promised me that he will play in the premiere – the songs naturally depend very much on the pianist. It seems that Miss Hinnenberg-Lefèbre is to sing them. I would most favour Vienna as the site of the premiere; either the cycle organized by Steuermann and Kolisch or the International, where I am at least known. The only question is whether the International would employ an external singer at all. Do you know? And is there anyone else in Vienna, man or woman, who would be suitable for the songs? These questions are naturally only relevant in the case that the songs meet with your approval; if they do not, I shall have them neither published nor performed. I cannot tell you how eagerly I await your verdict this time; for I consider the songs the first truly satisfactory composition that I have produced. Incidentally also the first piece in which one can see clearly how much I owe to you, even more in attitude than technique. The third song in particular would be *inconceivable* without you. I hope you will not feel that the work's originality has been impaired by this.

I have also been looking for an opportunity to publish the songs,[3] and wrote a letter of casual inquiry to Stein. But received a strangely reserved response; that U. E. cannot enter any commitments to new authors, with regard to, in view of,[4] you are familiar with all that. And this after Heinsheimer had approached me in 1926 concerning the quartet, and, as I recall, made more or less definite promises, also to you. But, as U. E. has meanwhile – i.e. since the correspondence with Stein – approached me regarding a restructuring of Anbruch, and I have, upon their request, sent them a large abstract relating to Anbruch,[5] my chances are perhaps better now; this must transpire soon, as I am to speak with Heinsheimer concerning Anbruch in Leipzig (which I shall pass on my holiday route). But if you feel that the songs merit the effort, then I would be infinitely grateful to you for a word of authority to U. E.; for this time, I, who was really in no hurry to find my way into print, would set great store by it and as I am about to reach the age of 25, it is now gradually becoming time for it, if I am not to live forever among the ranks of the music writers, whom, incidentally, the devil may gladly take.

If it seems advisable to you, and you are willing to dispense with it for a time, you could also send your copy to Stein, as I do not have a second that would be sufficiently presentable for the publisher. But only if you like and if it causes you no inconvenience; I do not even wish to request it of you, simply to leave it to your independent judgement. If you wish, I could have a new copy made, though this would cause a certain delay on account of my leaving for 4 weeks at the end of next week.

I have meanwhile concluded a second song cycle: that is, I have augmented the two George songs,[6] which I wrote while I was with you in Vienna that time, by a further two. The start of one of them was still composed in Vienna: 'darfst du bei Nacht und bei Tag',[7] you found it very convincing at the time, and I have now been able to finish it three years later. The final song[8] is completely new and *the strictest twelve-tone music*, stricter than the wind quintet,[9] i.e. other than in the introductory and closing bars without any 'free' complementary notes, but rather with every note formed from the two note-rows or their inversions, retrogrades or retrograde-inversions. Paralysed the note-repetitions by making them thematic! I think one will recognize in the work that I did not study with you, of all people, without reason. If it interests you, and above all, *if it does not disturb you in your own composing*, I can also send you the George cycle; in the course of the next week. Otherwise I shall send it to Vienna, Stein requested it, but you naturally take thousandfold priority.

Am I not a burden to you with all my wishes, and with the attention that I, a composer who composed nothing until now, am suddenly demanding for my works? But I am only daring to do so because I have no one but you: because I know that you are genuinely appreciative of my work, and ultimately out of that egoism which sets in with a certain brutality when one senses the ability to express oneself for the first time. Please understand this, and do not count me among the parvenus of the industry, for I do not – least of all now, among the Reichsdeutschen – belong there.

I will certainly be in Vienna, autumn or winter, and see you again at last. I am now utterly exhausted, and am taking 4 weeks of holidays before I return to composing; 14 days Dolomites or Lake Como, 14 days southern Italy. Then I shall write the quartet finale and some orchestral pieces, I already have a good deal of both.

Might I ask you which text you have now chosen for the twelve-tone opera, or would you prefer, out of a superstition I can very well understand, not to speak of it? At any rate, I wish you the very best for it with all my heart – above all good working conditions, for in your case it then goes without saying that something beautiful will come of it.

Once again, forgive the letter's busyness, do not engage with more of it than you feel is justified, but let me know soon concerning the songs.

My very fondest regards to you and Frau Helene,

your devoted

Teddie W.

Original: typescript with Adorno's own signature.

1 In his *Erinnerung* (Recollection), Adorno relates: 'He [Berg] once gave me tuition in clear note-writing for an entire afternoon' (*GS* 13, p. 341).

2 Adorno's song cycle was premiered on 19 January 1929 by Margot Hinnenberg-Lefèbre and Eduard Steuermann in Berlin.

3 According to a message from Adorno to Siegfried Kracauer from 29 August 1928, Heinsheimer had promised Adorno during their meeting to 'publish his songs'.

4 Two figures (translator's note: originally *hinsichtlich, rücksichtlich*, this being a satirical allusion to Austrian bureaucratic jargon) from Karl Kraus's *Die Unüberwindlichen* (The Invincible Ones), published in May 1928.

5 The abstract 'Zum "Anbruch"', in which Adorno laid out his ideas for a restructuring of the journal, whose editorial team he joined in 1929, was first published in 1984 (see *GS* 19, pp. 595–604).

6 On the two songs from op. 1, see letter no. 37, note 9.

7 The manuscript of the first song from op. 1 is annotated: 'Vienna, summer 1925 – Frankfurt, 2 August 1928'.

8 According to the manuscript, the composition of 'Wir schreiten auf und ab' was concluded on 13 August 1928.

9 This is Schönberg's op. 26.

81   BERG TO WIESENGRUND-ADORNO
     SATTENDORF, 26.8.1928

Gut Berghof
Post office: Sattendorf 9 $26./_{8}$ 28.
Lake Ossiach
Carinthia

My dear friend, in sending me your 'Four Songs', you have fulfilled – nay, surpassed my joyful anticipation. I thank you with all my friend's & artist's hearts for it & for the affectionate dedication. I not only 'approve' of this music entirely, I in fact know that I shall one day 'enjoy' it. If that is not yet the case, then only because of the slowness of my perception of all kinds of music & the impossibility of occupying myself for many hours & half-days with your music, as it deserves, at the moment. I have not yet got beyond admiring the entire structural fabric, which I do not hesitate to term masterful, the wealth of forms that is apparent at the first glance, and the almost playful manner in which you have mastered recent developments (in the good sense, of course); but I know that all the rest will follow, even if it does not until the performance!

Concerning this, Miss Hinnenberg-Lefèbre seems a reasonable choice. I shall send a letter to Steuermann with the same delivery as this. I would consider it better for the premiere to take place in the context of his (& Kolisch's) concerts. The Vienna *I.S.f.k.m.a.*[1] lies entirely outside of the music industry, while the St.-K. concerts are sold out every time & already have an excellent reputation. Should Miss Hinnenberg be unavailable (e.g. for financial reasons), one should still be able to find someone in Vienna whose voice is equal to the task of your songs (also in terms of pitch-accuracy); though the presence of mind with which Miss Hinnenberg approaches such things (& with which she compensates for her somewhat modest means) is admittedly not easily found. So we would just have to *search!* –

U. E.: More than any 'word of authority', which I shall incidentally supply, the *songs* themselves will testify to the necessity of printing them. This is why I decided – *as much as it saddens me* – to send them to Stein with this same delivery. I think they will definitely *appear.* Though when? U. E. is so inundated (for weeks & months) with printing (of enormous volumes) that they are putting everything else on hold. (E.g. I was unable to have the '7 Early Songs' printed before winter despite urgently needing them for various performances. (6.11. premiere by Heger in the V$^{na.}$ society concerts.))

I am very pleased to hear of your other musical productivity. And even one in the 12-tone style. But it is a false assumption on your part that there is anything stricter than Schönberg's 5^{tet}, where not a single 'free' note appears (aside from printing errors). But we would do better to speak, not write about this & many other things, which shall hopef. be possible soon (as you are coming to Vienna). Therefore I shall close now by expressing once more my heartfelt thanks & *our* best wishes for your well-deserved recovery!

Yours Berg

P.S. I am working on 'Lulu' with diligence and enjoyment. But this is an absolute secret for now. For *various* reasons!

Original: manuscript.

1 See letter no. 35, note 7.

Vienna, 30 August 1928.

Dear Alban!

I can confirm to you immediately that I have received the *songs by Wiesengrund*. I have not yet been able to look at them. I expect my letter will meanwhile have reached you.

Best wishes to you and your wife

Yours

Stein

31./8.28. Dear friend. This has never happened to me before: I found the letter enclosed[1] – unsent – just this moment. But the card from Stein on which I am writing proves that I indeed wrote to you (& Stein & Steuermann) on the 26th. Now also my thanks for the splendid card from Toblach[2] & once again warm greetings fr. your *Alban Berg*[3]

Original: manuscript on a postcard of the journal *Pult und Taktstock* that Erwin Stein had sent to Berg.

1 This is letter no. 81.

2 This seems not to have survived.

3 Berg underlined his name on the sender's address of the postcard.

Frankfurt, 17 December 1928.

Dear master and teacher,

you must think me terribly disloyal once again, and yet once again unjustly, for not writing for so long. But your letter concerning my songs was a source of great joy and affirmation to me, greater than I can express, and at the same time one that I was urgently in need of: and I can only hope that, as you write, a direct relationship with my music will truly ensue once you hear them; and thus that you do not secretly have reservations or an initially negative reaction to them, which you wished to keep from me out of consideration, whereas it would in fact show the greatest of consideration to tell me, as it would prove to me that these songs had penetrated the dialectic of your artistic consciousness. I feel all the more entitled to ask you this because Steuermann indeed had reservations which I had to engage with thoroughly, admittedly without being able to accept them; they stem from a consciousness that has not entirely liberated itself from the idea of tonal functions, and which sees free construction as arbitrary, to the extent that it is not psychologically founded; and my songs are not especially so, the music rather moving away from the words along its own very particular path. Having said this: if, of course, you were to have the same reservations, they would take on a far more threatening guise, and I must therefore insist that you voice them.

If my silence is hard to forgive, it is above all due to your having written a letter to U. E.[1] that I was not shown, but which must have been of such a kind that I cannot thank you enough for it. I am sure you can understand how important it is for me today to see my things being printed and performed, and to avoid the danger of being buried in public as a music writer; and you have helped me in this with all your initiative; this is my greatest comfort in a time that is generally – both musically and personally – hardly rosy for me. The delay in my thanks should thus be attributed only to that situation, not to any lack of warm gratitude.

You will have heard about the misfortune of my songs and the peculiar behaviour of U. E., who first, under the impression of my work for Anbruch, requested officially that I send them the songs, and then rejected them despite your letter and the exceptionally favourable reference from Stein, or rather did not even reject them, simply speaking of publication at some indefinite point in the future. Do you think they shall ever be printed and how do you view the situation? Stein is remaining silent in all languages living and dead – even in Mecklenburgish and dwarf-jargon.[2] The matter is beginning to embitter me quite thoroughly, when I think that U. E. are sending me home reams of songs by Křenek that are nothing but wastepaper.[3] They print his every note. What is more, misfortune is also otherwise remaining loyal to my songs. Margot Hinnenberg, who had intended – and was supposed to – sing a cycle (the George one, which you have not yet seen) in Berlin at the International, refuses, saying that it has been written too low for her, although the range goes no lower than in Schönberg's George songs[4] (to A). Now she has been sent the second cycle, and I am only curious whether this one will not be too high for her. What makes this a sad matter for me is that Steuermann is to accompany in that concert, and I am of course absolutely dependent on him as an accompanist.

Yet I am not actually writing you all this to complain, as much reason as there is to do so, but rather concerning an official matter, as holding a share of the responsibility for Anbruch, whose editorial staff

I have now joined after all. Today I received word from U. E. that you have decided not to contribute a response to Casella,[5] which *greatly* saddens me. The issue stands or falls with your article; without it, it will lose the thread that I had finally hoped to maintain with a long essay by Ernst Bloch[6] and my revised essay dedicated to you, 'Nachtmusik'. I *most urgently request once again* that you write the article. I cannot accept your arguments.[7] In principle: for Casella has made efforts to exterminate modern music, which after all Anbruch, if it is not from the outset to appear as a mere supplement to the 'press',[8] must energetically represent, and it is only just if the defence leads to Casella's own destruction. Practically: from the outset, U. E. had expected a devastating polemic from you, Heinsheimer himself wrote to me that you wanted to write something like the Pfitzner.[9] And one need hardly be more cautious towards the gentlemen than they are themselves. And furthermore: Casella, whose article I have not yet been sent, but who seems by all accounts to have produced the utmost that a villain can, has of course, by attacking modern music, attacked the most important part of U. E.'s production, and sought to ruin their business. So no one can seriously demand consideration towards him. In practical terms, the consequences of your refusal are very sad. The whole issue is already arranged around your article, I refer explicitly to it in my introduction,[10] in such a manner that the editors are seen to identify with it. And if you do not write it, it will not, as you probably suppose, be I myself who shall write against Casella, but rather Herr *Křenek:* Heinsheimer wants 'a truly renowned man' for the job; it seems that I am not renowned enough for him, and you can imagine what will come if Křenek, who is himself no better than Casella, writes it. And this would in any case only be for the second issue, in the first the Casella would stand on its own with an editorial note from Heinsheimer, which would no doubt be phrased quite carefully. In short: if you do not write, it will be a disaster, and I must ask you most urgently to consider this. It goes without saying that I, now having after all a certain say in the journal's activities, after supplying all the ideas for it, will insist without consideration that U. E. include your article, even if your tone intimidates the gentlemen. I need hardly tell you that my abstention from a response to Casella does not stem from cowardice. But firstly, quite aside from the effect of your name, I believe that you can do it incomparably better than I, who cannot nearly address a polemical object with such grim devotion and care as you do. What is more, it is an ungrateful task for me to insist on writing myself, if I am being recommended Herr Křenek after *you* had officially suggested me. Křenek must be prevented at all costs and I beg you to help me do so! But more important and urgent than the negative request is the positive one: that you might write after all! Please also discuss it with Soma and tell him my arguments! I am certain he will agree with me! U. E. will not dare to say anything against your article.

How is Lulu faring? I hope you are making good and quick progress, and that you can continue to compose in the city in winter, which is after all, as I myself have ample occasion to attest, no easy thing! Please do write to me how the matter stands. – And please also see to it that the early songs are sent to me for review in Anbruch,[11] I am afraid that Stein will snatch away the review, which I – if you approve – most definitely wish to write myself!

I am working on 2 cycles of orchestral pieces,[12] 3 large and 6 small ones. The small ones are studies towards the large ones, 3 of the small ones are finished. The large ones, which mean a great deal to me, are progressing only with difficulty. Walter Herbert[13] intends to do one of the cycles in Berlin in February. Otherwise, I am involved considerably with the local arm of the International, whose programme I have more or less managed to fix (in the 2nd concert Kolisch with the lyric suite, Schönberg op. 30, Webern op. 9), and with similar matters. The *Habilitation* business is still not progressing, but is not entirely hopeless.

How is Frau Helene? I wish I could come to Vienna at last, at long last! How it saddened me to learn from Horenstein that you had stayed in Duisburg and Düsseldorf without calling on me! – Once again, please write against Casella. Fond regards your devoted Wiesengrund.

Original: typescript with handwritten conclusion and signature.

1 Berg's letter of 12 December 1928, of which he enclosed a copy in his letter to Adorno of 27 December (no. 84); see appendix II, letter no. 2.

2 Stein's wife came from Mecklenburg, and he himself was a very short man; see also *GS* 18, p. 489.

3 Probably a reference to the *Vier Gesänge nach alten Gedichten für Mezzosopran und Klavier* op. 53, which were published around that time, and the Three Goethe Songs for Baritone and Piano op. 56, copies of which have survived among Adorno's belongings.

4 His op. 15.

5 The January 1929 issue of *Anbruch*, as the *Musikblätter des Anbruch* was called from that point on – the first with which Adorno was substantially involved – contained Casella's reactionary manifesto 'Scarlattiana'; Křenek's response followed in the February issue, together with an open letter by Gian Francesco Malipiero and Schönberg's statement 'I find Casella too sympathetic in other respects to want to respond to him in a theoretical context.' Adorno's polemic, entitled 'Atonales Intermezzo?' (see *GS* 18, pp. 88–97),

concluded the controversy in the May issue. See also Anna Maria Morazzoni, 'Der Schönberg-Kreis und Italien: die Polemik gegen Casellas Aufsatz über "Scarlattiana"', in the report from the second congress of the International Schönberg Society: *Die Wiener Schule in der Musikgeschichte des 20. Jahrhunderts*, Vienna, 12–15 June 1984, ed. Rudolf Stephan and Sigrid Wiesmann, Vienna, 1986, pp. 73–82.

6 See Ernst Bloch, 'Rettung Wagners durch Karl May', *Anbruch*, 11 (1929), pp. 4–10.

7 See appendix II, letter no. 2.

8 This refers to the *Neue Freie Presse*, one of Karl Kraus's primary targets.

9 Berg's article 'Die musikalische Impotenz der "neuen Ästhetik" Hans Pfitzners', first printed in *Musikblätter des Anbruch*, 2 (1920), pp. 399–408.

10 Adorno's introduction 'Zum Jahrgang 1929 des "Anbruch"', printed without his name; see *GS* 19, pp. 605–8.

11 Adorno reviewed Berg's Seven Early Songs twice: see *Anbruch*, 11 (1929), pp. 90–2 and *Die Musik*, 21 (1928/29), p. 761f. (*GS* 18, pp. 465–8 and 469–71).

12 The cycle *Six Short Orchestral Pieces* op. 4, composed between 1925 and 1928 – the conception of the final piece dates back to 1920 – was printed in 1968 by the Milan publisher Ricordi (see *Compositions 2*, pp. 29–54), after U. E. had contented itself for decades with loaning out the fair copy procured by Adorno in 1929. Nothing can so far be ascertained concerning the fate of the '3 large orchestral pieces'; no manuscript – even of sketches – has survived, nor are there any indirect references to the state of the composition; see also letter no. 87.

13 Walter Herbert (see also letter no. 68 and note 8 there) conducted the premiere of Adorno's *Six Short Orchestral Pieces*, which are dedicated to him, in Berlin on 16 February 1929.

84   BERG TO WIESENGRUND-ADORNO
     VIENNA, 27.12.1928

Alban Berg, Vienna, XIII.
Trauttmansdorffgasse 27   27.12.28

My dear friend, many thanks for the book.[1] I have already cast a few glances at it and I think it is my sort of book. I sense these things! As soon as I have read Ginster (whereupon I shall first write to Kracauer),[2] I shall begin your book. For until now I have been prevented from reading by a ghastly influenza and headaches. That was also my reason for having to leave your kind letter of the 17th unanswered. As I cannot decide on writing the Casella article after all, however – although it continues to float around my brain –, I have done my utmost to persuade Heinsheimer to let *you* write it. For like-minded people, as we: you and I are, the case is clear. You will therefore say *the same* as I would have. And it is only fortunate for Anbruch that you will say it differently than myself (who have only one model, namely Karl Kraus). Only *thus* would the response be possible. For it can never be *mine*! But Křenek is a *true* outrage: the only successful European composer that Casella acknowledges, and his views are practically identical to two-thirds of Casella's article!

I told Heinsheimer all this on the telephone and by letter. I hope it was not in vain! However he may act, I would advise you to write the article in your own manner. I cannot imagine that you would be prevented from printing it in 'Anbruch'; whether Křenek ultimately writes – or not.

Unfortunately, I have neither seen the songs you dedicated to me since the summer, nor do I know the other cycle. So I have nothing new to say on the matter. But I have such fond recollections of my ones that I have often longed to have them. Where are they? Will I soon receive them back? So the others are definitely to be done on January 19th in Berlin by Miss Hinnenberg. I know this from Steuermann, who would like to have the music soon! Under these circumstances the performance cannot but be successful, and I am thus most curious as to the effect of this work. You will surely be in Berlin for it?! Perhaps you will then stay until the 31st, when Horenstein is premiering the 3 lyr. string pieces. Your presence would mean a great deal to me; the score, incidentally, has long been published.

I am inordinately disgruntled that your songs were not accepted at UE, for many reasons. One of these is of course that my recommendation, which was of *such* a kind that there was no option *but to print them immediately*, was quite simply ignored, and this is almost enough for me to send you to Schott. I think a recommendation from me – and I would certainly formulate it accordingly – would have *more* success *there*, and then we would have reached the point that I – almost as an invocation – had warned UE of, namely that they have missed out on you! What do you say to the idea? Or would you rather wait until the concert?

I am very pleased that you are also so keen in other areas of work, and am most curious to see how a piece of yours for *orchestra* will turn out.

I have nothing truly pleasing to report. For I am not getting around to any composing here, and everything else is more or less insignificant. And I have a great deal to do, so I console myself with the thought that I will perhaps be able to return to 'Lulu' at the start of next year (by Lake Ossiach).

Today I am up for the first time, but still not entirely well. Especially my head, which you can tell by the fact that I am starting to repeat myself. Therefore finish. I would have liked to give you a little Christmas treat in the shape of a – new typewriter ribbon[3] . . .

And now warmest greetings from
your old Alban Berg
And also fond regards from my wife!
HAPPY NEW YEAR to you and your dear family!!!

Original: typescript with the 'copy' of Berg's letter to Hans Heinsheimer from 12.12.1928 as a supplement (see appendix II, letter no. 2).

1 It is not known what book Adorno gave Berg for Christmas.

2 Berg wrote to Kracauer on 31 December 1928 concerning *Ginster*; the letter has survived among Kracauer's belongings, and now lies in the Deutsches Literaturarchiv in Marbach am Neckar.

3 Berg is alluding to Adorno's previous letter, which had been written with an 'expiring' ribbon.

85   WIESENGRUND-ADORNO TO BERG
     COLOGNE, 27.12.1928

Cologne, 27 Dec. 28.
Dear master and teacher, I cannot tell you how happy I was to receive your early songs, which I am to review for 'Musik' and Anbruch!! Today I *heard* my songs,[1] the ones that belong to you, for the first time. Affectionately yours,
Teddie W.

  Warmest regards
  Yours Margot Hinnenberg

Original: picture postcard: 'Die Bastei', Köln am Rhein; stamp: Köln / Ehrenfels, 29.12.28. Manuscript with an additional note by Margot Hinnenberg-Lefèbre.

1 Adorno worked on his songs op. 3 with Margot Hinnenberg at her house in Cologne.

6.3. Yesterday I received *Anbruch* with your truly wonderful words about my 7 songs. My thanks, a thousand thanks!

And warmest congratulations on your orchestral pieces & your well-deserved success in Berlin. When shall I see them? And see *you* yourself?

Oh, if only you had been here yesterday! This performance[1] here is a miracle, a veritable miracle. A 2nd miracle: it being taken on at all.

More soon from your

Berg

Fondest best wishes for the orchestral pieces! Yours
Helene Berg

Original: picture postcard: Oldenburg, theatre; stamp: Oldenburg, 6.3.29. Manuscript with an additional note by Helene Berg.

1 The Oldenburg premiere of *Wozzeck* on 5 March 1929, conducted by Johannes Schüler. Berg held his 'Wozzeck lecture' there for the first time on 3 March (see Hans Ferdinand Redlich, *Alban Berg: Versuch einer Würdigung*, Vienna, Zurich and London, 1957, pp. 311–27). Adorno read this lecture for the recording of the opera by Pierre Boulez.

Frankfurt a.M.-Oberrad
8 April 1929.

Dear master and teacher,

returning from the Riviera, where I stayed for a few weeks in order to recover, I found your letter,[1] to my great joy. In order to prevent my debt from growing inordinately, I should both thank you and ask you to take into account my dying typewriter – it is certainly the last letter that you shall receive with its help, I am in the process of buying myself a new one, but cannot decide on the model, which you can perhaps also empathize with.

I cannot tell you how pleased I was to hear about Oldenburg. What force a work must have to break down all the walls that stand between it and the people there. I never doubted that it would be able to do so, even today, but it is gratifying to find this confirmed so clearly and unambiguously.

I hope I need not tell you how much I would have liked to have been there – and naturally also at Horenstein's performance of the lyric suite.[2] But it was truly not possible. The winter was the most strenuous I have ever had. First I had to work on my songs with Frau Hinnenberg in Cologne, then work on Anbruch here; then I was in Berlin for the premiere of the songs,[3] which, purely between the two of us, was very poor, as there was insufficient time to prepare and develop them and I had extraordinarily underestimated the difficulties. The success corresponded to this, i.e. a 'succès d'estime' before the spiteful audience of the Berlin International. I was already disappointed, but what pained me was the feeling that the performers too, i.e. Steuermann, did not believe in the matter. Steuermann made numerous objections that I was unable to accept, which presumably only served to reinforce them. So I came home very depressed, and had lost all my courage to write the orchestral pieces. They would not have been completed had not Kurt Weill, who was really the only one who genuinely appreciated the songs, strongly urged me to do so, and then also Walter Herbert. I composed them here and wrote the score in Bern, where I studied them straight away with Water Herbert. The performance of the pieces in Berlin was excellent, Herbert, who could play them from memory, did them twice, and this was the deciding factor in their success. Only one thing was missing: your presence. Even your approval for the pieces, though it makes me proud and happy, cannot compensate for that. Could you not get the pieces off U. E. and look at them a little more closely? Or is this too egotistic a wish on my part; are you composing? One thing I must confess to you: the songs, your songs, are far more to my liking than the pieces. For now I am more or less alone in this, but my instinct tells me that you will not think any differently. The songs shall be returned to you very soon, as well as the other cycle, from which you know only two songs that were written when I was still in Vienna, and can perhaps stand up to re-examination. – Nonetheless, I would not go so far as to deny the orchestral pieces. Through them I have overcome my fear of the orchestra, which you are familiar with, once and for all, I think they are decent enough and everything sounds as intended (a few parts of the first and third pieces are pointlessly difficult and could probably be orchestrated more clearly, but I hope this is precisely what I have learned from them, and now it may remain as I imagined it).

I was particularly happy that you were pleased with my review of the Early Songs. Especially as I was a little fearful of that article, and did not know beforehand how you would react: I had attempted to utter such delicate, hidden things in it that I was unsure whether it is actually legitimate to speak of them. Is there not always something shameful in speaking of shame? Now Proust, whom I did not speak of without reason, and whom I repeatedly found coming to mind during the songs, was in this sense also shameless, and your agreement removed all my scruples. A little sister to the article will appear as a review in 'Musik'. The Kolischs played the lyric suite here at the International,[4] once again I heard some rehearsals and was as deeply struck by the piece as ever. I would soon like to write something longer about you again; I think I could do so differently and at the same time more concretely than 4 years ago. Perhaps the opportunity will arise.

How far is Lulu? Are you getting around to work? what is finished? The most important thing to me is to hear about that. I hope the winter in Vienna did not impede you too severely. How is your health? Was there no trace of asthma during the cold winter?

As for myself, I have truly recovered well, which is normally not achieved through holidays of recovery. First of all I am planning something smaller, chamber songs,[5] to get a bit of writing done. Probably pure twelve-tone music after all. Then I hope finally to take up my grander plans; but I am delaying it until there is no choice, so as to learn as much as possible beforehand.

How do you like the new Anbruch? Does one sense my initiative in it at all? I know well enough that it is no temple, and never will be; but I still consider it possible to get some reasonable things done there and hope to train a small team of colleagues such as Redlich,[6] Westphal and Goldbeck,[7] with whom something can be achieved. Above all, the musical reactionaries can today *only* be fought in Anbruch, for Melos has devoted itself completely to them. Certainly things are difficult enough with Anbruch too, as long as U. E. is making money out of the reactionary stuff. But it is still possible to shock people from within it, as shown in particular by the Bloch essay on Wagner, which one can certainly have reservations about, but which definitely has a revolutionary perspective and cannot be mistaken for new functionality. My long essay against Casella will appear in the April issue.

I have not heard from Soma in a long time. I had Heinsheimer invite him to contribute to Anbruch, and he agreed; but I do not know if his article has been written and do not even know his address at present. It is possible that we were in Berlin at the same time without knowing about each other.

I intend to stay here over the summer months to compose, it is now the best time for it in every respect. But then I hope finally to come to Vienna again. What I would like most is then to stay there for a few weeks and live in Hietzing, in order to be near you. When would I find you there?

Of my compositional plans, there is one that I cannot keep to myself after all: to write a piano concerto.[8] I have occupied myself sufficiently with problems of writing for the piano, the combination with orchestra tempts me, and this presents me with the problem of large-scale form using a material in which I feel at least somewhat at home. What do you think? I also wish to complete the second cycle of orchestral pieces, the three 'large' ones, which I have already got quite far with. The first an allegro, the second a full-grown adagio, the third a sort of Tarantella.

How is Frau Helene? Have the early songs, now that they have been printed so beautifully, induced her to sing again? Is she quite healthy? Give her my very warmest regards!

To you, my dear master and teacher, fond, warm regards from your ever devoted

Teddie.

Original: typescript with Adorno's signature.

1 This letter, assuming Adorno did not mistakenly refer to the card of 6 March 1929 as a letter, has not survived among Adorno's belongings.

2 On 31 January in Berlin, Jascha Horenstein had conducted the premiere of the three movements from the *Lyric Suite* arranged for string orchestra.

3 See letter no. 80, note 2.

4 In the April issue of *Anbruch*, Adorno published the review of this concert, in which the Kolisch Quartet played, besides the *Lyric Suite*, Schönberg's Third String Quartet op. 30 and Bartók's String Quartet no. 3; see *GS* 19, p. 148.

5 The plan seems not to have been carried out.

6 The musicologist, conductor and composer Hans Ferdinand Redlich (1903–1968), who emigrated to England in 1939, published the monograph *Alban Berg: Versuch einer Würdigung* in 1957.

7 Fred (Frederick) Goldbeck (1902–1981), born in Holland, spent his youth in Frankfurt and was a close friend of Adorno; like him, he also studied composition with Sekles, as well as conducting with Josef Willem Mengelberg. From 1925, Goldbeck lived mostly in Paris, where he worked for various music journals. From 1936 to 1939 he was in charge of an orchestral class at the Ecole Normale de Musique in Paris. He was married to the pianist Yvonne Lefébure.

8 This seems to have remained an idea only.

Frankfurt a. M.-Oberrad.
Seeheimer Strasse 19.
29 April 1929.

Dear master and teacher,

these lines are not simply intended to introduce to you my new type-writer, an Underwood, which would provoke technical delight on your part, for I am rather coming to you with a substantial request. I am applying for Weissmann's post,[1] and am to go to Berlin tomorrow for this reason. The idea was not mine, but rather that of Weill and Klemperer, who have set everything in motion for this reason. For reasons known to you, however, their direct influence upon Ullstein is not very great, they can only help me indirectly. This is why I must ask you, who certainly have better things to do than stage such business for me, to help me. I do not know whether you are directly acquainted with the Ullsteins, but your name counts for so much that there is surely some possibility of intervention. Especially if it were possible to make *Kleiber* approach Ullstein himself, this could be of the greatest conceivable importance. Kastner,[2] whom I know rather well, is out of the question for this, as he evidently has aspirations to that post himself. Miss Voss, on the other hand, has been taking conspicuous notice of my articles for some time. As there are also social connec-tions of all kinds there, I am thus sure of at least getting to the Ullsteins. A word from you in the right place and above all from Kleiber, who is surely more to their taste than Klemperer, could decide the matter.

Perhaps my plan amazes you. But I am acting after thorough con-sideration and according to precise information. The post is extremely agreeable, merely evening visits to concerts and the opera and a weekly report, no editorial meetings, no editorial work, so with com-plete freedom to compose, far more than I would have as an outside lecturer, as well as financial independence and finally the chance gen-uinely to do some good as a critic. This is what made me take the ini-tiative. I hope you approve of it. It seems unlikely that I will succumb to the Ullstein plague. – My primary rivals are Stuckenschmidt,[3] Aber from Leipzig,[4] Schnoor from Dresden.[5]

Unfortunately, I have not yet had the chance to compose in peace here, and have only sketched chamber songs.[6] But I hope it will finally happen.

I enclose the proof copy of my Anbruch essay against Casella, whose publication there is causing such difficulties that I am still not

143

sure if it will appear at all. Perhaps it will be of interest to you, having occupied yourself with the same matter. The cuts were made by Stefan and Heinsheimer, so I would ask you to read the cut passages too.[7]

Did you receive my long detailed letter?

My Berlin address: Berlin W, Joachimsthaler Strasse 17, Guesthouse Violetta. I would be most grateful to hear from you.

Please also let me know roughly when you will be in Vienna. And tell me of your work, which I await most eagerly.

Fond regards to you and Frau Helene

from your faithful

Teddie W

Original: typescript with Adorno's signature.

1 Adorno's efforts to gain the critic's post previously held by Adolf Weissmann (1873–1929) at the *B.Z.* were fruitless.

2 See letter no. 76, note 5.

3 The critic, music writer and composer Hans Heinz Stuckenschmidt (1901–1988) succeeded Weissmann at the *Berliner Zeitung am Mittag*.

4 Adolf Aber (1893–1960), a friend of Herman Scherchen, was musical correspondent for the *Leipziger Neueste Nachrichten* from 1919 to 1933.

5 The music writer Hans Schnoor (1893–1976).

6 No sketches for chamber songs seem to have survived.

7 See the bibliographical reference for 'Atonales Intermezzo?' in letter no. 83, note 5. The proof copy of the essay has survived in Berg's library in the Alban Berg Stiftung; the following passage on the first page was cut: 'Certain radical-conservative theorists, such as Below, behaved similarly during the war, not concealing their goals of conquest from the start as the mainstream nationalists did, but quite simply invoking the politics of power in recollection of their feudal legacy, and thus involuntarily helping to unmask nationalist ideologies, because they operated with even more regressive ideologies. Their achievement is equalled by that of the musical politician Casella.' Written in the right-hand margin is the note: 'Please, as tempting as it might be – no fascism, no politics! Best wishes!', with the initials of Stefan and Heinsheimer. In the edition in the *Gesammelte Schriften*, vol. 18, p. 90, the passage that was cut should be inserted in the fifth line from the top, after 'im Rausch neuer Sachlichkeit entzaubert er die eigene Ideologie.'

Alban Berg, Vienna, XIII.
Trauttmansdorffgasse 27   3.5.29

My dear friend, I am writing this only in haste for your information: I am afraid your request for me to intervene at the B.Z. has come too late. I have already done the same for someone else,[1] and indeed directly to Ullstein (whom incidentally I do not know personally), so I cannot now repeat this. The one I had recommended is not among the candidates you named, however. This effort of mine for his sake (which would evidently have been fruitless in any case,) has thus at least not endangered your application. But Hertzka will immediately speak to the representative of the house of Ullman here about you. A recommendation of this sort would also be far more effective than one from Kleiber, who has lived very reclusively in recent years & – as one who is under criticism practically every week – will hardly be able or willing to help *one of those* involved in producing such criticism. I could do that far more easily – and I would have done so with the greatest vehemence, and naturally with an entirely different conviction than for the person on whose behalf I intervened almost a week ago. A shame, a great shame!

But I hope nonetheless that you will be given this post. I hope so for your sake, for music's sake and even for the paper's sake! And need not tell you that I find the idea a very good one. Please keep me informed as to the state of play; I am immensely curious as to the outcome. I congratulate you on your typewriter; but the left-hand margin stop appears not to work. For the left margin of a letter should not look as jagged as in your letter and as I have so far attempted to imitate in mine, but rather as uniformly vertical as I will maintain for the rest of this letter of mine. But otherwise the machine seems fabulous. The characters are already so sympathetic.

I almost came to Berlin, and that would have been a pleasant meeting, there of all places now with you. Unfortunately, I received Kleiber's invitation too late.[2] I would only have been able to attend *one* rehearsal. And I would only have come for the rehearsals, not to take a bow. In Berlin *itself* I would perhaps also have been able to find a way of assisting in your matter. It would all have fitted in place so well. It really is too bad that I am not there now. The early songs are being played there right now & you are no doubt there. Please tell me at some length about it. I am glad to know you are there!

I certainly did receive your lengthy letter, but for lack of time I must postpone my response to it, as likewise my reaction to your Casella essay, which I have not yet been able to read.

In any case many thanks for everything, my best wishes for the *B.Z.* and Voss and fond regards from your
Berg

Original: typescript with Berg's signature.

1 Unknown.

2 To the repeat performance of *Wozzeck* or the performance of the Seven Early Songs in the ninth symphony concert at the Lindenoper on 4 May 1929; Claire Born sang under Kleiber's direction.

90 WIESENGRUND-ADORNO TO BERG
   BERLIN, 5.5.1929

> Berlin W, Joachimsthaler Strasse 17.
> Guesthouse Violetta.
> 5 May 1929.

Dear master and teacher,
    a thousand thanks for your letter and your kind efforts: I shall respond immediately. I came just in time for the early songs. It seems that concert was Kleiber's first since the illness, and it did not benefit from his obvious weakness. But the beauty of the songs, in particular the unbelievable mastery and confidence of their instrumentation, became utterly clear. One finds in them something similar to the third part of the Gurrelieder[1] (or, if you will, in certain drawings by Ingres which van Gogh paraphrased):[2] an early substance entering into a dialectic with an eminently late, knowing technical experience that wholly sublimates it. The orchestral sonority of the first song in particular is fantastic, as if the instruments were enchanted; this piece only comes out fully in the orchestral version. The use of the muted brass as a form of unreal bass group is completely new. I have once again learned an infinite amount from all this, and have an egotistic desire to see and study the score very soon. Could you see to it with U. E.? I would like to write something about the orchestration of the songs for Stein.[3] Incidentally: it did fill me with a little pride that the sound of my short pieces[4] is genuinely reminiscent of your songs; this is not only my own wishful thinking, for impartial listeners came to me with that impression – considering the complete difference in melodic-harmonic substance, this is indeed most peculiar, and shows that apprenticeship can reveal itself in very indirect and latent ways.
    Performance: Miss Born is quite a good singer, pretty voice, seemingly also very musical and intelligent. But she lacks the necessary

146

character, that is to say the immediacy and authenticity of expression that the songs call for, as well as having an inadequate breathing technique, and the manner in which she handles her voice is not always appropriate. This led to a certain dullness. The songs were all rushed, evidently out of consideration for Miss Born, and thus did not speak so fully, there was not as much breath as they, more than some other works, require. I am certainly in favour of quick tempi, often too much so for your taste, but these tempi must of course be filled, they must not degenerate into a rushing about. In addition to this, I do not find that Kleiber's present work remains on a par with the Wozzeck premiere. He has a certain tendency to orient everything towards delicacy of sound and to neglect immediacy; in the songs, which are in any case deliberately orchestrated not with a view to clarity in Mahler's or Wozzeck's sense, but rather a transparent permeability for the voice, this made some things less clear, for example the marvellous counterpoint of the nightingale could not be heard, neither could the imitation in the second verse of Traumgekrönt; the final song very rushed. So the performance was not ideal (I am being honest), but it nonetheless produced as great and pure an effect as only these wonderful songs can. They would have to be done by someone from our musical circle who understands how to bring their construction to light.

Concerning my affairs: I am naturally extremely sceptical, as I could only gain access to Ullstein through a chain of misunderstandings and errors, and can hardly imagine that I still have any chances if anyone has read a line of my writing. But this chain has indeed continued until now, the personnel manager, Hess, is in favour of me thanks to social connections, preparatory work has also been done in the editorial offices, and certain informed persons believe I have a chance. So it is now all the more important to give a decisive push. A thousand thanks for your efforts with Hertzka. Perhaps you can inform him of my chances; for it would also be in his interests for me to be given the post, and I am sure he can undertake something. His influence is especially important because one hears repeatedly about U. E. and Ullstein being financially allied. So if you could persuade him to take serious action, this would mean a great deal. After learning more closely about the situation with Kleiber, I would also find it wiser to dispense with his help, as he is not popular in the house of U. In my letter of application, I named you as a reference for my 'musical and specialist qualification', and I would be most grateful if you could respond to any inquiries, which is all the more possible without harming the person you have already recommended because I have declared myself your student, so it need not be any more than a teacher's account of his pupil, not a 'recommendation', which is of course impossible after intervening on the other man's behalf. Practically speaking, it would perhaps be good if you were to speak not only of me as a composer, but also of my technical understanding and ability, and my well-founded critical faculty, or whatever one wishes to call it, as the publisher is naturally wary of giving the post to someone who is essentially a composer. A thousand thanks in advance.

My primary reason in waiting for a response to my other letter is that I would like to hear at last about your well-being and your work. Should matters here be decided more quickly than expected (at present it seems that they will drag on until autumn), I would come to Vienna at once. I am well here, I am hearing a great deal of music, some of it quite fine, and seeing people, some of them decent. But as ever, I long to be permitted finally to exist in your company, in depth and over a longer period.

Fond regards to you and Frau Helene from your faithful
Teddie W.

Original: typescript with Adorno's signature.

1 Schönberg only completed his orchestration of the *Gurrelieder* in 1911 – ten years after beginning work on them.

2 Unknown.

3 In the weeks that followed, Adorno wrote the essay 'Die Instrumentation von Bergs Frühen Liedern', though this was not printed in Stein's journal *Pult und Taktstock*, but only in March 1932 in issues 5 and 6 of the *Schweizerische Musikzeitschrift und Sängerblatt*; see the revised version in GS 16, pp. 97–109.

4 These are the *Six Short Orchestral Pieces* op. 4.

91 WIESENGRUND-ADORNO TO BERG
    FRANKFURT, c. MID-MAY TO MID-JUNE
    1929

ANBRUCH
MONTHLY JOURNAL
FOR NEW MUSIC
KARLSPLATZ 6
VIENNA I.

Dear master and teacher,

I am replying immediately,[1] not merely to show you that my machine now finally knows where to begin, or to exhibit the new constructive Anbruch letter-paper. I am very glad to be able to write about your songs' orchestration (and the connection between that instrumentation and the compositional substance, which it will also be good to refer to for the tactical reasons you mentioned), and am now only awaiting the score before I set to work at once, which I would ask you to report to Stein. In the same issue, I also hope to have a general essay I have long planned on problems of orchestration.[2] It is only a shame that I will not be able to keep any of the scores;[3] but I shall at least refrain from returning this one until I am sent an urgent reminder by U. E.

I went to hear Wozzeck,[4] not Toscanini's Rigoletto – together with Křenek, whom I had invited. Once again the work made as overwhelming an impression on me as it did the first time I heard it; and today, partly because I have examined it repeatedly, partly because I am simply better trained, it is completely transparent and evident to me in all its parts. I have only now fully grasped its developmental curve: from the first tavern scene onwards an incessant escalation. But it would be wrong to conceal from you that the performance suffered considerably. My impression that Kleiber, perhaps due to his illness, is not his old self any more has been confirmed only too clearly. He really dispensed entirely with shaping, contenting himself to hold the orchestra and the ensemble together more or less successfully. Yet often he is unable to attain even the minimum level of clarity that can be expected, so that for uninformed listeners, important leading voices are entirely lost, and the whole music is submerged in a sort of diffuse sound and atmosphere that falsifies it and creates the appearance of 'expressionism', which really no longer has anything to do with your work. There is even less singing than before. Only the new Marie,[5] who is probably superior to Miss Johannsen in acting and intellect, makes an exception; she sings, but I did not hear many right notes. I feel it is in your best interests, and absolutely necessary for the work, for the whole thing to be learned thoroughly from scratch. It is now finally time to put an end to this constant speaking (which also cancels out the contrasting effect of the genuinely melodramatic passages) and to bring out the musical line in its pure state. There is no point in supplying those reactionaries with ideologies who would most like to push the dangerous work backwards by calling it im- or expressionistic as they choose. In my essay on the songs I wish to do my utmost to combat this, but I observed through the work's effect on all sorts of people that there truly is a danger in the performance. Perhaps you can do something about it. A music in which one cannot follow thematic events always seems impressionistic, so the most important thing is to force clarity without reservation. It would be good if someone with musical expertise, such as Rankl,[6] could hold preliminary rehearsals

149

and study the work; then Kleiber, for God's sake, could restrict himself to those few things that he does.

Two days earlier I heard Toscanini's Falstaff: a miracle. This is how Wozzeck should be done, it need not be with such sets and direction. And the work is magnificent. Schreker's Der ferner Klang,[7] on the other hand, conducted by himself, palatable only to maidservants; a series of kitsch postcards.

There has still been no decision on Weissmann's successor, and this will not change before autumn. My chances are still good, I have heard that I am now in the final selection from countless applicants with Stuckenschmidt, after Hertzka, Kestenberg[8] and others intervened on my behalf. But I more than doubt that I can compete with Stuckenschmidt, who has all the qualities of a con man (also the good ones). And, to be honest, I would almost prefer if nothing came of it, for the quagmire one becomes entangled in there exceeds even the most audacious imagination, and I am also very much afraid that I shall no longer find time to compose, which is more important to me [than] everything else. But I would ask you to maintain the utmost discretion, as the matter is still undecided, and for the sake of etiquette I cannot sabotage it. If something does come of it after all, admittedly, I think that remaining there for a long time would be out of the question. Especially as it now seems that it would not even genuinely be Weissmann's post, for old Urbar[9] is evidently attempting to inherit it himself and relegate the new man to a clearly [subordinate rank].

I am glad [that you are now once more] at work, and I eagerly await the concert aria.[10] [What is the text?] And what singer? Herlinger, Fuchs-Fayer?[11] Or an American? And what about Lulu?

My dramatic plans are now also gradually gaining definition,[12] but I shall now first write some chamber songs, as exercises, which are intended to be quite artful, of the sort that people will cry 'artiste' – which troubles me little if I learn from them what I hope to learn.

Are we to see each other again at last? I long so much for it; but cannot leave here for the next few months, so that I can finally get some decent work done.

Fond, loyal regards from your old
Teddie W.

Original: typescript with printed letterhead and Adorno's signature. Berg cut out the sender's address; the words thus lost on the back of the paper were added by Berg above the lines; they have been placed in square brackets by the editor.

On the dating: The letter must have been written between Adorno's return to Frankfurt from Berlin in mid-May and the start of his work on the essay

'Die Instrumentation von Bergs Frühen Liedern', which was finished by 23 June.

1 Adorno's replies apply both to Berg's letter of 3.5.1929 (no. 89) and to one that was evidently lost, in which Berg clearly requested an essay on the Seven Early Songs for *Pult und Taktstock*.

2 Not written.

3 Probably the score of the Seven Early Songs published in 1928, as well as Berg's own hand copy (see letter no. 94, note 1).

4 Adorno's account of this performance is part of 'Berliner Opernmemorial'; see *GS* 19, pp. 273–5.

5 Marie Veselá sung the part of Marie during the 1928–9 season in Berlin.

6 Karl Rankl (1898–1986), a student of Schönberg and Webern, was employed at the Krolloper in Berlin at the time.

7 This opera by Franz Schreker (1878–1934) had been premiered in Frankfurt in 1912. See Adorno's review (*GS* 19, p. 272f.) and his lecture 'Schreker' from 1959, *GS* 16, pp. 368–81.

8 The pianist and musical pedagogue Leo Kestenberg (1882–1962) was in charge of music in the Prussian Ministry of Science from 1918 onwards.

9 Unknown.

10 See *Der Wein / Le vin* (Baudelaire–George), Concert Aria with Orchestra; the composition, for which Berg completed the short score on 23 July 1929, was dedicated to the Viennese singer Růžena Herlinger (1893–1978), who had commissioned it.

11 Unknown.

12 It could not be ascertained what Adorno meant.

92   WIESENGRUND-ADORNO TO BERG
     FRANKFURT, 24.6.1929

24 June 1929.   DR. TH. WIESENGRUND-ADORNO
                                       Frankfurt a. M.-Oberrad
                             Seeheimer Strasse 19 Tel. Spessart
                                                          62480

Dear master and teacher,

I am pleased to be able to enclose here a copy – albeit not a superb one – of my long essay on the early songs.[1] The original already went out to Stein yesterday. The delay in the essay's completion is due to my only receiving the two copies of the score 14 days after your letter, as they were at the customs office for so long, and not to be got away from there. But I hope that the manuscript is still in time for the next issue of Pult. My only fear is that the essay is now too long for dear old Stein (I would reckon about 12–14 printed pages, but I would ask you not to disclose this), and that he will therefore either cut it, which I could never allow, or publish it in episodes in the manner of a Courths-Mahler novel, which I would also consider very undesirable. I would ask you both sincerely and urgently to use your influence to ensure that the essay appears *uncut and in one piece*, it is already justified by the content, as the insights of the first part only gain concretion in the second, without which they would appear completely unfounded.

The essay deliberately stays very close to material-technical concerns and I hope this will appeal to you. Perhaps its factuality will compensate for my early, abstract sacrileges against you, but without lacking a clear intention. – On the contrary, I think that this infinitesimal crafting of the sonic sequence, this 'functional sound-mixture', is a new discovery, and that this makes it above all the first time that the connection between composition and instrumentation has truly been explained precisely. I await your opinion most eagerly.

Soma has been here since yesterday; he is having difficulties with the paper again,[2] but these will hopefully be solved in the best way. We were together yesterday evening, and I hope to see him again today. I was glad to hear good things about you from him, and also the texts for the concert aria[3] for Miss Herlinger, which seem most suitable – not least as texts for a work of *yours*.

How far is Lulu? Can one assume, as it has already been announced in the newspapers, that it has already reached a very advanced stage?

I am still being detained by onerous academic matters, two large presentations on the philosophical content of psychoanalysis, but after Tuesday week I shall be free to compose. Though I may be faced with a revision of my psychoanalysis book[4] for a *Habilitation* with the new professor,[5] as he has definitively agreed on the latter as such. But I hope that I shall be spared the worst regarding the reworking.

For the time being I am remaining here, having long been kept from continuous work this year by all my travels. I expect to travel to South Tyrol at the end of August and then to the Upper Italian lakes – if I can bear to return to Italy, of which I am not yet sure.

Did you receive my last letter, already from Frankfurt? The Ullstein matter is still unresolved, but I am not making any great efforts now – I have found a hair in my soup, and will shed no tears if nothing comes of it –, though I would ask you to keep this change of heart to yourself.

I wish you all the best for your work, you and Frau Helene a good recovery, and remain with my warmest greetings
your devoted
Teddie W.

Original: typescript with sender stamp and Adorno's signature.

1 This has been preserved among the documents at the Alban Berg Stiftung.

2 See Morgenstern, *Berg und seine Idole*, p. 219, n. 2.

3 Berg had sent Morgenstern the texts of the 'Wein-Gedichte von Baudelaire–George' with his letter of 12 June for him to check various 'enigmatic passages' (Morgenstern, *Berg und seine Idole*, p. 219); Morgenstern evidently showed Adorno these texts.

4 This is Adorno's first *Habilitation* thesis, *Der Begriff des Unbewussten in der transzendentalen Seelenlehre*.

5 This is Paul Tillich (1886–1965), who had succeeded Max Scheler in 1929.

93   WIESENGRUND-ADORNO AND SOMA MORGENSTERN
     TO BERG
     FRANKFURT, 25.6.1929

Dear Alban, I have not yet had the time to write to you: I have been travelling. Tomorrow I shall finally go to where the air is fresh. I will write soon. Fondly yours,
                    Soma

                    Fond & warm greetings
                    Annemarie v. Klenau

You have the misfortune, dear master and teacher, of encountering yet again the writing and the greetings of your devoted Teddie W.

· *Please* forward.

Original: picture postcard: Frankfurt University; stamp: Frankfurt am Main, 25.6.29. Manuscript with an additional note by Annemarie von Klenau. Morgenstern's text and the note by Annemarie von Klenau first printed in Morgenstern, *Berg und seine Idole*, p. 221.

Gut Berghof
     Post office: Sattendorf
     by Lake Ossiach
Carinthia   28.6.29

Only very briefly, my dear friend, concerning a matter of my own: your article about my songs is fabulous! I did not think it possible that someone could discover the – I can only say: secrets of my manner of instrumentation as you did. For the conductors (except Webern of course) have no idea, and it should be easy for them, as they *hear* all those things there that are not found in other scores, good or bad. But perhaps I am treating them unjustly: one isn't *supposed* to notice! Which makes your sensitivity all the more baffling!

But: I think the essay will be too long for P & T. It is almost a whole double issue. And I am the last person who would be in a position to demand that from U. E. and succeed; leaving aside the fact that they will not even ask me.

I can therefore only give *you* a word of advice: accept the possibility of having the middle section (i.e. the analysis, which you marked off for me with +) appear *in very small print.* If UE refuse, one could also spread the essay over two issues (à la Courths-Mahler) Finally – and do not now be cross with me: I would even consider abridging the large analysis that takes up 4/5 of the entire article. & even for artistic reasons. No one who is not in possession of the songs is in the know, even someone who has only the *piano* version will not always be able to follow (I myself, not having the score here with me, often lost the thread while reading) And the result would be that such a reader – i.e. 99% of the readership – would skip over all this and then perhaps not even get an idea of the important *general* aspects. And that would indeed be *a great shame!* And the many, many details concerning things that one cannot *see*, let alone *hear*, will tire even the patient and enthusiastic reader.

So would it not be possible to shorten the middle section with this in mind. For example by leaving all your general comments, also in the individual analyses, discussing one song or another (e.g. the first) in its entirety, (as you have done,) while emphasizing only certain *particularities* of the others. E.g. with 'Im Zimmer' the final, the only *low* note[1] at the end of the song, which I am very proud of! (I am thus bringing a terrible omission to your attention in a subordinate clause!)

I think it would be not simply from the perspective of P & T, but also in your interests and those of the songs, i.e. also in mine, if the article – as it is appearing for now in a *journal*, not a book, were cut by about a third. Do not be cross with me at this imposition, & also not for writing only about myself. You will shortly receive a lengthier and more altruistic letter. Yours with warmest greetings & heartfelt thanks for all the fine things

Alban Berg

Where is Soma? What did he actually do in Frankfurt. And at the 'Frz.'?[2]

Original: typescript with Berg's signature and a note in Adorno's hand along the left margin: 'Verkäufer Verteidiger Verführer Diplomat' (salesman defender seducer diplomat), as well as a marginal note at the top of the second page: 'Kollektivmonolog'.

1 In his hand copy of the Seven Early Songs, Berg had made the following note after the double-barline of this song: 'Dear Teddie, I am almost proud of this low note (the only one!)!' (Berg archive in the music collection of the Österreichische Nationalbibliothek, F 21 Berg 3286, leaf 26ᵛ).

2 This is the *Frankfurter Zeitung*.

95   BERG TO WIESENGRUND-ADORNO
     TRAHÜTTEN, 8.8.1929

Trahütten in Steiermark
Post office: Deutsch-Landsberg
     via Graz   8.8.29

My dear friend, I kept on having to postpone the long-announced letter. Now I am making use of a break from work to commit at least the most important things to paper. A break from work to the extent that I, having come home a week ago, have fallen ill with the inevitable asthma, whose attacks are now slowly petering out. But also a break from work to the extent that I am near finishing the fair copy of the 'Wine-aria', and then hope finally to get back to 'Lulu'.

For now, let me say what I have long wanted to tell you: your Casella essay is really quite, quite excellent. Firstly as a snub, but then on account of the general part, where you say everything about the current state of music that can be said at all, and which no one had said before you, and *therefore* thirdly again: as a snub! Though it will not receive the attention it deserves; & for the same reason as all polemic that cannot be rebutted, and which is therefore hushed up. In contrast to such lightly and loosely written argumentative essays as

155

the Karl May article,[1] for example, which the likes of Korngold[2] – even with a certain success – can pounce on. Which does more harm than good. So one really cannot know how to go about it to achieve the desired effect. Perhaps like Karl Kraus, whose last Offenbach Fackel[3] (no. 811–19) you absolutely must read?

But, at any rate, I personally – and the few people who matter – see it as a blessing that this, the only possible position in the Casella affair, has been set down as you have done.

To speak directly of another article: what is to happen to the one about the 7 early songs? I have not heard one word about it from U. E. or P & T. I would certainly be sorry if it were suppressed. Not only for *my* sake! (NB the score arrived as required. My thanks!)

What have you heard about Weissmann's post? Well, my respect for Berlin's music critics may well have dropped further since reading Einstein's hymn to 'Der Maschinist Hopkins'*[4] . . . I cannot quite imagine how *you* could live in this atmosphere. But this should not, for God's sake, keep you from trying it nonetheless. Even if it remained only an attempt, it would not be in vain. But if it does not, then one could expect something extremely interesting.

Will this season pass once more without our seeing each other? I can imagine that Vienna does not tempt you; but perhaps some time one of the cities I am likely to visit soon for 'Wozzeck' premieres:[5] especially Cologne start of Nov. Later Königsberg, Lübeck, Essen . . .

For the time being I am remaining here. Perhaps you can write to me some time, even if my replies come so late and are so short. I unfortunately have so much *business* correspondence to take care of that I quite simply do not get around to friends' letters. But I nonetheless think a great deal about them, in fact about you, my dear Teddy!, to whom warm greetings (also in the name of his wife) from

his old Berg

Original: typescript with Berg's signature.

1 See letter no. 83, note 6.

2 Allusion to Julius Korngold, the music critic of the *Neue Freie Presse*.

3 On the occasion of the 110th anniversary of Jacques Offenbach's birth, from 3 to 10 June, Karl Kraus had arranged a reading of eight operettas, accompanied at the piano by Georg Knepler. Schönberg's student Paul A. Pisk (1893–1990) then criticized, in the *Arbeiterzeitung* of 9 June – 'Vorgelesene Operetten' – the musical reduction of Offenbach's works to one voice and

---

* Incidentally, your Frankfurt also chooses to put on 'Der Maschinist Hopkins' instead of the repeatedly announced 'Wozzeck' – just like Moscow, who do not find the latter sufficiently revolutionary.

piano (see *Die Fackel*, no. 811–19 [1929], pp. 85–7). In the same issue of *Die Fackel* (pp. 91–3), Kraus published a letter by Eduard Steuermann in which he emphasized, also in the name of Berg and Kolisch, the musical significance of the Offenbach readings.

4 The premiere of this opera by Max Brand (1896–1980), a student of Schreker, had taken place on 13 April 1929 in Duisburg; Alfred Einstein wrote his review – 'Opern-Woche im Industrie-Gebiet' (*Berliner Tageblatt*, 10 July 1929) – after the 7 July performance during the fifty-ninth Tonkünstlerfest of the Allgemeiner Deutscher Musikverein (Musical Artists' Festival of the General German Music Society), which had taken place from 2 to 7 July in Duisburg.

5 The Cologne premiere took place only on 11 October 1930, those in Königsberg and Lübeck both on 13 May 1930. In Essen, *Wozzeck* was premiered on 12 December 1929 in Berg's presence.

96 BERG TO WIESENGRUND-ADORNO
     TRAHÜTTEN, 4.9.1929

Trahütten in Steiermark
Post office: Deutsch-Landsberg
   via Graz   4.9.29

Today, dear friend, just briefly the following: 'Der Scheinwerfer', the programme magazine for the Städtische Bühnen Essen (editorial office. Essen Theaterplatz 10), has asked me for a picture, article etc. (for the perf. of 'Wozzeck' there), and goes on:
   'Could you furthermore name someone suited to writing about you, and in particular about "W."?'[1]
   Of course I can! And mention your name.
   Perhaps it is already tedious to you, as it is to me! But on the other hand, perhaps different things could be said *today* than years ago. For example the connection to so-called 'objectivity',[2] and here I would like to add that *I myself* consider 'W' no less objective than romantic. I know – if I look at the score – *how* objectively it was written, albeit always in the attempt that the listener would not notice, and feel as romantically snug as in a good armchair, where the nails do not stick out and there is no stench from the glue that holds it together. And you can also repeat or incorporate that infinitely pleasing one from one of the last issues of Anbruch (on the occasion of the Berlin reprise in June).[3] And after all, you are constantly coming up with something new!
   I expect you received my last letter of the 7.8.?[4] When you next write to me, then please here for now, where I hope I can remain until

157

late Sept. early Oct. But please BY REG. MAIL, as I might have to leave here suddenly after all: the Vienna 'Wozzeck' perf. seems to be getting serious . . .

(A discreet question: what is *Sievert* in Frankfurt like?[5] It is possible that he might come into consideration for me) I have not felt at ease here for a long time. Nonetheless, I am at least composing the 'Aria' *score* and am now busy with 'Lulu'. But the disturbances keeping me from it are increasing all the time!

How are you faring and where are you during this superb late summertime?

Fond regards from your

Alban Berg

Original: typescript with Berg's signature.

1 Adorno subsequently wrote the essay 'Die Oper Wozzeck'; see *Der Scheinwerfer: Blätter der Städtischen Bühnen Essen*, vol. 3 (1929–30), pp. 5–11 (*GS* 18, pp. 472–9).

2 Translator's note: the original term *Sachlichkeit*, while having the meaning of 'objectivity', most likely refers to the *Neue Sachlichkeit* movement, which is commonly translated as 'New Functionalism'. As Berg subsequently uses the word in its more general sense, however, and this would not be communicated by continuing to use 'functional' or 'functionality', I have chosen to use 'objectivity' and 'objective' throughout.

3 See 'Berliner Opernmemorial', *Anbruch*, 11 (1929), pp. 261–6; *GS* 19, pp. 267–75.

4 This should be the 8.8.

5 The premiere in the Viennese State Opera under Clemens Krauss took place on 30 March 1930; the stage set was designed by Oskar Strnad (1879–1933), not by Ludwig Sievert (1887–1967), who made the set for the Frankfurt production of *Wozzeck*.

97   WIESENGRUND-ADORNO TO BERG
     BELLAGIO, 4.9.1929

Bellagio, Hotel Genazzini
4 September 29.

Dear master and teacher, accept my warmest greetings from this glorious peninsula. Your letter was very pleasing to me, and I am proud that you liked my things. I hope you are satisfied with the 12–tone essay.[1] Stein did not print the one about your songs!![2] And U. E. in

general. – Is the Baudelaire finished? Where has Lulu got to? Thank you for the recommendation to Holland![3] – We must at last meet somewhere. All my best to you and Frau Helene
Yours Teddie W.

Original: picture postcard: Bellagio; stamp: Bellagio / Como, 5.9.29. Manuscript.

1 Adorno's essay 'Zur Zwölftonmusik' appeared in the September/October 1929 issue of *Anbruch* (see *GS* 18, pp. 363–9).

2 See letter no. 90, note 3.

3 In a letter of 30 July 1929 to the Dutch composer Daniel Ruyneman (1886–1963), who was preparing two concerts with 'Viennese chamber music', especially from the Schönberg circle, Berg had recommended compositions by Adorno: 'I advise you to put on one of the two song cycles with piano by Wiesengrund-Adorno. You should also contact him directly regarding this [. . .]. Incidentally, he has also written a very fine quartet' (Paul Op de Coul, 'Unveröffentlichte Briefe von Alban Berg und Anton Webern an Daniel Ruyneman', *Tijdschrift van de Vereniging voor Nederlandse Muziek Geschiednis*, 22 [1972], pp. 201–20; for the quotation, see p. 206f.). Adorno's *Four Songs for Middle-Register Voice and Piano* op. 3, which were to be performed in the first of the two concerts on 24 March 1930, were presumably taken off the programme owing to Margot Hinnenberg-Lefèbre's sudden cancellation.

98 WIESENGRUND-ADORNO TO BERG
    FRANKFURT, 9.10.1929

DR. TH. WIESENGRUND-ADORNO
Frankfurt a. M.-Oberrad   9 October 1929.
Seeheimer Strasse 19 Tel. Spessart 62480

Dear master and teacher,
forgive me for replying to your kind letter only today and now immediately accosting you with my own affairs. I am only doing so in the belief that the things I am telling you are of some significance also for you – and perhaps even in general.
So: I have given up the directorship of Anbruch, which I had in effect had for half a year (for Stefan did nothing at all apart from his stupid essays, it was only Heinsheimer who meddled) and am leaving the editorial committee. You can see why from the letter I have enclosed from Herr Heinsheimer,[1] who admittedly only showed his true nature between the red cover pages of Die Fackel. It is obvious

159

that I must go, and today, after this disclosure, it almost seems suspect that I ever had dealings with the villains. I would not trouble you further if the letter did not contain that passage about 'Schönberg and his closest circle', which could not but deeply hurt me.

I shall leave open the question of whether it is truthful, or simply stems from the imagination of Herr Heinsheimer, who sought thus to deal me a deadly blow. And I have no illusions whatsoever about the Anbruch I experienced as an editor. I know the paper is bad. I was compelled, in order to achieve at least some of the things I felt were necessary, to print poor stuff forced upon me by the publisher, the idiotic essay by Felber on Szymanowski,[2] the poor one by Preussner on Křenek,[3] the waffling of the directors Wallerstein and Graf,[4] the utter boredom of the radio essay by Szendrei[5] and much more. But as clearly as I can see all this, I still know that, in spite of it all, the paper under my initiative was at least an attempt to speak the truth in musical matters and to address those grave realities that are suppressed everywhere else (naturally also in Melos) today. My concrete measure in this was the work of 'Schönberg and his closest circle'. I take no credit for this, there is no other proper music today and I was simply compelled by this insight and by the most basic decency to act as I did. I requested no support and received none; not one line was printed to aid my endeavours by those with whom I feel solidarity. I accepted this, and attempted to enforce my Schönberg policy alone and with the entirely inadequate assistance of such people as Redlich and Westphal.[6] If now, after all this, Schönberg too is stabbing me in the back and sabotaging the little that I undertook in the interests of the cause that he himself embodies, this can only outrage me. This is a case of that stupid and solipsistic 'sovereignty' that considers itself exempt from all human obligations on account of its genius and achievements; the same disloyalty that he also showed towards you, according to your own account, when the Altenberg songs gave rise to a scandal and he uttered not one word in your defence. He, who boasts that everything he says has several meanings, would in such a case have done better to find unambiguous words. He did as little as he had done in the Casella case.[7] Even if he always said that Anbruch was a filthy rag – which I communicated to the publisher time and time again –; he should have added that he recognized I was seeking to cleanse it, instead of even supplying the likes of Heinsheimer with pretexts for foiling my efforts. To say nothing of the fact that I cannot recognize someone who asks Mummy what modern people are[8] as an authority on literary matters, even if he were a Beethoven, which he is not, however, as he would not ask such questions otherwise.

This is what I wish to ask of you: to discuss the matter with Webern and Steuermann, who aside from you are the only ones I can count on,

160

perhaps also with Stein (if he has not been entirely bought by U. E.), and also to show them Heinsheimer's letter, and, if it is possible, to take a step that would make it irrefutably clear that at least Schönberg's 'closest circle' is not against me. It will be good to undertake this with Hertzka personally and to show him Heinsheimer's letter, which after all, at least as far as your stance and Steuermann's are concerned, contains a *direct untruth*. Incidentally, Rudi *Kolisch* spoke very positively of my achievements at Anbruch when I saw him a few weeks ago. So the statement in question must come from Schönberg himself. I shall inform myself through Kolisch. – I thank you in advance for your efforts. I feel entitled to ask you this because in this case, the person and the matter are truly identical.

The loss of Anbruch is a particular blow to me, coming at a moment when I had managed for the first time to produce an issue corresponding at least to some extent with what I hoped to accomplish in Anbruch,[9] although here too the quality of the individual essays is not consistent. At any rate, I would sincerely ask you to take a look at this issue, which will most likely have come out by the time you receive this letter. And finally another request. The November issue will be the last issue under my direction and it is naturally especially important to me for it to turn out well. Would you help it ad maiorem gloriam by making available the revised version of your Wozzeck essay that Heinsheimer requested from you?[10] You would truly be doing me a great favour. In this context I would also like to tell you that not only Pult und Taktstock but also Anbruch itself turned down my essay on the orchestration of the early songs on the grounds of lack of space, though said lack does not prevent the publication of the most harebrained essays by Felber, Stefan etc. Equally, my repeated request to publish detailed reviews of the orchestral variations by A. S.,[11] the string trio and the symphony by Webern[12] has in part been ignored, in part openly rejected. I must ask you to also inform Webern and Steuermann of this.

I shall gladly write the Wozzeck essay for Der Scheinwerfer in Essen, although it is much more difficult for me today, as I know the work much better and more profoundly than 4 years ago, and therefore feel an entirely different responsibility towards the work. At any rate, I promise you that this time the essay will be very concrete, and cleansed of a philosophy that is useless as long as it formulates itself abstractly, rather than proving itself through its material. By this I mean that I feel a need to make up for some of what I wrote in my *Anbruch* essay on Wozzeck in 1925. I hope I shall succeed.

One hears wondrous things about the Schönberg opera.[13] The music apparently surpasses everything that has come before it. But why apply that to a text that is seemingly so crassly bourgeois and arch-reactionary? *How much better your instinct is in choosing Lulu!* I cannot tell you how I long to hear it, as also the Baudelaire aria. It seems it will be premiered in Frankfurt by Scherchen.[14] Will you come? Then *naturally* as my guest.

I am finding no time to compose properly on account of the Kierkegaard book,[15] but this will now definitely be the last stop. I am working on 2 chamber songs in strict twelve-tone technique. – U. E. have of course done nothing for my orchestral pieces.

Concerning your question about Sievert: he is a very gifted decorative painter, though he is caught within an impressionism that has been shifted towards artisanship, which is in truth not appropriate to Wozzeck, but would be favourable for the audience. Similar to Aravantinos.[16] But the only one who should really produce the sets for Wozzeck is Moholy-Nagy. His Hoffmann's Tales[17] made an extraordinary impression upon me. Only: as a Bauhaus man he is a risky choice in a practical context. Someone far more dangerous is Wallerstein,[18] who has a colourful directorial warehouse, and deprives everything of its seriousness with his ghastly playfulness and ideas. You must watch him very, very closely. Will Krauss really do Wozzeck? Have rehearsals started? I questioned Steinberg here about Wozzeck,[19] and he was quite certain that he would do it next season, it being impossible this season due to the incredibly difficult Schönberg. Steinberg certainly made a serious impression in his attitude, and I believe that he will carry out his plan.

This much for today. Once again, do not hold it against me that I have drawn you into the démarche with U. E.; I would not trouble you with it if it did not seem truly urgent – and if my authority in relation to U. E. did not depend on it. You can safely show Hertzka Heinsheimer's letter yourself.

I hope you and Frau Helene are well, and that work on Lulu is going well in spite of everything. Also extend my greetings to Soma, whose address I unfortunately do not have, otherwise I would write to him. Please also inform him of my conflict with U. E.

With fond regards and the hope that we shall soon meet again,

Devotedly yours,
Teddie W.

Original: typescript with sender stamp and Adorno's signature, as well as an enclosed copy of a letter to Adorno from Hans Heinsheimer.

1 See appendix II, letter no. 3.

2 See Erwin Felber, 'Karol Szymanowski', *Anbruch*, 11 (1929), pp. 206–11.

3 See Eberhard Preussner, 'Ernst Křenek', *Anbruch*, 11 (1929), pp. 154–9.

4 See Lothar Wallerstein, 'Aufgezben der Großstadtoper', *Anbruch*, 11 (1929), pp. 252–6, and Herbert Graf, 'Oper im neuen Russland', ibid., pp. 238–50.

5 See Alfred Szendrei, 'Fünf Jahre musikalische Volkserziehung', *Anbruch* 11 (1929), pp. 194–206.

6 The following articles by Kurt Westphal appeared in that year's volume (11) of *Anbruch*: 'Die Harmonik Scrjabins' (Scriabin's Harmonic Language) (February), 'Die Sonate als Formproblem der modernen Musik' (The Sonata as a Formal Problem in Modern Music) (April) and 'Grenzen der motorisch-rhythmischen Gestaltung' (Limits of Motoric-Rhythmic Shaping) (September/October).

7 See letter no. 83, note 5, where Schönberg's statement on Casella is cited.

8 At the end of Schönberg's opera *Von heute auf morgen* (From One Day to the Next), the child asks: 'Mummy, what are these modern people?'; Adorno is also alluding to the fact that Gertrud Schönberg had written the libretto to that opera under the pseudonym of Max Blonda.

9 Adorno means the September/October issue, whose theme was 'problems of compositional technique'; the contributions and their authors were: Hanns Gutmann, 'Über die Möglichkeit der Kompositionskritik' (On the Possibility of Compositional Critique); Ernst Křenek, 'Freiheit und Technik: "Improvisatorischer" Stil' (Freedom and Technique: 'Improvisatory' Style); Kurt Westphał, 'Grenzen der motorisch-rhythmischen Gestaltung'; Hans F. Redlich, 'Neue Probleme der Chorkomposition' (New Problems in Choral Composition); Adorno's contribution to the issue was 'Zur Zwölftontechnik'.

10 Berg does not seem to have prepared a revised version of the large lecture on *Wozzeck* (see Hans F. Redlich, *Alban Berg: Versuch einer Würdigung* (Attempt at a Tribute), Vienna, Zurich and London, 1957, pp. 311–27) that he had written in January 1929 for the Oldenburg premiere of the opera. Willi Reich relates (*Alban Berg, Leben und Werk*, Zurich, 1963, p. 72): 'As he had not been able to treat the individual parts of the opera in equal detail, he forbade any publication of his text. When, however, a brochure on the work was ordered from me for the American premieres of *Wozzeck* (Philadelphia and New York, 1931, conductor: Leopold Stokowski), I was allowed for this purpose to rework the lecture under his supervision, in such a way that all parts of the opera were considered as uniformly as possible, and most of the musical examples eliminated.' The February 1930 issue of *Anbruch* subsequently contained two pages under the heading 'Wozzeck: Bemerkungen von Alban Berg' (Wozzeck: Remarks by Alban Berg) that are in no way a revised version of the lecture on *Wozzeck*.

11 Schönberg's Variations for Orchestra op. 31.

12 These are op. 20 and op. 21.

13 *Von heute auf morgen* op. 32 was premiered in Frankfurt on 1 February 1930.

14 The concert aria *Der Wein* was premiered in Königsberg on 4 June 1930 at the sixtieth Tonkünstlerfest des Allgemeinen Deutschen Musikvereins; Růžena Herlinger, who had suggested the composition, sang the solo part under Hermann Scherchen. The performance planned for 18 November 1929 at Frankfurt Radio with the same musicians had to be cancelled because Růžena Herlinger had fallen ill.

15 Adorno's second *Habilitation* thesis, 'Kierkegaard: Konstruktion des Ästhetischen', with which he completed his *Habilitation* in February 1931; the revised version was published in 1933 (see *GS* 2, pp. 7–213; English translation: T. W. Adorno: *Kierkegaard: Construction of the Aesthetic*, trans. Robert Hullot-Kentor, Cambridge, MA, MIT Press, 1993).

16 Panos Aravantinos (1886–1930) had designed the stage set for the Berlin premiere of *Wozzeck*.

17 The painter László Moholy-Nagy (1895–1946) had designed the stage set for the production of Offenbach's opera at the Krolloper in 1929; Alexander von Zemlinsky conducted; for Adorno's report, see *GS* 19, p. 268f.

18 The conductor and opera director Lothar Wallerstein (1882–1949), who had worked alongside Clemens Krauss in Frankfurt since 1924, took over the direction of the Vienna *Wozzeck*.

19 The premiere of the Frankfurt production of *Wozzeck* took place on 19 April 1931 under the musical direction of Hans Wilhelm Steinberg.

99   WIESENGRUND-ADORNO TO BERG
     FRANKFURT, 17.10.1929

DR. TH. WIESENGRUND-ADORNO
Frankfurt a. M.-Oberrad
Seeheimer Strasse 19 Tel. Spessart 62480   October 17th 1929.

Dear master and teacher,
   10 days ago I wrote you a long letter with the copy of a document by Heinsheimer and as I have so far heard nothing from you, and the matter is certainly important, I wish to ask you if you received the letter, as I would otherwise like to write to you and send the Heinsheimer again. I would be most grateful for a card of confirmation.
   Incidentally, I believe one can indirectly observe the effects of an intervention on your part at U. E., who somehow seem to be giving way. First I received a letter from Stefan, then one from Heinsheimer, then Redlich sought to mediate with me at H.'s behest. I subsequently clarified my position in a short and very firm letter to U. E. My only compromise was to be willing to expand the circle of contributors somewhat, as I myself have the feeling that there is a danger of

inbreeding. If I can maintain my own position in Anbruch, I consider this sufficient justification for perhaps letting in things that are not at my own level, and which, at least as long as I am myself writing and setting the direction, take care of themselves as naturally as the contributions of Stefan and Felber have done until now. Anbruch is our only bastion in the domain of musical publications, and this does seem so fundamental after all that I – also on the advice of Kracauer and Holl – do not want to give everything up, now that I have seen that U. E. do not want to lose me there. It would naturally be of the *utmost* importance to me to know what you think of this and how you assess the whole situation. The publisher has still given no direct reply to my second, fundamental letter. I had categorically demanded in it that the journal should not be turned once more into an advertising paper, and furthermore that, if I am still to play a deciding part in it, I could not do so as an external adviser, but only as an editor with the necessary jurisdiction; I rebuffed the attacks levelled at me sharply, and naturally refused (on principle, the figures are unimportant) to accept any cuts in payment. This for your information.

I would like to thank you most warmly for arranging a performance of my songs in Amsterdam. Yesterday I received a letter saying that this is certain. Unfortunately I was unable to reach Steuermann, so someone from Amsterdam will play it.[1] I am moved that you thought of me on this occasion.

When will you come to Germany? – I am now beginning the Wozzeck essay. Otherwise, I am entirely immersed in the Kierkegaard, which would also interest you – if only because of Karl Kraus, who, I am increasingly realizing, would be inconceivable without Kierkegaard. I have now made sufficient headway with the preliminary work that I can think of composing once more.

Fond regards to you and Frau Helene from your devoted
Teddie W.

Original: typescript with sender stamp and Adorno's signature.

1 Unknown.

100   BERG TO WIESENGRUND-ADORNO
       VIENNA, 20.10.1929

VIENNA XIII. Trauttmansdorffgasse 27   20.10.29

My dear friend, I received your first letter 10 min. before leaving for Venice,[1] and found the 2nd here yesterday upon my return. But much of what I wanted to write to you regarding the 1st letter has now been made obsolete by the 2nd. So I can be very brief, which is rather convenient for me in this particular case, as I have returned after almost 5 months of absence from Vienna to find more horrendous amounts of work *than ever before*.

So. The proper solution to the matter would naturally have been to leave Anbruch altogether. And UE would have deserved it too! But for the cause, for *our* common cause it is admittedly very good that you have found a way to continue working there. I would only ask that you do this in a manner that does not seem like a capitulation. In my opinion it would almost suffice if you were to be guaranteed the status of a 'collaborator', so that everything *important* you have to say about music, and which no one but you says and can say as you do, is guaranteed a place in the pages of Anbruch. Until you find a more sympathetic platform. I.e. a music paper that is not a *publisher's* paper. For believe me: that is the only reason for the behaviour of UE. If they were honest, they would have written: 'We are a publisher's paper, not an art journal, and as our financial situation is not the best (which is genuinely *true* Discretion please!), we cannot afford the luxury of an *art* journal, but at most only a pure *publisher's* paper in which every line aids us materially. As we can naturally not expect this of you, Herr Wiesengrund, we cannot hold it against you if you take action accordingly.' *That* would have been honest, and everything else claptrap that you should not for God's sake get worked up over. Nor over the passage about 'Schönberg and his closest circle'. As far as the *latter* about the 'closest circle' is concerned, Heinsheimer confessed immediately to me that this was an untruth and that he had done you an injustice with it. As far as *Schönberg* is concerned, however, he did make a remark *in conversation* with Heinsheimer to the effect that Anbruch 'serves the other authors at UE but not him' (it must have gone something like that), but certainly no criticism of your activities. Schönberg lives in perpetual conflict with UE, constantly feels disadvantaged by them and happens to draw Anbruch into the accusations he constantly levels at them. But it is beyond doubt to me that – to the extent that he reads it at all – that he, who already praised your essays to me some time ago (you know that he initially thought them too difficult), can only be and will indeed have been highly satisfied with your recent articles, e.g. the Casella essay. I will be able to offer you certainty about this when I finally meet with Schönberg again, which should certainly happen at some point this season. But you too must speak to Schönberg about Anbruch when he comes to Frankfurt for the premiere,[2] and you will see that there is nothing personal. And then surely also regret, in secret, the words you wrote to me in an understandably heated state about him.

Perhaps we shall see each other in mid-Nov. in Frankfurt at the premiere of the 'Aria'. We could then speak further about all this, and reach a clarity that is almost impossible to attain in letters. But I shall also keep an eye on your matter with UE here & perhaps inform you when I consider a particular action on your part to be diplomatically favourable. For the time being, the matter seems to be progressing well.

This, my dear Wiesengrund, in *great* haste.

Accept my very best wishes and also many thanks for your other news from your old

Alban Berg

Original: typescript with Berg's signature.

1 Berg had visited Alma Mahler-Werfel in her house in Venice.

2 To the premiere of his opera *Von heute auf morgen* on 1 February 1930.

101   WIESENGRUND-ADORNO TO BERG
        FRANKFURT, 23.10.1929

DR. TH. WIESENGRUND-ADORNO
Frankfurt a. M.-Oberrad
Seeheimer Strasse 19 Tel. Spessart 62480   23 October 1929.

Dear master and teacher,

many warm thanks for your most kind letter – I cannot tell you how glad I am that in this situation, which burdens me so terribly and probably quite disproportionately, I have at least not been forsaken by the only ones who matter to me. I too am up to my neck in work, and you must therefore forgive my egotistic brevity in addressing two points which, however, are very important ones.

Firstly: a 'capitulation' on my part is *absolutely* out of the question, and it would be quite incomprehensible to me if U. E. had gained such an impression from my extremely sharp and firm letter. I only insisted upon an editorial position because of the attempt to force me into a form of advisory function, where I would have been expected to offer my ideas without any guarantee that they would be properly carried out. And *that* is definitely out of the question for me. If U. E. thought that they could keep me among their editorial staff and still turn the journal into an advertising paper, I would leave *immediately*. I was, and still am, entirely *serious* about my resignation.[1] And I have still received no answer from U. E., and thus have no notion of what course the matter will now take. But in *personal* terms, it is extremely important to me for you to know that I am doing nothing that cannot be justified truthfully and without With regard to or In view of.[2] My *only* concession is the expansion of our base of employees, and I consider this necessary in any case if the paper is not to die of boredom, which is perhaps a nobler but no less agonizing death than one brought about by open malice.

Then: the claim that Anbruch has done things for other composers, but not for Schönberg, is plainly contradicted by the facts. Schönberg must not have read Anbruch at all. I certainly do not hold that against him; but then he should not presume to comment on it. I could mention Motive II and III,[3] in both of which A. S. had a central role; the song essay,[4] which was entirely devoted to him; the Westphal essay on the problem of the sonata;[5] Atonales Intermezzo[6] and the twelve-tone essay[7] (what do you think of it?), Westphal's article on the limits of rhythmic-motoric shaping.[8] These are only the ones that occurred to me immediately, and I think that it is a great deal in one year. For Schönberg is hardly likely to confuse me with the head of propaganda at Universal Edition. Indeed, that very head of propaganda has quite simply *ignored* my request – repeated countless times – to send me the orchestral variations for review[9] (just as my essay on the orchestration of your early songs was dropped without further ado). Perhaps it would at least interest Schönberg to know this. Incidentally, I shall be seeing Rudi Kolisch within the next few days.

When will you be in Frankfurt? I ask so that I can arrange my time accordingly, as I have to go to Göttingen for a few days in November concerning my Kierkegaard. And I definitely want to arrange this in such a way as not to miss you. For you shall be staying with me!!!

This much for today. Fond regards to you and Frau Helene from your devoted

Teddie W.

Original: typescript with sender stamp and Adorno's signature.

1 In a letter of 8 October 1929 to Adorno from Paul Stefan, the latter already assumes that Adorno has withdrawn from 'editorial work', and hopes that he can rely on Adorno's 'private and occasional assistance'. This suggests that the publisher and *Anbruch* had already decided early on to remove Adorno from his position as the head of the editorial staff.

2 See letter no. 80, note 4.

3 The collection of aphorisms entitled *Motive II* had appeared in the June/July 1928 issue, and *Motive III* in the August/September issue.

4 See 'Situation des Liedes', *Musikblätter des Anbruch*, 10 (1928), pp. 363–9 (*GS* 18, pp. 345–53).

5 See letter no. 98, note 6.

6 See letter no. 83, note 5.

7 See letter no. 97, note 1.

8 See letter no. 98, note 6.

9 Adorno's review of Schönberg's op. 31 appeared in the January issue of *Anbruch*; see *GS* 18, pp. 370–5.

DR. TH. WIESENGRUND-ADORNO
Frankfurt a. M.-Oberrad
Seeheimer Strasse 19 Tel. Spessart 62480   3 November 1929.

Dear master and teacher, in great haste, the large Wozzeck essay is finished and already in print. But I made so many corrections to the proof copy that I am reluctant to send you a duplicate of the type-written manuscript – I would have to send you a copy so entirely defaced by corrections that you would derive little insight or enjoyment from it. I would therefore ask that you wait until you can read the final printed version.

Concerning the essay itself – which above all deals most extensively with 'objectivity'[1] and cites a passage from a letter of yours[2] – I shall today reveal only its denouement to you: it attempts to grasp Wozzeck as a passion.

On 12 November I shall have your clarinet pieces[3] – which I have never heard – played here in the 'Music Studio'[4] founded by Soma's uncle Heinz Simon,[5] and which I am now in charge of. I am greatly looking forward to it.

When will you come? Is the performance of the aria in November certain? Please do let me know.

Fond regards to you and Frau Helene Your old
                    Teddie W.

Original: typescript with sender stamp and Adorno's signature.

1 See letter no. 96, note 2.

2 See *GS* 18, p. 476; the passage is from letter no. 96.

3 The Four Pieces for Clarinet and Piano op. 5.

4 See also Adorno's essay of the same name from 1931, *GS* 19, pp. 520–4.

5 Heinrich Simon (see letter no. 61 and note 1 there) was an uncle of Inge Morgenstern.

$^{17}/_{11}$29

My dear Wiesengrund, your article in 'Der Scheinwerfer' was an immense source of joy to me. I thank you for it with all my heart! I would have liked to do so in person, and kept hoping to go there for the Frankfurt perf. of the aria. But never quite knew, which is why I left your repeated questions on this matter unanswered. Until, that is, the utterly unexpected cancellation of the perf. removed all doubts. A shame! We could at last have had a good chinwag once more. When will the opportunity arise? Perhaps in Essen, where the premiere will take place on 7 December.[1] And where I expect to hold a 'Wozzeck' lecture a few days beforehand.[2] – *Now* you should be seeing Webern soon. You could almost certainly make it possible for Webern to be *put up* during his stay in Frankfurt.[3] Explanation superfluous: In case *you* are not able to do so, the Seligmanns would surely be an option. If they hear that Webern is coming to F., I am sure they will invite him to their house. As you – so I hear – are picking him up in any case, you could no doubt arrange that easily. I expect you shall then also discuss the Amsterdam concert with Webern. Steuermann's participation is still entirely uncertain, though we all desire it so very, very much, and Ruyneman has already made arrangements for it.[4]

But the people there cannot pay anything, and – even if this does not appear to be the main reason, one can hardly expect Steuermann to pay for himself to travel somewhere (primarily) as an accompanist!

Please write to me at length about Webern's concert, and perhaps I shall also find the time to report at greater length myself. I have to practise the piano this week, as I am accompanying the early songs in Vienna.[5] And otherwise I also have so much to do that I often do not know if I am coming or going.

Once more warmest thanks for the splendid article and fond regards from us both.

Your Alban Berg

In the next Bach issue of 'Musik' you shall read something of mine![6]

Original: typescript with Berg's signature.

1 In fact, it did not take place until 12 December.
2 This is the major lecture on *Wozzeck* written for the Oldenburg performance and first held there; see letter no. 98, note 10.

3 On 24 November, Webern conducted Mozart's Divertimento (no. 11) in D major, K 251, *Kindertotenlieder* by Gustav Mahler (sung by Josef Hueber) and Mozart's Symphony in G minor, K 550, at Southwest German Radio. Furthermore, Webern rehearsed his *Four Pieces for Violin and Piano* op. 7 and his *Three little Pieces for Violoncello and Piano* op. 3 with Erich Itor Kahn (piano), Licco Amar (violin) and Maurits Frank (cello) for an ISCM concert on 27 November. (See Adorno's review in *GS* 19, p. 169, and Anton Webern, *Briefe an Theodor W. Adorno: Transkribiert und mit Anmerkungen versehen von Rolf Tiedemann*, in *Musik-Konzepte*, special issue: *Anton Webern I*, Munich, 1983, pp. 6–22). While in Frankfurt, Webern stayed at the house of Milton Seligmann.

4 See letter no. 97 and note 3 there.

5 Berg accompanied Stella Eisner, who sang his Seven Early Songs at a chamber music evening of the Österreichischer Klub on 27 November 1929 (see *The Berg–Schoenberg Correspondence*, p. 391, n. 10).

6 See 'Credo', *Die Musik*, 22 (1929–30), p. 264f.; in it, Berg cites phrases from the Bach entry in Hugo Riemann's musical encyclopaedia, making small changes so that the homage to Bach is at the same time also one to Schönberg.

104 WIESENGRUND-ADORNO TO BERG
   FRANKFURT, 30.11.1929

DR. TH. WIESENGRUND-ADORNO
Frankfurt a. M.-Oberrad
Seeheimer Strasse 19 Tel. Spessart 62480   30 November 1929.

Dear master and teacher,
   it was sorely disappointing indeed for me to learn suddenly that you were unable to come. The devil take that stupid Herlinger woman for falling ill precisely when I have hopes to see you again at long last. I had thought it certain that you would stay with me, and for that reason not taken Webern in, instead putting him up with Seligmann (long before your letter arrived), where he felt most exceptionally at ease. We were together the whole time, and it was wonderful with him. I have completely discarded the reservations I once had about him, and must absolutely agree with you. He is a wonderful person, of a kind that is truly in scarce supply today, and so utterly substantial and authentic that certain ties of his in fact carry no significance. And what an artist! The performance of the Kindertotenlieder, but also the G minor symphony were among the most beautiful things I have ever heard. They would have been a source of joy also to you, and you would have been proud – for outside of our closest circles there is no one who can make music in such a way. – Unfortunately, my attempt

171

to have the radio here employ Webern in the long term initially proved fruitless[1] (through no fault of Schoen, the excellent new director).[2] But I shall not give up and the concert certainly did a great deal to pave the way. – I also played Webern my things, the two song cycles and the orchestral pieces, and had the impression, especially from the severe manner in which he insisted that I should do nothing other than compose, that he was genuinely satisfied. He will no doubt tell you himself. I only hope that I shall soon indeed be far enough in my external circumstances that I shall not have to do anything other than compose.

It was also much to my regret that you did not hear the performance of your clarinet pieces in the 'Studio', which I had prepared thoroughly and was decent, I think (unfortunately not the Webern songs, though his violin and cello pieces at the International were excellent). The clarinet pieces are wonderful,[3] especially the quick one, and it was only upon hearing them in their real instrumental sound that I grasped what is so uniquely Bergian about them (that is, their expansive force, which certainly does set them noticeably apart from analogous things by Webern). The clarinet and its combination with the piano sound fabulous.

To know that my Wozzeck essay gave you some pleasure is, to me, the only success for it that counts. Though I did have the feeling, after the brevity of your response, and after you did not comment on any of the essay's aspects, that you have certain objections, which for the sake of leniency ('as he's already written the essay anyway') you preferred not to reveal to me. I would like – *assuming that you have the time and consider it sufficiently important* – urgently to request that you voice these objections openly and without reservation. Not least for the sake of the matter itself. For the essay contains some quite audacious interpretation, and if you felt unable to acknowledge it, I would be forced to undertake a thorough revision of my arguments, though I believe that I have been as conscientious as is within my powers (I cannot be held responsible for a typographical error on the first page, *per*ceived rather than *con*ceived by me). I hope I need not tell you how *personally* important it must be to me to know your true verdict. So, be open; even if there were grave charges, I would rather know about them than live in the uncertain fear of having fallen short of you and your work.

A further word on the essay. Anbruch intend to reprint it in January[4] (in place of your lecture, which you are evidently unwilling to hand over to the paper, which indeed I cannot hold against you), I hear, with your consent. But they want to abridge it for that purpose, which in *this* case is quite impossible. You need only cast a glance at it to see for yourself; the few sentences that could perhaps be removed are meaningless in terms of space, and their absence would disturb the delicate balance of the essay's overall form. I spent an evening with Kracauer attempting to abridge it – in vain; he too considers it out of the question. So I would ask you to persuade U. E. (to whom I have already written in the matter) to publish the essay uncut. Naturally, it makes no difference financially.

A certain Herr *Reich*[5] has sent me an essay on twelve-tone technique[6] that I find exceptionally interesting, and which was evidently influenced directly by you. I have meanwhile heard from Webern that he is a student of yours. I tried to have him taken on by Anbruch, but (please do *not* tell Herr Reich this) encountered the most vehement resistance from Heinsheimer, who 'warned' me about Reich. As the man struck me as uncommonly talented, I would like to know what is behind this, and would be grateful to you for any information.

As Pult und Taktstock continues to exist, I could perhaps give them the essay on the orchestration of the songs. What do you think? Perhaps you could also speak to Stein.

I hope you and Frau Helene are well and at work. I am up to my neck in mine – – I wish I could return to what matters.

Devotedly yours   Teddie W.

Original: typescript with sender stamp and Adorno's signature.

1 According to the account of Josef Hueber, the attempt failed because, during the reception after Webern's concert on 24 November, the director of Southwest German Radio, Hans Flesch, despite being prepared, did not want to be the first to ask the question for reasons of prestige, and Webern was for his part awaiting the director's initiative; see Hans Moldenhauer and Rosaleen Moldenhauer, *Anton von Webern: Chronik seines Lebens und Werkes*, Zurich and Freiburg in Breisgau 1980, p. 305.

2 Ernst Schoen (1894–1960), a composition student of Edgard Varèse and lifelong friend of Walter Benjamin, was artistic programme director at Southwest German Radio in Frankfurt from 1929.

3 Webern's Six Songs on Poems by Georg Trakl op. 14 and Berg's Four Pieces for Clarinet and Piano op. 5 were performed on 14 November in the Musikstudio des Verbandes konzertierender Künstler Deutschlands (Music Studio of the Union of German Concert Artists).

4 This never occurred.

5 The music writer Willi Reich (1898–1980) was a student of Berg from 1928, and later editor of the magazine *23*.

6 Unknown.

Pontresina, 21 August 1930.
Dear master and teacher, after almost completing my Kierkegaard book, I broke down and fled to the mountains, and have come to my senses again in the presence of their beauty. Forgive the long silence of one who for months has not been human for work! In 14 days the book will be finished, then I shall conclude the chamber songs[1] – and hope to be with you soon in Vienna. Ever your faithful
Teddie W.

Original: picture postcard: Tschierva Glacier with Piz Bernina and Roseg; stamp: Pontresina, 30.VIII.30. Manuscript.

1 Adorno seems not to have composed them.

DR. TH. WIESENGRUND-ADORNO
Frankfurt a. M.-Oberrad
Seeheimer Strasse 19 Tel. Spessart 62480   16 January 1931.

Dear master and teacher,
it has already been so shamefully long since I last wrote to you that I hardly dare begin. But I shall swallow this shame as my well-deserved punishment and write nonetheless – simply because it is otherwise an unbearable condition that pushes me down further each day. I suppose I must go back quite far to begin my account. You knew that I was preparing a Kierkegaard book. In February last year, these preparations had progressed sufficiently for me to begin with the manuscript. For this purpose I withdrew from the city to Cronberg, a small, very pretty town in the Taunus, and worked in complete isolation. So intensively that I had a complete breakdown at the start of August – something that I had not yet experienced in my life – and, before my book was finished, went to the mountains, first to the Dolomites, then to the Engadin. At the start of September I was in Frankfurt once more and completed my book, which was now only missing the final chapter; then went back to Cronberg for another 3 weeks for corrections and revisions; have now been here again since October and await my *Habilitation*, which – admittedly as a by-product this time – is to follow from the book.[1] The faculty representatives have accepted it,

the committee has been formed, by human reckoning nothing can prevent it this time and the matter should at all events have been concluded within this term, i.e. in February at the latest. This is all the more likely as – the best thing in such cases – I am depended on, in so far as the two professors are so overburdened that I have to relieve them of a part of their work, and have long done so in practice. But of course your pessimism concerning all things institutional and official will remain justified until I have the venia legendi in written form. The book, whose exact title is 'Konstruktion des Ästhetischen in Kierkegaards Philosophie', is this time quite unconnected to its official function and purely a philosophical matter of my own intention, and I think that it is, *despite* having to serve as a *Habilitation* thesis, truly of some worth and something new and original. If you would like to enter the peculiar maze of the book, which of all my literary works so far is surely the one most profoundly connected to my, I hope I may say our, music – then I hope to be able to send you a copy in a few weeks. Perhaps it will amuse you to hear that much the same arguments are being levelled at it as those we are so accustomed to hearing from the music world: over-intellectuality, incomprehensibility, madness, dissolution; and that can even offer some consolation for having to go through the *Habilitation*.

At the moment I am composing once more. Initially, to work my way back in, a piano sonatina,[2] *tonal!!!*, entirely carefree and by no means for public listening, simply because I am dissatisfied with my technique, and wish to prove one or two things to myself. I shall have to see if I can even show it to you. Then I have a big radio commission, incidental music for Cocteau's Voix humaine,[3] a wonderful piece, which I have already set to work on. Since writing my short orchestral pieces, I cannot keep my hands off the orchestra; incidentally, I believe and hope that my apprenticeship with you is nowhere more evident than in the orchestral sound. And I hope to take half a year off as soon as I can, and go to you in Vienna to work on instrumentation. Nothing else.

The 'Wein' aria is wonderful, even just from the piano reduction – I can only dream of what the full score must look like. I shall review it in Anbruch[4] – who have incidentally still not printed the large analysis of the orchestration of the Early Songs. I expect you heard of my leaving the editorial staff after much wrangling.[5] It had of course been clear to me from the start that I was fighting a losing battle – and this time I had to lose it in the end. Were you in agreement with the last things of mine in it, the polemics against Stuckenschmidt and Křenek,[6] the essays on Mahler and Ravel,[7] the Schönberg reviews[8] and aphorisms?[9]

For next week, Miss Herlinger was to sing the 'Wein' aria and my long George songs (only part of which, and precisely not the more important ones, you know) here at the radio.[10] But she did not learn my songs in the 6 weeks that were at her disposal, refers to Webern (!!!), who supposedly called them the most difficult songs in the whole literature, is demanding countless further rehearsals and only intends to do them in March. Subsequently the radio programmed all the Herlinger, also 'Der Wein', for March. On the one hand I regret the postponement of 'Der Wein', but on the other I am naturally glad to be allowed to appear under your wing. I had passed a request on to Miss Herlinger to study my songs with you or, should you (which I of course thought highly likely on account of Lulu) be indisposed, with Webern or Steuermann. She did not do this, however, preferring to stay with Pisk.[11] I daresay they will have made a fine mess of them. Should your unlucky star ever bring you into the vicinity of this couple, you could perhaps have a listen. For the songs' sake – I can more or less imagine the pleasure to be derived from the interpretation.

I have now gone on at terrible length about myself and my own matters, but what else am I to do when appearing before you other than report. I might add that I was together with Schönberg a great deal at the premiere of the opera 'Von heute auf morgen', which, despite the atrocious libretto, is a *masterpiece*, and got a great deal out of seeing him, without the slightest friction between us. Personal interaction with him can even stand up to his music.

On Monday the Wozzeck rehearsals shall begin here, and I greatly hope that you will come for them some time soon. The final date for the premiere, as the singer for Marie told me today (very good and reliable; the same one who sang the woman in the Schönberg),[12] looks to be in mid-April, at the latest. Then you will of course be here.

Now let me ask you: how you are, above all, with the asthma and your health; in reactionary Vienna;[13] and musically? How far has Lulu progressed? I assume that you have quietly gotten very far. There was an announcement in the press that it would certainly be finished this year. Might one ask anything about this? I have heard a few things about the new form of twelve-tone technique you are using in it, with the serial permutations.[14] How glad I would be to see and hear some of all this soon.

I have also heard about your car,[15] and can well imagine what a source of joy it is to you, and that, as all things technical do in your hands, it shall come to life and become a peculiar form of pet. To say nothing of the exquisite rage that the idiocy of the traffic wardens or even the lights will cause you.

What does Frau Helene say to all this, and how is she? Does she curse me a great deal? Or will she take a stroll with me in honour of Wozzeck some time?

In terms of health, everything is in the best possible order here.

Admittedly, life in Germany is becoming more problematic every day for a thousand reasons, and I often consider it a blessing that you have not yet come to Berlin after all,[16] but remain in Austria, where in spite of all, the people, as the last elections show, are a little more human than the Germans, who have succumbed to a demonic stupidity.[17]

I ask you sincerely not to repay evil with evil and soon send a word to your faithful, yearning and Berg-hungry
Teddie.

Original: typescript with sender stamp and Adorno's signature.

1 It followed on 16 February 1931; the assessors were Max Horkheimer and Paul Tillich.

2 The 32–bar fragment of a sonatina for piano has survived among Adorno's belongings.

3 Adorno seems not to have carried out his radio commission; nor have any sketches been found to indicate that he ever started work on it. Cocteau's 'Pièce en un acte' for one person had been published on 13 February 1930, and was premiered four days later in the Comédie Française.

4 This never occurred.

5 The January 1931 issue of *Anbruch* (p. 31) contained the following editorial note: 'Dr. Theodor Wiesengrund-Adorno has left the editorial staff of "Anbruch", to which he belonged for two years, in cordial agreement. He will continue to supply "Anbruch" with his valuable contributions.'

6 See H. H. Stuckenschmidt and Theodor W. Adorno, 'Kontroverse über Heiterkeit' (Controversy About Gaiety), *Anbruch*, 12 (1930), pp. 18–21 (*GS* 19, pp. 448–52); Theodor W. Adorno, 'Reaktion und Fortschritt' (Reaction and Progress), *Anbruch*, 12 (1930), pp. 191–5 (*GS* 17, pp. 133–9); on this essay, see also Ernst Křenek, 'Fortschritt und Reaktion' (Progress and Reaction), *Anbruch*, 12 (1930), pp. 196–200.

7 See Theodor W. Adorno, 'Mahler heute' (Mahler Today), *Anbruch*, 12 (1930), pp. 86–92 (*GS* 18, pp. 226–34); Theodor W. Adorno, 'Ravel', *Anbruch*, 12 (1930), pp. 151–4 (*GS* 17, pp. 60–5).

8 Adorno's review of the Variations for Orchestra op. 31 by Arnold Schönberg had appeared in the January 1930 issue of *Anbruch*, and that of the opera *Von heute auf morgen* in the February issue; see *GS* 18, pp. 370–5 and pp. 376–80.

9 See Theodor W. Adorno, *Motive V*: 'Hermeneutik', *Anbruch*, 12 (1930), pp. 235–8 (*GS* 16, pp. 269–71, and *GS* 18, pp. 19–24).

10 The concert with Adorno's *Vier Gedichte von Stefan George für Singstimme und Klavier* op. 1 (see Adorno, *Compositions 1*, pp. 8–23) and Berg's *Der Wein* took place only on 8 April 1931, and the programme also included Paul Hindemith's *Konzertmusik für Klavier, Blechbläser und Harfen*

op. 49 (1930). For the incomplete typescript of Adorno's introductory lecture preserved among his belongings, in which he discusses Berg's composition, see GS 20.2, pp. 793–6.

11 Paul A. Pisk had studied piano with Julius Epstein.

12 This role of Marie was sung by Erna Recka in the Frankfurt premiere on 19 April 1931; the part of the woman in Schönberg's opera was taken by Else Gentner-Fischer.

13 Following the treaty of friendship signed by Austria and fascist Italy in February 1930, fascist reaction had increased in Austria itself.

14 Willi Reich lists the procedures used 'according to statements made by Alban Berg' in his essay 'Zur Texteinrichtung und musikalischen Einheit der Oper "Lulu"' (On Textual Disposition and Musical Unity in the Opera 'Lulu'), in *Alban Berg, Lulu: Texte, Materialien, Kommentare*, ed. Attila Csampai and Dietmar Holand, Reinbek near Hamburg, 1985, pp. 220–4.

15 Berg had bought a Ford sports coupé in the summer of 1930.

16 Berg had been elected an extraordinary member of the Akademie der Künste in Berlin; he rejected an offer of a post from the Hochschule für Musik there, however.

17 In the Reichstag elections on 14 September 1930, the Nazis had gained 107 seats, 95 more than they had had previously.

107   WIESENGRUND-ADORNO TO BERG
     FRANKFURT, 20.1.1931

DR. TH. WIESENGRUND-ADORNO
Frankfurt a. M.-Oberrad
Seeheimer Strasse 19 Tel. Spessart 62480   20 January 1931.

    Dear master and teacher,
    I forgot to send you with my last letter the copy of a large essay on you and Webern,[1] which I wrote for the American magazine 'Modern Music', and which you will perhaps find pleasing. In enclosing it here, I would like to append a request. 'Modern Music' would like one photograph each of you and Webern to complement the essay; but not one from real life, rather one of a *portrait*. Do you own one of the picture by Schönberg depicting you?[2] If it were available, I would be most grateful to you for sending it to:
Modern Music
113 W. 57th Street
New York City
U.S.A.

Many thanks in advance for your efforts and dearest greetings from your faithful

Teddie.

Original: typescript with sender stamp and Adorno's signature, as well as a note in the margin alongside the address of the American journal in Berg's handwriting: 'was sent in directly'.

1 See Adorno, 'Berg und Webern', *GS* 20.2, pp. 782–92; an English translation appeared under the title 'Berg and Webern – Schönberg's Heirs' in *Modern Music*, 8 (1931), pp. 29–38.

2 See the reproduction of this painting as the frontispiece of the Alban Berg catalogue of the Österreichische Nationalbibliothek (Vienna, 1985).

108 BERG TO WIESENGRUND-ADORNO
VIENNA, 26.1.1931

ALBAN BERG VIENNA XIII/I
TRAUTTMANSDORFFGASSE 27   26/₁31

To be honest, dear Wiesengrund, I ~~am~~ was cross with you. And have been for a long time: the 1929/30 season, during which I was near you three times, Essen, Aachen & Düsseldorf & hoped each time to see you, to see *a great deal* of you – and was disappointed. To say nothing of the fact that you could have come to Vienna at some point – & that you did not sense it & were content to send a postcard after months of silence, before subsequently continuing to be silent for months . . .

But your kind, lengthy letter and the wonderful essay are to blame for the crossing-out at the start of this epistle and also for my further assurance:[1]

Yes! I particularly liked your article this time. Presumably because you know that an ordinary mortal American could never translate the German that you normally write, you write much more simply this time & just imagine: *I* understood every word and was able *for this reason* to derive such enjoyment from it. Never before was the problem of the Schönberg *school* so correctly pinpointed & solved, never before was it made so clear why one still speaks today – and rightly so – of the 'Schönberg pupil' Berg (or Webern etc) *That* – and everything else in your article was certainly most pleasing to me & I am only sad that it will not be published in German! (Please also send it to Webern!)[2]

Naturally I want to have your book on Kierkegaard – even if I was jealous of him for years (for that is also a part of my Schönberg-pupildom!) Please send it to me as soon as it is published.

But let us speak at greater length of all that & about your composing, *which I am very pleased about*, in the spring, or as early as *the end of February*, when we are invited to the Wozzeck premiere in Darmstadt.[3] And then also about the Herlinger case.

She is to give a big concert in Vienna in a few days (in the Musikverein) and has now naturally put everything else on hold.

What a shame!!! that I was unable to do anything for your orchestral pieces in London.[4] The Berlin section did *not* send them in –, in fact hardly any *concert* music, which supposedly 'no longer exists seriously in Germany!!' We must also speak *a great deal* about that! –

Since having a car, I no longer have asthma. And the former is as marvellous as the latter was ghastly. More also about this in person, indeed perhaps more than you would like –, for this is now *all I talk about!*

Your comparison to a pet is so close to my wife's own thoughts that she too is no longer cross with you . . .

And now accept the warmest of greetings from your meanwhile aged

Alban Berg

When are you coming to Vienna?? Fondly H. B.

Original: manuscript with sender stamp and an additional note by Helene Berg on the reverse of the envelope.

1 'Ich grolle nicht' (I do not grumble): Berg cites the opening of the vocal part of no. VII from Robert Schumann's song cycle *Dichterliebe* op. 48.

2 Webern had already received the essay, and thanked Adorno in his letter of 23 January 1931; see Anton Webern, *Briefe an Theodor W. Adorno: Transkribiert und mit Anmerkungen versehen von Rolf Tiedemann*, in *Musik-Konzepte*, special issue: *Anton Webern I*, pp. 6–22; the letter in question is on p. 19f.

3 It took place on 28 February.

4 Berg was in London and Cambridge in mid-January in his function as a jury member of the International Society for Contemporary Music, in preparation for the ISCM's Oxford festival in July 1931.

109   BERG TO WIESENGRUND-ADORNO
       SATTENDORF, 7.6.1931

ALBAN BERG
GUT BERGHOF
POST OFFICE: SATTENDORF
BY LAKE OSSIACH   7.6.31
CARINTHIA, AUSTRIA
TEL. VILLACH 1395

Dear Wiesengrund, in haste the following:[1] I have not yet spoken to U. E. concerning the 'publishment' of one of your works, 1.) because – with the situation as it currently is – it would most certainly have been a futile request 2.) because I prefer to do so in writing (from here, where I have been for a few days) & 3.) because I would first ask for your consent to what I intend to – & *can* – demand from Hertzka:

The times are currently such that U. E. (& no other publisher either, I think [e.g. Bote & Bock have lately put their brakes on to a colossal degree!]) cannot think, *may* not think [they are under observation from the bank: utmost discretion!!!] of undertaking anything costing money that is not *guaranteed* to flow back *soon*. Where this is assured, they publish of their own accord (e.g. the 'Wein' aria, for which they suddenly had the score printed without the slightest involvement on my part, purely due to the American prospects etc.), where this security is not guaranteed, no suggestion, urging or vouching is of use.

I nonetheless consider it important & right (for you, for our music*, even for the publisher) that you should 'appear' in U. E. as soon as possible. Are you prepared to carry the cost yourself? That is, to do what we have all done ourselves (whether directly or through a patron: Schönberg's op 1–3, op 10 Berg's op 1, 2, 3, 4 & 7, Webern's large orchestral pieces etc. – Etc etc. . .)? Then I shall write to Hertzka at once with the utmost emphasis, and a chance of success, as there is no one among his authors of whom he currently thinks more highly than of me.

Then: so I am – also for your sake – a juror in the A.D.M.V.[2] – Deadline for score 1 Sept 31 at the latest. –

* that is, for *that* music which begins with Schönberg

181

Opera & orchestral works	{	Berg
		Gál[3]
		Toch[4]
Choral & chamber music	{	Jarnach[5]
		Holle[6]
		Dr Stein[7]

So please send in 2 kinds of works: orchestral works *&* chamber music![8]

    & now I must hurriedly end with warmest greetings from
your Berg

Original: manuscript with sender stamp.

1 Berg is here probably following on from his conversations with Adorno in Frankfurt – Berg held his introductory lecture there before the Frankfurt premiere of *Wozzeck* – about the problem of finding a publisher for Adorno's compositions.

2 From 1929 to 1933, Berg was a jury member for the Allgemeiner Deutscher Musikverein (General German Music Society), founded in 1861 and dissolved in 1937.

3 The composer and musicologist Hans Gál (1890–1987); Berg had written 'Gall'.

4 The composer Ernst Toch (1887–1964).

5 The composer Philipp Jarnach (1892–1982).

6 Hugo Holle (1890–1942), musical pedagogue and music writer.

7 The musicologist Fritz Stein (1879–1961).

8 Adorno did not send in any compositions; see letter no. 111.

ALBAN BERG
GUT BERGHOF
POST OFFICE: SATTENDORF
BY LAKE OSSIACH   21.$/_{7.}$31
CARINTHIA, AUSTRIA
TEL. VILLACH 1395

Dear Wiesengrund, what is the matter with you? where are you? Out in the country, I hope! But I would appreciate a sign of life from you.

I wrote you a letter over 6 weeks ago with important questions: concerning the publishing of your songs. Did you receive the letter?

I have been here since the start of June & am working on 'Lulu'.

While the summer before last stood under the sign of the typewriter, and the last under that of the car, the current one is under the sign of the 5-tube device, which works perfectly & passes our lonely evenings for us & brings the distant world closer. I can more or less listen to the whole of Europe & am already well versed in the operation of this mechanism. I recently heard the records of Schönberg's Frankfurt lecture with parts of the 'Variations'.[1] –

But now you must write to me soon, and tell me what is the matter!

Fondly yours,
Berg

Just now I received a call from Dr. Graf,[2] who is spending 14 days by Lake Millstadt (1 hour by car from here).

Original: manuscript with sender stamp.

1 See Arnold Schönberg, 'Vortrag über op. 31', *Gesammelte Schriften 1: Stil und Gedanke: Aufsätze zur Musik*, ed. Ivan Vojtěch, Frankfurt am Main, 1976, pp. 255–71. Schönberg's analysis of his Variations for Orchestra was recorded on 22 March at Frankfurt radio; Hans Rosbaud conducted the work two days later. A gramophone record of parts of this lecture is to be found among Schönberg's belongings.

2 The director Herbert Graf (1904–1973) had been responsible for the Frankfurt production of *Wozzeck*.

DR. THEODOR WIESENGRUND-ADORNO   FRANKFURT A. M.-OBERRAD
OUTSIDE LECTURER AT THE UNIVERSITY OF   19 SEEHEIMERSTRASSE
FRANKFURT A. M.   TEL. SPESSART 62480
23 September 1931.

Dear master and teacher,
whenever a long time has passed without my writing to you, my guilty conscience builds up to such a degree that, rather than stimulating my impulse to write, it inhibits it; and the inhibition is reinforced by the fear that you might – and rightly so! – be cross with me, and feel only annoyance at the finally completed epistle. This time, my guilt is now particularly severe: after you had sought, with such love and friendship, to do something for my music, without receiving the slightest response on my part. So I really do not know if I can even gain your forgiveness this time, and must invoke all your Johannic spirit to retain any hope thereof. Nonetheless, do not think me a monster, do not banish me from your space of consciousness and unconsciousness, and be, as the holy Baudelaire puts it, not mère but père, même pour un ingrat, même pour un méchant.[1] For my obstinate silence and your initiative on behalf of my music – which, along with your recognition in the spring,[2] made me happier than I have been for a *very* long time – are actually connected. To tell the truth: I would not be able to justify appearing at one of the large festivals today with one of my things. Firstly: I am not satisfied with them. I am not suffering from any false modesty, and know only too well that they are better than most of what is done there. But this is no standard, and as I learnt the highest from you, you will pardon me for now also applying it myself. I am sure that I, who find it so *very* difficult, shall one day write much better things than I am able to now; which can perhaps hold up the earlier works. But to this day, I have been unable to carry out my true compositional ideas. After you and Webern waited for so long, why should I be impatient? The printing of my things is a different matter; but if I am to appear in the programme of a music society or the International for the first time, then this should really show the whole artist, and prevent even the likes of Stefan from speaking of a talent show and such. What makes matters worse is that, as a composer, I am currently experiencing, to put it charitably, a crisis, or, to put it uncharitably, stagnation. I have not completed anything substantial for two and a half years. But until I have proved conclusively to myself once more that I am a composer, I cannot expect others to believe it. I cannot tell you how heavily this weighs upon me,

it actually sours my whole existence, it has filled me with hatred for the university, which steals my time, and is also the most fundamental reason for my inability to write to you. I am ashamed, and look to you as a moral authority. For it is laughable, of course, to seek to blame it on the university. It can only be my own doing, and the only proper excuse that I have is the miserable breadth of imagination which one is confined to in Germany today, and which robs me of all freedom and thus of all true productivity. If I tell you that I nonetheless consider myself nothing in the world if not a composer, and would be happiest of all for everything else to be sent to the devil, you will find this hard to believe. But nonetheless, this is how it is for me – I cannot assess whether it is also objectively true – and I know for certain that it will come through completely once more. I think of nothing else, feel no joy, for as long as I am not at it again, and yet I cannot make it happen by force now. If you can put yourself in my place, then perhaps you will judge me more leniently. – One thing could lessen my worries: the publication of my songs, if you truly consider it legitimate, would be a great joy to me. But I am currently on such bad terms with U. E. that I am certainly not prepared to make any concessions to them as long as they refrain from coming to me with such a request. I had a different idea: Doblinger.[3] They have published a piano sonatina by Otto *Jokl*,[4] for example, evidently a student of yours, which was yesterday performed on the radio (I gave the introductory lecture).[5] So perhaps the publisher is not averse to the school, and would decide on a book of my songs. What do you think? Otherwise, I am having more theoretical dealings with music than ever. Tomorrow I am to have a discussion with Strobel, the enemy, on the radio, about neo-classicism;[6] then I have also written a big article to settle the score with Hindemith and his ilk, 'Kritik des Musikanten',[7] two new larger series of musical aphorisms besides, of which one shall appear in the Frankfurter Zeitung, the other probably in Anbruch;[8] and between these a great deal of critical work. I can see increasingly clearly how one must compose and how one may not – only I myself lack the courage, probably because I know it only too well. – I heard *all* the performances of Wozzeck in Frankfurt, I think there were six, and the work is now as familiar to me as a Beethoven symphony, but without losing an iota of its power for it. On the contrary, it has become more and more clear to me; as on a mountain hike, where one sees more peaks the longer one climbs. If the aesthetic of speculative idealism, which regards a work of art as essentially infinite, is right, then it can certainly support its claim with reference to Wozzeck, where there is no end to the perspectives in sight. The performance, in my opinion, was not very good, Steinberg was soon enough content to 'hold things together', and he was not able to fill anything out. But ultimately the work is so filled-out and through-composed that it is largely untouched by the fortuity of performance. And so it made a very strong impression nonetheless, even on neutral listeners.

I was away during August, only three weeks due to bad weather, 14 days in Berchtesgaden, without being able to go on any tours, a week in Salzburg. I heard Das Lied von der Erde under Bruno Walter. Musically speaking, there is certainly a great deal that one can object to about the interpretation, which tends towards the generic and the melodically sugary, as well as the expressively distorted. And yet it has something, which must come from the Mahlerian atmosphere, that is authentic, and for this reason it touched me very deeply. And of course the work, which becomes ever more beautiful. I also saw the famed Reinhardt performance of Der Schwierige[9] and thought of you both all evening. It really is an excellent play, and I will not let any Kraus take this away from me (incidentally, I was greatly disappointed by Karl Kraus's response to Benjamin's essay[10] – not understanding is no excuse, understanding things that are clear is certainly a *moral* issue; just as with Schönberg's music, which can hardly be criticized on the grounds that Strobel does not understand it. But with Kraus the case is of course different, and in fact precisely confirms Benjamin's hypothesis – his behaviour is like that of a ghost being called by its name!).

As far as the Lohengrin that Helene spoke of is concerned – the second act is overwhelming and the whole piece, on the stage, contains a demonism that even the swan cannot whitewash. Only: reading it, in the score, it pales, especially the first act, like an enchanted land-scape that glows only at its magical hour. One shall never reach the end of it. – Tannhäuser has a very strong effect on me today, the change in the second act, the Rome narrative, and above all its con-tinuation with the invocation of Venus and of course the composi-tionally depicted bacchanal. In a certain sense, it forms the centre of Wagner.

How far has Lulu got? You have been silent on the matter, but I am sure that you are now very far, after having the entire summer by your-self. I have been reading a great deal of Wedekind, and have found it extremely rewarding. Also the posthumous works, where one finds the most foreign and outlandish things.[11] It anticipated all of surrealism and also some of Kafka, a fantastic landscape at once absurd and utterly real. Do you know the prose piece 'Mine-Haha oder über die körperliche Erziehung der jungen Mädchen'? It is in the first volume of the collected works. If I am not mistaken, it is among the most important works to be produced in the German literature of the last 50 years. For all its great simplicity, even banality, it remains completely mysterious, and I am far from having understood it. But if there is such a thing as a dowsing-rod in the arts, it is pointing very clearly to this.

How is your health? Has your asthma spared you, with such bad weather? Did the actions of the home guard greatly disturb you, or did you conduct yourself like Balzac?[12] He was visited by a friend, I think it was the time of the July revolution, who told him the latest news. He listened briefly, then said 'let us return to reality', and continued writing.

You must thank Helene especially warmly for her card.[13] She broke into my fearful silence like an angel with a flaming sword.

Warm, fond regards to you both from your in spite of all *most* devoted

Teddie W.

Original: typescript with printed letterhead and Adorno's signature.

1 Adorno is citing from the second 'Chant d'automne' from *Les Fleurs du mal*.

2 Berg had evidently spoken very positively about Adorno's compositions during their time together in Frankfurt in April 1931.

3 A Vienna music publisher.

4 The composer Otto Jokl (1891–1963) studied with Berg from 1926 onwards; his Sonatina for piano op. 21 had been published by Doblinger in 1930.

5 This seems not to have survived.

6 The radio discussion with Heinrich Strobel (1898–1970), editor of the journal *Melos*, about 'Neo-classicism in music', took place on 24 September 1931.

7 The essay first appeared on 12 March 1932 in the *Frankfurter Zeitung*; Adorno later incorporated it in 'Ad vocem Hindemith: eine Dokumentation' (see GS 17, pp. 222–9).

8 The former sequence appeared under the title 'Schräger Rückblick' (Oblique Retrospect) in the *Frankfurter Zeitung* of 17 October 1931 (see GS 18, pp. 31–7); the other collection of aphorisms, intended for publication in *Anbruch* but not printed there, is 'Kleiner Zitatenschatz' (Little Quotation Compendium), published in the July 1932 issue of *Musik* (see GS 16, pp. 271–5 and GS 18, p. 24f.).

9 Max Reinhardt had staged Hofmannsthal's comedy in 1924 for the Theater in der Josefsstadt; the production was subsequently also taken on for the Salzburger Festspiele, and finally in 1930 for the Berliner Komödie.

10 Kraus had responded to Benjamin's essay 'Karl Kraus', which appeared in March 1931 in the *Frankfurter Zeitung* (see Walter Benjamin, *Gesammelte*

Schriften: Unter Mitwirkung von Rolf Tiedemann und Hermann Schweppen-häuser, vol. 2.1, Frankfurt am Main, 1977, pp. 334–67), with the following words: 'I was able to gather little more from this piece, which is no doubt well meant and well thought-out, than the fact that it is about me, that the author seems to know various things about me that I previously did not, although I still cannot quite tell, and I can only voice the hope that other readers have understood it better than I have. (Perhaps it is psychoanalysis.)' On Benjamin's essay and Kraus's reaction, see Benjamin, *Gesammelte Schriften*, vol. 2.3, pp. 1078–86.

11 See Frank Wedekind, *Gesammelte Werke*, vol. 9: *Dramen, Entwürfe, Aufsätze aus dem Nachlaß*, Munich, 1921. See also Adorno's radio lecture from 4 February 1932, 'Über den Nachlass Frank Wedekinds', GS 11, pp. 627–33.

12 The *coup d'état* attempted by the Steierische Heimwehr (home guard of Steiermark) on 13 September was unsuccessful.

13 It has not been preserved among Adorno's belongings.

112   BERG TO WIESENGRUND-ADORNO
      VIENNA, 24.12.1931

ALBAN BERG VIENNA XIII/I
TRAUTTMANSDORFFGASSE 27
(AUSTRIA) TEL. R 34–8–31

24.12.31, My dear Wiesengrund I now not only owe you a long letter but also many thanks. *These* thanks are for the Wedekind letters you sent, which have truly been a *most especially great source of joy* to me.[1] But your letter too was *tremendously* pleasing to me: it has been lying on my desk for exactly 3 months, I keep returning to it, read it & show it to one or two very good friends, in the way that one likes to share something that affects one. I have only failed to answer it: not only for lacking the time that such an extensive reply would demand, but also for lack of the necessary high spirits. For the compositional inactivity of the last 3 months has pulled me down ever further. Most lately, to such a degree that I was on the point of despair. I overcame this, or at least my primary doubts, by recently getting out the compositional sketches for 'Lulu' made so far and the *amazement* at the things I found there – and had long, by God,: forgotten was so great that I found new courage – & the conviction that, whenever it might be that I finally return to my work, . . . that it shall 'work out'.

     And I nonetheless intend, now that the plan to spend the winter at the Riviera has come to nothing after all, to compose again soon. &

scnd by going first to Gastein (c. 10 January), staying there until I have to go to Brussels (Wozzeck 1ère).² And after that – and then by car – going to the French Riviera³ & staying there until it is too hot there & warm enough in Carinthia again (c. April): in this way forcing an almost uninterrupted period of work from January to October (1932).

I have now told you the most important things concerning *me*. How I would like to respond to all those things that you wrote about *yourself* & *other things*: Karl Kraus, Lohengrin, Wedekind etc. But I *must* conclude, or the letter shall stay lying around again, like a previous one that I then threw away. Thank you again, truly thank you & Fond regards from us

Yours Berg

How are your family? *All* well, I hope!

Original: manuscript with sender stamp.

1 See Frank Wedekind, *Gesammelte Briefe* (2 vols), ed. Fritz Strich, Munich, 1924.

2 The premiere of *Wozzeck* in the Théâtre de la Monnaie took place on 29 February 1932; the conductor was Corneil de Thoran.

3 The Bergs did not travel there.

113 WIESENGRUND-ADORNO TO BERG
      BERLIN, 21.5.1932
      JOINT CARD

LINDNER & SEIDEMANN
TIERGARTENHOF
NEAR TIERGARTEN TRAIN STATION

CHARLOTTENBURG 2, Friday[?]¹

Dear master and teacher, after a wonderful performance of the Chamber Concerto² (*completely* transparent and meaningful *in all parts*) we are sitting together and thinking loyally of you. Warm regards Yours Teddie

Were you able to hear any of it?³ I would like to hear from you! Fondly yours Kolisch

I think it went quite reasonably – what a shame you were unable to come – certainly, you had and have more important things to do – Give my regards to Frau Helene Yours Stiedry

189

Your work is really *very* fine.   Gräner[4]

Dear friend, it is a shame you were not here, I think (and hope) that you would have been satisfied. Warmest regards – Yours Eduard.

Best wishes Rose Gielen-Steuermann[5]   Felix Khuner[6]

Original: postcard with printed restaurant address; stamp: Berlin, 21.5.32. Manuscript with additional notes by Rudolf Kolisch, Fritz Stiedry, Paul Graener[?], Eduard Steuermann, Rose Gielen-Steuermann and Felix Khuner.

1 Difficult to read, as the first syllable has been lost through the card being hole-punched.

2 The conductor of this unidentified performance was evidently Fritz Stiedry (1883–1968), and the soloists were Rudolf Kolisch and Eduard Steuermann.

3 The concert was evidently broadcast on the radio.

4 Presumably the composer Paul Graener (1872–1944), who became vice-president of the National Socialist Reichsmusikkammer in 1933.

5 Rose Gielen-Steuermann (1891–1973), one of Eduard Steuermann's two sisters, was married to the Dresden musical director Josef Gielen (1890–1968).

6 The violinist Felix Khuner (1906–1991) was a member of the Kolisch Quartet.

114   BERG TO WIESENGRUND-ADORNO
       SATTENDORF, 11.9.1932

ALBAN BERG
GUT BERGHOF
POST OFFICE: SATTENDORF
BY LAKE OSSIACH   11.9.32
CARINTHIA, AUSTRIA
TEL. VILLACH 1395

My dear Wiesengrund, 1000 thanks for your offprint.[1] I find it quite wonderful. No one could see the state of today's music any better than you have, & what has happened could not be described more clearly & unambiguously. It is *good* that this has now been said! Thank you, dear friend!

But thank you also for something for which I have long been meaning to express my agreement to you: for the Handel gloss from your 'Kleiner Zitatenschatz' in one of the last issues of 'Musik'.[2] You *well and truly* took the words out of my mouth & I am glad that the thoughts I have had on the matter for 4, 5 years have now also been stated in public. –

I have had – despite the unprecedentedly *fine* weather – a *bad* summer. After an exceedingly productive June (as far as work is concerned) then interruption through the V^{na} music festival.[3] And then a July with constant disturbances of a familial nature (Helene's mentally ill brother!),[4] an August that began with small annoyances: twice I had to have teeth pulled after days of toothache, a throat infection with a high fever, an attack from a swarm of wasps (where I sustained 20–30 stings to the head, nape of the neck, neck, arms, legs), before finally ending in disaster on 31 August: through the carelessness of our maid[5] a terrible petrol explosion which left Helene, who was standing just next to it, with frightful burns in the face & on the hand. It will take weeks, even months, before she is quite back to normal again. You can imagine what we have been through (then & in the last 11 days) . . .

For now we are staying *here*. Write me a few lines: no doubt (& hopefully) you have better news for me of yourself and your loved ones.

Warm greetings from us

Your old, really very old

Berg

Original: manuscript with sender stamp.

1 Of Adorno's essay 'Zur gesellschaftlichen Lage der Musik' (On the Social Situation of Music), which had appeared in issues 1/2 and 3 of the first volume (1932) of the *Zeitschrift für Sozialforschung*; see GS 18, pp. 729–77. English translation: T. W. Adorno, 'On the Social Situation of Music', trans. Wes Blomster, in *Essays on Music*, ed. Richard Leppert (Berkeley and Los Angeles, University of California Press, 2002).

2 See GS 16, p. 274f.

3 During the Zehntes Internationales Musikfest in Wien, from 16 to 22 June, works by Schönberg, Berg and Webern were performed alongside other compositions, as well as some by their students; Berg's concert aria *Der Wein*, with Růžena Herlinger and under the direction of Anton Webern, was on the programme of 21 June, together with Schönberg's *Friede auf Erden* and *Begleitmusik zu einer Lichtspielszene*, and Mahler's Second Symphony.

4 This is Franz Josef Nahowski.

5 The Bergs' long-standing maidservant Anna Lenz.

Alban Berg
'Waldhaus'
in Auen by
Lake Wörther
Post office Velden
Austria

in our possession since a few weeks ago & as soon as snow & ice have melted the half- or three-quarter-yearly stay of your Berg, who sends you a thousand thanks for Bloch's Spuren[1] which he is greatly looking forward to following.

    Best wishes for the remaining 360 days of 1933
Yours once again Berg

                              5.1.33

Original: picture postcard: Waldhaus in Auen am Wörthersee. Manuscript with typewritten sender's address. Berg probably sent the unstamped card in an envelope from Vienna.

1 The book had first been published in Berlin in 1930. Translator's note: *Spuren* means 'trails'.

Dear master and teacher, we are sitting here, conscious of guilt and loyalty, and thinking of you – the poet en suite. Fond regards Yours Teddie

I still owe you the programme from a performance in *Osnabrück*.[1] Perhaps the last one in Germany for some time – sadly. Fondly yours Rudi

Most devoted greetings Gretel Karplus[2]

Original: picture postcard: Atelier, Restaurant und Bar. Berlin W 50. Tauentzienstr. 123; stamp: Berlin-Charlottenburg, 26.3.33. Manuscript with an additional note by Gretel Karplus.

1 Unknown.

2 The PhD chemist Margarete Karplus (1902–1993) married Adorno in England in 1937.

ALBAN BERG
'WALDHAUS'
IN AUEN BY
LAKE WÖRTHER
POST OFFICE VELDEN
AUSTRIA

28.7.33 My dear Wiesengrund, why have I not heard *anything* from you. I must receive some sign of life now & again.

I have been here for 1 month & am at work (Lulu). We purchased the house overleaf in the autumn & now have something for the rest of our lives. If I only knew *what* to live off (until Lulu is finished), we would be *most* content here.

So please just 1 line, also concerning the well-being of your family.
                              Fondly yours Berg

Original: picture postcard: Waldhaus in Auen; stamp: Velden, 28.VII.33. Manuscript with sender stamp.

DR. THEODOR WIESENGRUND-ADORNO   FRANKFURT A. M.-OBERRAD
OUTSIDE LECTURER AT THE UNIVERSITY OF   19 SEEHEIMER STRASSE
FRANKFURT A. M.   TEL. SPESSART 62480
8 September 1933

Dear master and teacher, I can hardly express how glad I was to receive your card, and really do not need to, as you will notice easily enough yourself, after hearing – I assume – something to the contrary.[1] I am now quite well. I did not give any lectures at the university last semester, and will hardly do so during the next, but must instead, as a 'non-Aryan', reckon with having the venia legendi taken away from me on account of the civil service law.[2] Once I had returned to my senses after the first weeks, however, I did not waste any time. On the contrary. You perhaps recall my writing to you one or two years ago that I knew exactly that sooner or later, whatever happened, I would return to composing with an explosion. Now this has happened, and the fulfilment of my prophecy has coincided with that of your old one: I am working on an opera. The libretto, my own, is finished, a dramatization of Mark Twain's 'Tom Sawyer' (but complete discretion on this).[3] As a 'lyrical drama', that is, not through-composed, but rather in an intermittent form with dialogue and music in alternation; but certainly no 'song' style, rather – I hope – decent and fully developed music. By my snail's standards, work is progressing quickly, and I have my expectations of the libretto, which has dug a few holes in the children's tale; not least, indeed especially in scenic terms. I have a certain hope that it can be put on at the Volksoper in Vienna through Walter Herbert – I would give everything at least to spend a *longer* stretch of time there and assist in the learning of it; all the more for having a greater yearning for Vienna, and that means: for you than ever before. Please, cross your fingers for me, and perhaps you can give me some advice!

I daresay Lulu will soon be finished now. Only 12 hours before receiving your card, I watched a silent film by Pabst entitled 'Büchse der Pandora' [Pandora's Box],[4] and even in so distorted a form, the parts from Lulu once again had a profound effect on me. The text is ingenious and accords incredibly well with your music. I can also see exactly why the part of Lulu must be sung by a coloratura; if one reads Wedekind's notes, it becomes clear that it corresponds entirely with his own intention (Lulu as a 'naïve').[5] When might I have the chance to see some of your work?

You imply in your card that you are having material difficulties. I would therefore like to ask you something: my friend Ludwig Carls[6] is making a (*very* serious and avant-garde) film of Storm's Schimmelreiter.[7] He asked me about the possibility of my writing some music for it, and, recalling your card, I mentioned your name, naturally as a possibility that could only be reckoned with by an enormous stroke of luck. He, or rather R. Fritsch (*not* Willi Fritsch) Film Inc., will write to you within the next few days. As these are not commercially oriented film people, their resources are of course limited; he named 2000 Rm as the highest possible fee. It would involve a short period of work (around 14 days), and I suppose the compositional effort would have to be judged accordingly. Necessary expenses, such as for the journey to Husum by the North Sea, would most likely be covered. You would only require the consent of the Ministry of Propaganda (Goebbels), as you are Austrian; but I think this could be obtained easily enough*. As I said, I only got into the whole business on account of the remark about your material situation, and I would ask you sincerely not to

* perh. through Kleiber.

hold it against me, should you reject the idea; I could simply imagine that the prospect of earning 2000 Rm in 14 days might mean something to you after all. I am convinced that, *artistically speaking*, the project can certainly be taken entirely *seriously*, and you will of course receive all the necessary documents beforehand. I expect you know 'Schimmelreiter'; the novella is wonderful.

Has Helene *completely* recovered again after the catastrophe? How is your own health, in particular your asthma? What about the car? I have also driven a good deal, but of course done considerable damage to the car. – Where is Schönberg? I spoke to him at the end of March, and it was not particularly enjoyable. How is Webern, what is to become of Jalowetz?[8] Is Heinsheimer still so impudent? – I should add that I have been carrying out some compositional studies these past six months that were quite substantial for me, in particular fugues and strict 4-part vocal counterpoint.[9]
Best wishes to you both – à bientôt, I hope
Your devoted Wiesengrund

Have you taken a glance at the Kierkegaard ⌢

Original: manuscript with printed letterhead.

1 Unknown.

2 This, his licence to teach, was taken away from Adorno three days later, on 11 September, his thirtieth birthday.

3 See Adorno, *Der Schatz des Indianer-Joe* (The Treasure of Indian Joe): *Singspiel nach Mark Twain, hrsg. und mit einem Nachwort versehen von Rolf Tiedemann*, Frankfurt am Main, 1979; only two songs of the composition were completed (see *Compositions 2*, pp. 63–72).

4 The film, directed by Georg Wilhelm Pabst, had been made in 1929; Louise Brooks played the leading role.

5 See Frank Wedekind, '"Was ich mir dabei dachte": kurzer Kommentar zu den Werken Frank Wedekinds von ihm selbst' ('What I was thinking': Short commentary on the works of Frank Wedekind by himself), in Frank Wedekind, *Gesammelte Werke*, vol. 9, Munich, 1921, pp. 419–53. The passage on *Lulu* reads: 'In my portrayal of Lulu, I was concerned with evoking the body of a woman through the words she utters. With each statement of hers, I would ask myself whether it made her young and pretty. Consequently, Lulu is a very easy and rewarding role once the right person has been found' (ibid., p. 427).

6 This is the pseudonym of Carl Dreyfus (see letter no. 54 and note 6 there).

7 Theodor Storm's novella was filmed by Curt Oertel and Hans Deppe (script and direction) with Marianne Hoppe and Matthias Wiemann; the music was composed by Winfried Zillig.

8 Heinrich Jalowetz initially worked as a freelance conductor following his return from Cologne in 1933, then from 1936 to 1938 in the Bohemian town of Reichenberg. He emigrated to the USA in 1938, and taught at Black Mountain College from 1939 onwards.

9 Studies in two- and three-part counterpoint, as well as a two-part fughetta, have survived among Adorno's belongings.

119 WIESENGRUND-ADORNO TO BERG
     FRANKFURT, 13.11.1933

DR. TH. WIESENGRUND-ADORNO
Frankfurt a. M.-Oberrad
Seeheimer Strasse 19 Tel. Spessart 62480

13 November 1933.

Dear master and teacher,
I have not heard from you for some time now – and am a little concerned that you might be cross with me on account of that film business. Since writing to you I have not received any information concerning this, and would therefore assume that the project has been aborted – especially as my friend appears not to have retained his position there. In any case, I would sincerely ask you not to hold the matter against me, whatever might have happened. I only wrote to you on the most urgent request of the Lothar Stark-Gesellschaft, and in the belief that it was something very positive, and this only in the belief that the plan might interest you for financial reasons. If nothing has come of it now, then I myself was taken in by an unsecured project – and therefore ask you not to be angry with me.

By an indirect route, I heard the news that Lulu is progressing very well, that it is approaching its conclusion and that Tietjen is planning to stage the performance in Berlin next season.[1] This is a source of great joy to me, and I would be happy to hear some authentic information on the matter.

As for my own work, it is not going so well at present. I have now lost my licence to teach after all on account of the Aryan paragraph, and I am spending much time and energy looking for a new lecturing post. This in itself would not be so bad, but for weeks I was generally so depressed that I lacked the freedom to compose, and I must now work hard to regain it. I have embarked upon a theoretical study on the side, but it should soon be finished.[2] But in spite of all this, I still believe that my libretto and the few songs I have completed (which already exist in full score) are of some worth. But such a wide-ranging task does ultimately require a more open imaginative horizon than I currently have.

In this context, I have a request to make today. I am currently nego-
tiating with the English Academic Assistance Council[3] to obtain a lecturing post or professorship, or whatever is equivalent to our terms
there. My father[4] was in London for a few days and spoke to the
people in question, and the chances are not bad, as I am not making
any material demands for now. Now, I once made Dent's acquaintance
(at Seligmann's, on the occasion of an I.S.C.M. board meeting), and
as I assume that he knows my name and possibly my publications
from Anbruch, I intend to write to him today and ask him to recommend me at the Academic Assistance Council. It would now be of the
utmost importance to me that you write to him about me and bring
me to his attention.[5] The mere authority of your name will suffice to
set him (whom I do not consider a particularly sympathetic person,
very skilled, but cold and probably essentially ill-disposed towards our
music) in motion, and I expect you know him in any case from the
jury. But to make one thing clear: I am after a lectureship[6] for philosophy and in particular aesthetics, not musicology or such like; but if
you could emphasize both my theoretical-aesthetic and my practical
musical achievements, and perhaps say that you would consider it
fruitful for philosophical-aesthetic research and teaching to benefit
from concrete artistic practice, this would not fail to have an effect –
as for the rest, you surely know much better than I do what is most
sensible to write. His address: Prof. Edward Dent, Kings College,
Cambridge.

My attempts to find work at a university abroad also extend to
Vienna. The uncle of my lady friend Gretel Karplus,[7] a certain
Professor Karplus, a neurologist, is doing what he can for me there,
and I also have connections to the 'Vienna Circle' of Schlick, Carnap,
Dubislav.[8] For today, I merely wish to ask you how you would generally assess the chances of transferring my *Habilitation* to the university in Vienna, and what advice you could give me in this matter; at
the same time I would ask you to maintain complete discretion. I need
hardly explain that this solution would be the most favourable one for
me – the only one that would not smack of 'emigration'. Otherwise,
it is quite possible that I shall end up in Constantinople,[9] where I have
the best prospects; but it goes without saying that it would give me
little joy to live there, and the isolation there would be no less than
here.

I hope you are both in good health, and that Helene has entirely
recovered once more. I myself have had a bout of tracheitis that hin-
dered my speech – now I can at least bark again. – Yesterday evening
I heard act 3 of Siegfried from Vienna on the radio, in a not very
impressive performance under Krips,[10] with that most notorious
Nemeth;[11] but still, what an orchestra! And what music!

197

When is Webern's fiftieth birthday?

I have not heard from Soma at all – I do not even know if he has received and read my Kierkegaard book; Claassen[12] told me that he is no longer working full-time for the Frankfurter Zeitung, and I fear that he is not in the best shape. Please ask him to write to me some time.

Fond regards to you and Helene from your devoted

Teddie Wiesengrund

Original: typescript with sender stamp and Adorno's signature.

1 Heinz Tietjen (1881–1967) was general director of the Prussian State Theatre from 1927 to 1945. In the autumn of 1933, it seems to have been genuinely intended that the opera would be premiered in Berlin during the 1934–5 season; in a letter written to Berg on 17 September 1933, Schönberg relates that Stuckenschmidt had written to him 'that the Berlin <u>Intendant</u> Tietjen told him that he definitively wants to do your new opera' (*The Berg–Schoenberg Correspondence: Selected Letters*, p. 445). In March 1934, Berg himself was still hoping to complete the orchestration in the summer of that year; despite increasing Nazi repression, he hoped to be able to arrange the performance, under the musical direction of Erich Kleiber, by writing identical letters to Tietjen and Furtwängler in which he informed them of 'the complete removal of my works from German theatre and opera programmes', and attempted to defend himself against the classification of his music as 'foreign to the race' (*artfremd*). See Volker Scherliess, 'Briefe Alban Bergs aus der Entstehungszeit der "Lulu"', *Melos / Neue Zeitschrift für Musik*, 2 (1976), pp. 108–14.

2 Adorno had been planning an essay on Ludwig Klages's book *Der Geist als Widersacher der Seele* (The Mind as the Soul's Adversary); he could also be referring to a critique of Heidegger that he was considering at the time. Neither of these projects was carried out then.

3 This institution helped emigrant scientists; it was Ernst Cassirer who established the connection for Adorno.

4 Oscar Wiesengrund (1870–1946) had lived in England for a considerable time before his marriage.

5 The musicologist Edward Dent (1876–1958) had been president of the ISCM since 1922, and had taught at Cambridge since 1926. Berg's letter of 18 November 1933 to Dent was published in the July 1997 issue (vol. 50, issue 3) of *German Life & Letters*.

6 This wish of Adorno's remained unfulfilled. Translator's note: the word appears in English in the original.

7 The neurologist Paul Karplus (1886–1936), after whom the Karplusgasse in Vienna is named.

8 Moritz Schlick (1882–1936) and Rudolf Carnap (1891–1970) worked in Vienna; Walter Dubislav (1895–1943) had been a professor at the Technische Hochschule in Berlin since 1931.

9 Further details unknown.

10 Josef Krips (1902–1974) conducted at the Vienna State Opera from 1933 onwards.

11 The Hungarian singer Maria Németh (1897–1967) had been a member of the Vienna State Opera since 1924.

12 Eugen Claassen (1895–1955) was director of the publishing house Societäts Verlag in Frankfurt until 1934; in the same year he founded the Henry Goverts Verlag with Henry Goverts.

120 BERG TO WIESENGRUND-ADORNO
     AUEN, 18.11.1933

ALBAN BERG
'WALDHAUS'
IN AUEN BY
LAKE WÖRTHER
POST OFFICE VELDEN $^{18.}/_{11.}33$
AUSTRIA

My dear friend, I sent a letter with the same delivery to Dent, whom I know very well & who (in this context I might as well mention it:) has a very high opinion of me; so my 'letter of recommendation', which speaks of you in the most effusive manner, could very well have an effect.

I am naturally not cross at all. I initially intended to put off answering your 1st letter until I had heard from the film company *itself*. And so the letter still lay there, until your 2nd – placed me in your debt once again. –

So: I was most pleased by the lengthiness of your letters. Especially your plans and work for the opera. Could you send me your *libretto*? I would very much like to become acquainted with it & perhaps I would have something useful to say to you about it.

Lulu (I am following your letters chronologically:) will only be finished in a few months. I am currently working on the scene next to the gambling-hall. I think I have done a particularly good job with Castipiani. But this work is the reason why I probably cannot come to Vienna at all, so it would be of little benefit to me if you were to be there during this season. And furthermore, I would advise you not to seek a professorship there. The situation is very questionable at present & it is to be expected that anti-Semitism will make its presence felt in Aust. too. I am afraid I must tell you this, as *much* as I personally would be glad for you to be in Aust.

I am extremely interested in 'sound films' & I hope that my next project will be one. Perhaps I can find someone fool enough to do that with *me*, & scnd *the way I* want to. –

Helene has completely recovered. *Nothing* to be seen!!! & this for over half a year now. Practically a miracle!

Schönberg is a prof. in Boston.[1]

Webern will be 50 years old on the 3.XII, is living in Vienna as always.

Jalowetz currently in Vienna, where he is working for the newly founded concert society (with Zemlinsky).

Your letter II.

Soma is living after a fashion in Vienna & is still with the Frankfurter Zeitung. The child is very sweet.[2] His father-in-law is expecting great success in Germany with his 'Kohlhaas'.[3]

Finally to myself: I hope I shall manage to 'keep going' until Lulu is completed. I have also heard that Tietjen & Kleiber are to do the prem. (Otherwise Clemens Krauss.) But will Rich. Strauss tolerate that?[4] And Graener? *My* situation under the new regime is in any case a quite peculiar one. In Germany, of course, *not a single note* of mine is being played. But what makes it worse is that I am – *Not* a Jew! For while the whole *non-German* world is endeavouring somehow to compensate for the injustice suffered by Jewish artists, it is making *no mention* of the fact that we (apart from myself: equally Webern, Hindemith,[5] Křenek, by whom *not a note* is to be heard in Germany!) are suffering the *same* injustice & is not lifting a finger (of those hands that e.g. in Vienna cannot get enough of celebrating 'martyrs' like Bruno Walter, Hubermann[6] etc etc in half-hour rounds of applause. –

Please send me brief confirmation of this letter & tell me once more about yourself (your family!!) & former Frankfurters (e.g. Schoen) some time.

Our fond regards

Yours Berg

Original: manuscript with sender stamp.

1 Schönberg taught at Malkin Conservatory, a rather small music school.

2 This is Dan Morgenstern (b. 1929).

3 Paul von Klenau's opera *Michael Kohlhaas* had been premiered on 4 November in Stuttgart.

4 Richard Strauss had been made president of the Reichsmusikkammer – i.e. the 'Führer' of German music.

5 Hindemith's compositions were still performed, albeit amid hostilities; in 1934, his position also became more problematic, and it was only in 1936

that the performance of his works was officially forbidden in Germany. Hindemith moved to the USA in 1937.

6 The Polish violinist Bronisław Huberman (1882–1947) taught at the Musikhochschule in Vienna from 1934 to 1936; in 1936, after moving to Palestine, he founded the Palestine Orchestra, which became the Israel Philharmonic Orchestra in 1948.

121 WIESENGRUND-ADORNO TO BERG
BERLIN, 28.11.1933

28 November 1933   Berlin N 20
                                          Prinzenallee 60b, c/o Karplus

Dear master and teacher,
a thousand thanks for your most kind letter, which caused me the greatest joy in many hopeless months, and for writing to Dent. He has now meanwhile replied to my first letter (i.e. before he could have received yours) in the most cordial manner, and offered me his support.[1] According to what he writes, it is possible that in England a university professor for musical aesthetics, for example, would also be expected to give practical composition lessons, which I would of course particularly like. So, should Dent ask about my ability as a composition teacher, I would be very, very grateful to you if you could inform him accordingly.

I am here primarily in order to effect my admission to the Reichskulturkammer,[2] which the possibility of publication depends on – but I seem to be succeeding. Incidentally, Stuckenschmidt told me today that the performance chances for modern music are improving. There are indeed certain indications that non-Aryan intellectuals will be able to retain their work. In any case: if I were you, I would send a letter to the Musikerkammer (to Ihlert,[3] or perh. directly to Strauss) and clarify the fact that, contrary to certain claims that keep being made in Germany, you are of pure Aryan descent. For if one is celebrating the likes of Hubermann and Walter in Vienna while forgetting you, then I do not see why you should still show solidarity with a Jewry to which you do not even belong, that certainly shows you none, and about which one should, after all, have no more illusions than about other matters. In this context, it might interest you that the 'Jüdischer Kulturbund',[4] founded amid great hullabaloo, forbade my co-operation in Frankfurt on the grounds of being of Christian confession and only half-Jewish by race.

The opera by Klenau is apparently not as bad as one would think, though this is admittedly not saying very much.

Frankfurt: Schoen is in London, but as far as I know he has not found anything definite yet, and is working in the record industry. The young Erich Kahn,[5] whom you also know and value, is searching in Paris. Steinberg also had to leave,[6] does not yet have anything, and looks to marry an infinitely rich woman. Turnau is in Vienna, I hear; Graf is chief director in Basle. Rosbaud has stayed and is continuing to work, though I have not seen him for a very long time.

I shall send you the libretto of my opera as soon as I am in Frankfurt once again; I do not have a copy here, only the original that I am working from. Naturally I shall be as glad and grateful to receive your – or indeed *any* – critical comments as one can be. Though it would be good if I could at least give you an idea of the style of the music at the same time. If you like, I could perhaps enclose one of my (*legibly* written) orchestral sketches.

When shall I finally set eyes upon the composed Casti-Piani! This scene in particular cries out for music, and it made me think (forgive my foolishness) of the great tavern scene in Wozzeck. Incidentally, an observation concerning that: the more faithfully the Büchner philologists restore Wozzeck, or Woyzeck, as they call it, the paler and worse it becomes; now they are even claiming to have found out that Wozzeck does not drown and other things – while Franzos' edition, the 'false' one[7] – the Wozzeck set by you remains eternally beautiful, and not to be improved on by any philology, or hopefully spoilt by the professors. Because: this is the one that burst in upon history, and it is not the abstract 'work-in-itself' that lives, but only the historical-dialectical Wozzeck, namely yours! What do you think about this? I should think that these reflections would be to your liking, and they would also be in line with certain of Kraus's insights (e.g. concerning Shakespeare translations).[8] – I have now returned to an old study on Wedekind's posthumous works that is unsatisfactory as a whole, but nonetheless contains a few interesting things – if I prove able to rewrite and 'save' it, I shall send it to you. Do you know the novella 'Mine Haha'? It is one of the most puzzling things – some of it is like Kafka's open-air theatre from Oklahoma.

I read Der Mann ohne Eigenschaften on your recommendation, and found some very beautiful and profound things in it, despite a certain resistance on my part; the head teacher is superb, as are the masks of Klages and Rathenau; I am less convinced by Agathe, and it is regrettable that there is a weak, amateurish philosophical theory running through it all, worth about as much as the poetic effusions of some philosophers. Although, on the other hand, the dissatisfaction with blind forms and the novel's striving for insight themselves have their rightful place. But this cannot be improvised from private reflections, any more than an amateur can construct counterpoint from musical moods, for example.

I would like to write a short congratulatory article for Webern.[9] With Webern one can at least rely on the diabolical consolation that things *could* not be any worse.

That film lot will have to apologize to you with all due formality, I promise you that. At the heart of their unqualified behaviour lies once again, it seems, the myth of your Jewish descent. This is one more reason for me to advise you to oppose this idle gossip most energetically.

I am awaiting, with great emotional ambivalence, the news of whether I shall become a professor in Constantinople. If only it were not so far away; one can have better sloppiness in Vienna, decay in Venice and the blue bay in Naples.

To you and Helene – Helenae redivivae – fond regards Your loyal Teddie W.

Original: typescript with handwritten ending and Adorno's signature.

1 Dent's letter has not survived among Adorno's belongings.

2 Adorno was denied admission to the Reichsschrifttumskammer (State Chamber of Letters) in a letter dated 20 February 1935.

3 The Nazi party member Heinz Ihlert (1883–1945) was presiding councillor of the Reichsmusikkammer (State Chamber of Music).

4 The Jüdischer Kulturbund (Jewish Cultural Association) had been founded on 11 May 1933.

5 The composer and pianist Erich Itor Kahn (1905–1956) was an employee of Radio Frankfurt and assistant to Hans Rosbaud; he emigrated first to France in 1933, then to the USA in 1941.

6 Wilhelm (William) Steinberg was now only allowed to conduct concerts held by the Jüdischer Kulturbund; he went to Palestine in 1936, and was principal conductor of the Palestine Orchestra for two years before moving to the USA.

7 Karl Emil Franzos (1848–1904) had deciphered the Woyzeck fragments in the context of his *Erste kritische Gesamtausgabe* (First Complete Critical Edition) of Büchner's works, including his handwritten documents, published in 1879; he was the first to attempt a reconstruction of a practicable sequence of scenes.

8 See Karl Kraus, 'Sakrileg an George oder Sühne an Shakespeare' (Sacrilege against George or Atonement for Shakespeare), *Die Fackel*, no. 885–7 (1923), pp. 45–64.

9 The article 'Anton von Webern' first appeared in the *Vossische Zeitung* of 3 December 1933 (see GS 18, p. 517f.) and – slightly revised – in '23' *Eine Wiener Musikzeitschrift*, no. 14 (1934), p. 9.

ALBAN BERG
'WALDHAUS'
IN AUEN BY
LAKE WÖRTHER
POST OFFICE VELDEN
AUSTRIA

3.11.33[1] My dear Wiesengrund, thank you for your kind letter. Concerning that, I must bring to your attention Dent's response to me,[2] some of which I presume is not intended for *your* eyes, which is why I would ask you not to give *him* any reaction to *this*. But I did want to inform you about the possibilities in England & without *copying out* 4 pages of type. Please get back to me once you have read this.

I shall at some point undertake something for my sake and for the sake of my Aryan descent. Perhaps indirectly via Kleiber; for I do not know Ihlert, and I certainly *do know* Strauss!

So I await your libretto & perh. comp. scenes.

I absolutely agree with what you say about literary historicism.

I shall read Mine Haha soon. –

'D. Mann ohne Eigenschaften': Just imagine: I certainly remember the title – but not the novel. Who wrote it? What happens? Did I not recommend to you 'Jude the Obscure' by Hardy, which I indeed enjoyed colossally, and which does include a head teacher but no Agathe etc. And now I *recommend* to you T.M. Joseph und seine Brüder.

Please do not undertake anything with regard to the film company. Incidentally, I have just read in a magazine that the film has been *made*.

Otherwise, I am still remaining in my self-imposed concentration camp, the only place where I can concentrate. But in fact I secretly yearn for the metropolitan bustle of Berlin. Enjoy yourself there!

Fondly yours Berg

Original: manuscript with sender stamp.

1 An error on Berg's part.
2 See appendix II, letter no. 4.

ALBAN BERG
'WALDHAUS'
IN AUEN BY
LAKE WÖRTHER
POST OFFICE VELDEN
AUSTRIA

Sincerely wishing you a Merry Christmas and a Happy New Year
Yours Alban Berg
I received Dent's letter back again. Thank you! Meanwhile I have
heard from Zillig that you put him onto Schimmelreiter. That is most
pleasing & no doubt turned out superbly. – *Where* are you *now*? We
are still here – in our self-imposed exile. –

The Lulu desk

Original: picture postcard: view from Berg's study in the 'Waldhaus' in
Auen; stamp: Velden am Wörthersee 22.XII.33. Manuscript with sender
stamp. At the top of the picture stands, written in Berg's hand: 'The Lulu
desk' and 'Merry Christmas and a Happy New Year'.

Warmest birthday greetings
                    fondly
                         Teddie Wiesengrund

Original: telegram.

ALBAN BERG
'WALDHAUS'
IN AUEN BY
LAKE WÖRTHER
POST OFFICE VELDEN
AUSTRIA

15.2.34 Many thanks, dear friend, for your telegram. – How are you?
Our correspondence broke off so suddenly (you merely sent me back

Dent's letter without a word) that I am now not at all up to date on you and your plans. Externally, I am well. But you can imagine my unease in these frightful days.[1]

Fondly yours Berg

Original: picture postcard: view of the 'Waldhaus' in Auen; stamp: [Velden am Wörthersee,] 16.II.34. Manuscript with sender stamp.

1 From 11 to 16 February there were street battles in Vienna and other cities between government troops and right-wing combat leagues, on the one hand, and the Republikanischer Schutzbund (Republican Defence Association), on the other. The Austrofascist Dollfuss, who had been ruling as a dictator since the abolition of the parliamentary constitution in March 1933, gave the order to open fire on the workers' estates; this was followed by a ban on all parties except Dollfuss's own Vaterländische Front.

126   WIESENGRUND-ADORNO TO BERG
OXFORD, 6.2.1935

Oxford.
47 Banbury Road, c/o Mrs. Nye.
6 February 1934.[1]

Dear master and teacher,

the guilt of my silence has once again grown to such a degree that it really requires such an act of force as your fiftieth birthday, which I hope provided what, according to tradition, such occasions offer: amnesty. And it is indeed an act of force; for you are not fifty years old like one entering the mature phase of his life, for if it was ever true of anyone that youth was native to their being, then of you; native equally to your face and your existence – youth as passion, as the undiminished ability to suffer, which I suppose alone wards off from all of us – at the most painful cost – what Goethe calls ageing,[2] namely the 'step-by-step retreat from the phenomenon', to which you remain completely and utterly devoted as only an artist of your kind can, like Baudelaire or Swinburne – knowing that there is no truth but in the phenomenon, and no happiness but the pain inflicted by appearance. If you, as one of this kind, of this kind through and through, were to confront your friend with the figure of fifty years – you, who still identify – and not by chance – with your *early* songs, who are able to conceive them anew – I could think of nothing better to wish you than that which you already have, beyond any wish, without any wish, indeed against any wish: youth as the undiminished force of suffering, which is no other than humanity itself. Let me add, as a sign, a few

206

lines by Rudolf Borchardt,[3] who would deserve to find your music one day: Handle nur, du opferst schon / Dich den Deinen, Überwinder: / Keinem ward es noch gelinder: / Lebe nur, es ist Passion [Only act, your sacrifice is done, / Conqueror, for your next of kin: / Greater mildness has never been: / Live: and it is passion].

You could now retort that this is not so fine a wish, that it is the one thing you do not lack, and whether I am in agreement with Herr Schloss, who, ten years ago, upon your asking him if he had perfect pitch, replied: 'No, thank God'. But do not misunderstand me: my wish that you retain your primordial capacity for suffering forever and at all times, this capacity that spawned Wozzeck and, I am sure, now also Lulu – this wish is joined with another, namely that this ability, which can find enough nourishment for a whole life in but one day, should bring as much happiness as one human life can hold; indeed such a surfeit of happiness as should be necessary for this capacity for suffering to bear life at all. So let me therefore, on the paradoxical date of your birthday, hope concretely and not so much sub specie aeterni, but all the more tenderly, that you be granted all the good things you desire; first of all a performance of Lulu that satisfies you; but then such great and copious works that you would have to reach the age of one hundred and fifty to transpose your sketches into the wondrous sight of your hand-crafted scores in your concentration camp. And if I might make a wish for myself, it would be the symphony slumbering in your 3 orchestral pieces and in act 2 of Wozzeck, and which of all the living *only* you can write in such extensive wealth and tectonic compaction – not even Schönberg, not today – and which such an immeasurable part of your work to date points towards. Let me wish you, alongside this, good health, a life without asthma, and to you and Helene, both of you, such an order in your outward life that all petty and meaningless things that would steal minutes of your composing time vanish from it.

The orchestral score of 'Lulu' should, I assume, also be finished now – it is a misfortune of the category 'thank God',[4] which is avoidable and should be abolished, that I was forced to miss the Berlin premiere of the Suite[5] through the strictures of the University of Oxford, and was recently also unable to tune in to the Swiss radio broadcast. But my lady friend,[6] who attended the premiere, told me wondrous things about it – in particular the film music and that accompanying the Paris scene, which she described as the true fulfilment of musical surrealism (she wrote that this is how Stravinsky and Weill should have been composing if they had understood their subject), the analysis by Reich also gives a vague idea[7] – I would be willing to endorse[8] the work, as one says commercially here, even without having seen a note of it. – But hopefully this state of ignorance will not last much longer. I hear from Reich that you will be coming to London for Wozzeck at the end of April.[9] I shall definitely see to it that I am there; and would furthermore like to show you the city, which I now know very well – and you must come to Oxford, which can only be compared to Venice, and is only waiting, so to speak, to be gazed at by you. Please be sure to let me know soon roughly when you will be in London so that I can already arrange things accordingly – I shall probably be on the Riviera in mid-April, but will organize everything so as to suit your plans; only with the further request that you show me 'Lulu'. If you are not to have private accommodation, then we could stay in the same hotel – the Albemarle Court, which I came upon through Rudi Kolisch, and which is not expensive (the two of you can get a room with full board for 7 pounds weekly) and in some respects quite pleasant, directly next to Hyde Park – albeit relatively far from Covent Garden, if that is where the performance will be (I do not know any details yet), but close to the BBC. And I promise to show you all there is to see in London, from the Whitechapel streets where Jack encountered Lulu to the finest restaurants in Piccadilly, from the Bloody tower to Hampstead, London's Hietzing – and to take as many technical matters off your hands as I can.

As far as the question of a Berlin performance of Lulu is concerned, I am rather pessimistic at the moment; reason: the more the Nazis are forced to compromise in their foreign and economic policy, the more fixated they become on the cultural domain, as the only one where they can wreak havoc without substantial consequences. And I certainly do *not* expect anything of Clemens Krauss[10] – but Kleiber will have great difficulty asserting himself against the new policy. How are things looking in Vienna – is Weingartner[11] *really* in charge there? The best chances at the moment would seem to be in America (Stokowsky).[12]

The plan to publish a laudatory article on your music,[13] which Reich (of whom I now have a considerably better impression than previously, through our correspondence and in particular through the journal's development) would so liked to have done together with me, could not be realized this time – may those who bear the responsibility rectify it. Perhaps it has the advantage that this time you will be spared having to read an essay of mine about yourself, which is probably starting to get a little 'bland' for you – although, on the other hand, *your* music is so unfathomable that I shall have no difficulty in seeking further ways to fathom it. Allow me today, as a very small gesture, to give you a – I hope – reasonably corrected copy of the songs dedicated to you;[14] the ghastly colour of the binding and the absurd title page are not my doing, and it would be too long a story to tell you how they ensued – so please look, if at all, only at the notes; for, whatever their quality, they were gazing towards you with every bar;

208

perhaps not always to your pleasure. But I know that I can *truly* thank you only with music, never with words, even the most incomprehensible ones – therefore take these bars for as little and as much as they are: a vow of the deepest gratitude.

I do not care to tell you about myself and my rather dreary life today, the life of a middle-aged student or a man whose worst nightmare came true – to have to return to school;[15] in London I shall be able to regard the matter with more humour. All I shall say is that I naturally did *not* write to Dent any more after you gave me access to his unspeakable letter.

May you and Helene have a beautiful, joyful day of celebration, play the Adagio,[16] of which, as Reich wrote to me, you made a birthday present to yourself (how one could see the whole Berg in this one move! what genius of suffering! but also what genius in coping!), drink the wine that you have sung, and as you do so, do not entirely forget your devoted

Wiesengrund

Original: typescript with Adorno's signature.

1 An error on Adorno's part.

2 See Goethe, *Gedenkausgabe der Werke, Briefe und Gespräche*, ed. Ernst Beutler, vol. 9, 2nd edn, Zurich, 1962, p. 669: 'Alter: das Zurücktreten aus der Erscheinung' (age: the retreat from the phenomenon). Translator's note: Adorno misquotes Goethe, writing 'von der Erscheinung' instead of 'aus der Erscheinung'; while the former suggests a retreat from the presence of the phenomenon, the original implies a retreat *out of* the phenomenal domain.

3 Adorno is evidently quoting the second half of the poem 'Einem Jüngern in den "Joram"' (To a Disciple in 'Joram') from memory; compared to the original, there are alterations which almost suggest an interpretation of its content. The complete poem reads:

> Nicht nur Gott von Gottes Thron
> Der Gepeitschte mit der Kron –
> Alle seid ihr seine Kinder,
> Keiner näher, keiner minder,
> Keiner dingt vom ganzen Lohn.
> Handle: und du opferst schon
> Dich für Brüder, dich für Kinder;
> Sprich: du bist mit jedem Ton
> Überwunden, Überwinder.
> Gottes Sohn ward es nicht gelinder –
> Lebe: und es ist Passion.'
> [Not only God from God's throne
> The flagellated with the crown –
> All of you are his children dear,

None are less, none more near,
No one claims the whole return.
Act: and your sacrifice is done
For brothers, for a child's tear;
Speak: you are with every tone
Conquered, o you conqueror.
No milder life for God's son here –
Live: and it is passion.]

(Rudolf Borchardt, *Gesammelte Werke in Einzelbänden: Gedichte*, ed. Marie Luise Borchardt and Herbert Steiner, Stuttgart, 1957, p. 118).

4 Thus also in Adorno's published recollections of Berg; see *GS* 13, p. 343, and *GS* 18, p. 489.

5 The *Symphonische Stücke aus der Oper 'Lulu'* were premiered by the Viennese singer Lillie Claus under Erich Kleiber on 30 November 1934. Owing to the campaign instigated against him following this concert, Erich Kleiber was forced to resign from his post and leave Germany.

6 Gretel Karplus, later Adorno's wife.

7 Willi Reich had enclosed the text of his 'short introduction for the programme of the Berlin premiere of the Suite' in his letter to Adorno of 4 November 1934, requesting that it subsequently be returned: the analysis appeared in *Anbruch* under the title 'Alban Bergs "Lulu-Symphonie": Beziehungen zur Oper – Das Berliner Erlebnis' (Connections to the Opera – the Berlin Experience).

8 Translator's note: this phrase appears in English in the original.

9 The planned performance at the Royal Opera House in Covent Garden did not take place; Adrian Boult conducted a concert performance at the BBC on 14 March 1934.

10 Clemens Krauss had been appointed musical director at the Berlin Opera in 1935.

11 The Swiss conductor and composer Felix von Weingartner (1863–1942) had taken on the directorship of the Vienna Opera for the second time in 1935.

12 Although Leopold Stokowski (1882–1977) had initially shown interest in conducting the world premiere of *Lulu* following the American premiere of *Wozzeck* in Philadelphia on 19 March 1931, he later expressed his indifference to the Wedekind plays upon which the opera is based (see *The Berg–Schoenberg Correspondence*, p. 450).

13 Willi Reich had – as he wrote to Adorno on 4 November 1934 – intended to publish a 'short guide to *Lulu*' with Universal Edition for Berg's fiftieth birthday in place of a festschrift (see Reich, *Alban Berg: Leben und Werk*, Zurich, 1963, pp. 147–68), and had invited Adorno to write 'an introductory essay on the textual basis and on Berg's manner of text setting'. An essay by Adorno on 'Twelve-Tone Music' for the issue of *23* planned for Berg's birth-

day was also discussed. Adorno seems to have turned down both suggestions. For financial reasons, the issue of 23 planned for Berg's birthday could only be published on 25 March 1935; it included, among other things, a photograph of the bust of Berg by Anna Mahler as a frontispiece, a welcoming address by Reich and Adorno's essay 'Zur Krisis der Musikkritik' (On the Crisis of Music Criticism) (see GS 20.2, pp. 746–55).

14 Adorno's op. 3.

15 Adorno, who had been an outside lecturer in Frankfurt since his *Habilitation*, had to lead the life of a postgraduate student at Merton College, Oxford.

16 Berg had scored the Adagio from the Chamber Concerto for violin, clarinet and piano.

127 BERG TO WIESENGRUND-ADORNO
VIENNA, 19.2.1935

19.2.35

My dear friend, your long letter and the dedication[1] were a very great source of joy to me Those are truly splendid songs and I am proud to have them dedicated to me & only wish I could hear them performed. I will certainly do my utmost to find an opening for them in Vienna.[2] Either in the Int. Soc. (Webern president) or 'Studio' (Křenek) or 'Konzerte neuer Musik' (Pisk).[3]

Now on to your letter, which I really found much more pleasing than some 'article' [you will think that this is easy for me to say, as I cannot after all judge how much a *new* 'fathoming' of my 'unfathomable' aspects would have pleased & excited me]

I would so like to respond to you at great length. But these days I have such an unbelievable amount of correspondence to take care of (thanks for congratulations etc.) that I must sadly be very brief.

Yes, *how much* I would like to compose a *symphony* next in the coming 1, 2, 3 years. But it is out of the question. 1. I have not yet finished orchestrating 'Lulu'. In Vienna, where I have been since November, I am not even able to secure my mornings for this work: and now I must even *interrupt* the work entirely. I must 'effectuate' a commission for a violin concerto,[4] as I require it to live; so I am set up until the autumn. Sadly only with work & not existentially. And this brings me to a gloomy chapter of my 50th (& now 51st) year. In order to secure my existence for the next months & thus the possibility of work, I am turning to unreasonable ideas, after the reasonable ones (a professorship in Vienna, bequeathing my entire past &

future output in exchange for a lifelong monthly pension) have proved impossible: the sale of my manuscripts. The Americ. National Library in Washington has already purchased the score of Wozzeck,[5] which has enabled me to live/work these last 9 months. Now I'm thinking of the score of the Lyr. Suite. Should you, dear Wiesengrund, happen by chance to hear something (re this) in England, please bear it in mind. Otherwise, this is not supposed to be a lamento letter. For that, I would have to go into much greater detail; would have to say that U. E. are doing *what they can* already, that everything will be in order again once better days come (& they *will* come!) & 'Lulu' is staged properly; in other words, that I now only have to see *how* to get through these next 1 or 2 years. The latter will certainly be aided by the performances of the 'Symphon. Pieces', which are being done *everywhere* (already: Berlin, Prague, Geneva (Ansermet) Soon: Brussels (Kleiber), Holland, Turin, London (BBC) Boston, N. York, Philadelphia)[6] & also *other* concert performances, of which I have many in non-German-speaking countries. Also as a result of my entering into old age, which thus brings me to a pleasing *chapter* once more.

It is still questionable *if* & *when* I shall come to London. The Lulu pieces are supposed to be performed on 20 March at the BBC & I shall perhaps (?) be invited.[7] Wozzeck in Coventgarden is to happen on 30 April & 2 May (?).

Whatever the case may be: I would be *tremendously* happy to see *you* again & talk for hours and days. Not simply to tell you about *myself*, but also to hear as much as possible about *you*. Hopefully we shall have the chance.

Once again many *thanks* & fond regards from us!

Your 'old' Berg

Original: manuscript; the start is written on a concert programme book from the Verein für Neue Musik dated Saturday, 9 February 1935, 5 p.m., Kleiner Musikvereinssaal (small hall in the Musikverein): 'Alban Berg / Anläßlich seines 50. Geburtstages' (On the occasion of his 50th birthday). The programme consisted of Berg's Piano Sonata op. 1 (played by Rita Kurzmann), three of the Seven Early Songs and the two versions of 'Schliesse mir die Augen beide' (Julia Nessy, Jakob Grimpel), the Four Pieces for Clarinet and Piano (Leopold Wlach, Eduard Steuermann), 'Lied der Lulu' and the Adagio from the *Symphonische Stücke aus der Oper 'Lulu'* in a version for voice and four-handed piano (Julia Nessy, Eduard Steuermann and Jakob Grimpel), as well as the *Lyric Suite* (Galimir Quartet).

1 It reads: 'Alban Berg / dem Meister / in liebender / Verehrung' (To Alban Berg / the master / in loving / admiration).

2 Berg showed the songs to Křenek, who subsequently performed 'Verloren' (Lost), to a poem by Theodor Däubler, and 'In Venedig' (In Venice), to a poem by Georg Trakl, with Hertha Glatz on 25 March 1935 in the Österreichisches Studio; see *Theodor W. Adorno und Ernst Krenek, Briefwechsel*, ed. Wolfgang Rogge, Frankfurt am Main, 1974, pp. 59–63. For Křenek's 'Ansprache zum Abend zeitgenössischer Musik im Österreichischen Studio am 25. März 1935 im Ehrbar-Saal, Wien' (Address for the contemporary music evening in the Österreichisches Studio on 25 March 1935 in the Ehrbar-Saal, Vienna), see ibid., pp. 199–204.

3 Paul A. Pisk had been secretary of the Viennese section of the ISCM from 1922 until 1934, when he resigned from his post for political reasons.

4 The violin concerto had been commissioned by the American violinist Louis Krasner (1903–1995), a student of Carl Flesch; Berg finished work on it in August 1935 and dedicated it to the memory of Manon Gropius, who had died on 22 April 1935 at the age of eighteen. See also Louis Krasner, 'The Origins of the Alban Berg Violin Concerto', in *Alban Berg Studien*, ed. Franz Grasberger and Rudolf Stephan, vol. 2: *Alban Berg Symposion 1980: Tagungsbericht*, ed. Rudolf Klein, Vienna, 1981, pp. 107–17.

5 Schönberg had put Berg in contact with Carl Engel (1883–1944), the director of the music library at the Library of Congress; Berg had to share the proceeds of the sale, which took place in June 1934, with Universal Edition, who had been granted ownership of the original score by contract.

6 Erich Kleiber conducted them once more on 9 February 1935; previously, Václav Talich had performed them on 9 January in Prague; the Geneva performance under Ernest Ansermet took place on 16 January. The Brussels performance took place on 22 February; no record has been found of performances in Turin or Holland. The Boston performance on 22 March was conducted by Serge Koussevitzky, who also performed the work in New York on 4 April.

7 The BBC concert under the direction of Adrian Boult took place on 20 March.

128 WIESENGRUND-ADORNO TO BERG
   OXFORD, 5.3.1935

Oxford, 5 March 1935.

Dear master and teacher,
a thousand thanks for your letter – I am only writing to you in haste today concerning various practical matters, and admittedly also with the firm resolution not to allow such long pauses to interrupt our correspondence from now on when it is my turn to write.

First of all the matter of the original score of the Lyric Suite: I started by attempting to win over a certain lady of serious musical interests and considerable financial means in London (whom I know through Kolisch).[1] She herself has decided against it, but wrote to me that the London newspaper *Sunday Times* had held an exhibition of modern music manuscripts in London (Grosvenor House – the site of the *exhibition*, not the *newspaper*) last autumn, and that the directors of this exhibition would know exactly who the interested parties are. The *Times* book club was also involved in the matter. So I would advise you either to contact the editorial staff or music editors of the Sunday Times directly and find out who the experts there are who would definitely like to procure your manuscript; or to assign this task to me; I shall be coming to London at the end of next week (on the 16th). – But then I also have another friend – also through Kolisch, the violinist André Mangeot,[2] who far exceeds the English musical standard and is a delightful person, interested in the cause, and he has contacted the pianist Cortot,[3] a friend of his, who he believes would like to buy the manuscript. Should this fail, he would know of other people (you need not worry that your manuscript might be 'offered' in any manner harmful to your prestige – it is simply a matter of coming into contact in the *most restrained manner conceivable* and you can rest assured that neither Lady Waterhouse nor Mangeot nor I myself will fail to ensure the proper treatment.). Only Mangeot has written me today that it would definitely be important for him to know what price you are asking for the manuscript. So if you have not meanwhile heard directly from Cortot, it would probably be best to let Mangeot know your price (sit venia verbo) immediately, best of all by telegram, as I believe he has to travel to the continent at the start of next week; his address:

André Mangeot, 21 Cresswell Place, London SW 10. – If you write or telegraph him, please do so in English or French, as he does not speak a word of German. I would also formulate the price in English pounds.

I have not yet heard anything about the Lulu performance at the BBC on the 20th. But please let me know whether it will take place and whether you are coming. I will definitely be coming to London for a few days on the 16th (on the same day as Kolisch, as it happens); but I would like to make the length of my stay depend on *your* coming; should you not be coming, I would, for certain reasons, make my stay in London as short as possible this time.

On the other hand, it is not out of the question (albeit not at all likely) that I might turn up in *Vienna* on the 25th. You were kind enough to show Křenek my songs, which had the surprising result that he wants to perform them as soon as possible, preferably on that same 25th, and accompany them himself, and I would naturally like to come if it proves feasible,[4] i.e. if I were to be exempted from paying the 1000 marks and were able to exchange currency.[5] At the same time, the period of 3 weeks strikes me as a little short to learn the songs; I know only too well what difficulties they pose for singers. So this is an awfully vague chance, but nonetheless one that I do not wish to withhold from you.

In any case, a thousand thanks for what you have done and are doing for the songs – but most of all for *appreciating* them – this is a greater moral support than I can express and immediately gave me fresh courage to compose.

How far has the violin concerto progressed, and what architectural idea might it be based on this time? The delay in the Lulu score is very, very troubling; but I think I am sufficiently familiar with your working method to console myself that it is only a matter of *copying out* the score, not the orchestration itself, which must be indicated in full in the short score. Do you have to do this copying work yourself? – And while I am asking, let me close by asking you about another matter extraordinarily close to my heart: you had said at one point that the whole of Lulu was to be developed from *a single* twelve-tone row. But Reich's analysis now seems to suggest that the Paris scene, at least, is not *consistently* twelve-tone music. So this means that you have departed from the twelve-tone principle in a fundamental respect, and I need hardly explain what this essentially means. Are you prepared to tell me about the matter? Please just a card, at no cost do I wish to steal your time, which God knows is there for more important things.

My work is proceeding well,[6] and I have no more reason for dissatisfaction than the general situation dictates. Though I admittedly consider it an ultra-dismal one.

Fond regards to you and Helene from your old and devoted
Teddie Wiesengrund.

Original: typescript with Adorno's signature.

1 This is Lady Waterhouse, as mentioned further down in the letter.

2 The French violinist André Mangeot (1883–1970), who lived in England, was first violinist of the International String Quartet. He was in charge of a chamber music class at the Oxford University Musical Club at the same time that Adorno was also a member of this club (see Evelyn Wilcock, 'Adorno in Oxford 1: Oxford University Musical Club', *Oxford Magazine*, Fourth Week, Hilary Term, 1996, pp. 11–13).

3 The pianist and conductor Alfred Cortot (1877–1962).

4 Adorno did not travel to Vienna.

5 Germans travelling to Austria had to pay a penalty of 1000 Reichsmark; this was intended to strike Austria, which had banned its own Nazi party, in a particularly sensitive area: its dependence on German currency.

6 Adorno is referring to the studies on Husserl which he worked on in England from 1934 until 1937, and with which he hoped to gain a PhD in philosophy from Oxford; the final result was the 1956 book *Zur Metakritik der Erkenntnistheorie: Studien über Husserl und die phänomenologischen Antinomien* (see *GS 5*, pp. 7–245). English translation: T. W. Adorno: *Against Epistemology*, trans. Willis Domingo, Oxford, Blackwell, 1982.

129 BERG TO WIESENGRUND-ADORNO
VIENNA, 8.3.1935
FRAGMENT

ALBAN BERG, VIENNA XIII/I
TRAUTTMANSDORFFGASSE 27   8.III.35
(AUSTRIA) TEL. R 34-8-31

My dear friend, 1000 thanks for your letter of the 5th and your many & various efforts regarding the mnscrpt of the Lyr Suite. I shall now skip directly to business matters.

I do not wish to write or telegraph Mangeot; nor the Sunday Times. If only for the reason that I cannot name a fixed price. I would therefore ask *you* to pursue the matter further, as I also asked Kolisch in a letter I sent to him in The Hague yesterday. And after your meeting in London on the 16th, that is very convenient for my business. I shall tell *you* what sort of figure I had in mind & the two of you can then discuss on the 16th whether & to whom you shall offer it.

For the score of Wozzeck (3 vols) the National Library in Washington paid me 6000 Au. shillings (which are c. 250 pounds). I have generally been told that this was *very* little & that this sc. (also seen in terms of the mnscrpt market) is worth twice (or even 3 times) as much. On the basis of these experiences, I would consider the sum of 3000 shillings* (i.e. c. 125 pounds) justified as the *minimum* offer for the 'lyr. Suite'. What do *you* & *Kolisch* think about that? Can one ask that much? Or perhaps even *more*? The mnscrpt is nicely bound, has 80 pages and is in immaculate condition.

[The sc. of the 'Wein' aria would also be 'available']

I therefore ask you, dear Teddy, to reach a decision yourself (on the basis of my information) as far as possible concerning the price and then offer it wherever you suspect some interest in it. I shall ask

---

* it is also the sum I require in order to get through the summer to some degree.

Kolisch to do the same. And write me a brief statement regarding my 'offer' & also your London address.

Original: manuscript with sender stamp; only one page has survived, the rest seemingly having been lost.

130   WIESENGRUND-ADORNO TO BERG
      OXFORD, 11.3.1935

Oxford, 47 Banbury Road,
c/o Mrs Nye.
11 March 1935.

Dear master and teacher, a thousand thanks for the letter of the 8th, to which I shall respond immediately.

I had indeed imagined a price in the region of £125–150. Whether this is feasible is another matter. I am no expert on the collectors' value of manuscripts (and the *true* value of the manuscript, *this* of all manuscripts, is of course inestimable –), but the people here are still moaning a great deal about the economic situation, and above all this sum, according to the inland value (i.e. the buying power), is almost twice as much as its equivalent in shillings. I shall do my utmost, as will Kolisch no doubt, but I cannot promise in advance that we shall be able to get this much. Without imposing any limit upon you, I would therefore simply like to ask you today whether, in the case that this sum proves unattainable, I should *refrain* from selling or perhaps *compromise* to a degree. It goes entirely without saying that we would only do this in the *utmost* emergency.

So from Saturday until the 20th incl. I shall be at the: *Albemarle Court Hotel*, Leinster Gardens, London W. 2. Rudi normally also stays there.

Lulu: I have not seen *any* of the score and would be most grateful if you could have UE send me what they can, best of all to London. I would like to write a report on the London performance for 23[1] – which would be advisable for a number of reasons – and would probably have opportunities with other journals, Auftakt or the Schweizerische (the Frankfurter has been acting very peculiarly since my friends stopped working there). I would naturally have an entirely different impression *with* the score, and would like most of all to hear a rehearsal too. Could you perhaps let Boult know, and give him my address?[2] Only if you are writing *anyway*! There is no point asking Clark,[3] as he is a charming fellow, but forgets everything. But please do so only if it causes you no inconvenience. The best option of all would be to follow the score in rehearsal, and then simply listen during the performance. I hope it will be a *concert* performance, and that we shall not have to depend on those infernal loudspeakers.

I shall equally be on the lookout regarding the 'Wein' aria; it should be easier to sell. The first person to consider would of course be Miss Herlinger; if she cannot sing it, then she can at least buy it; but with her ups and downs[4] one cannot even be sure of this. Or rather, it will most likely be a down. – Incidentally, have you thought of Walter Herbert? I am sadly not in a position myself, primarily because of the transfer difficulties;[5] otherwise I would at least have requested the 'option of purchase' in the case of the 'Wein' aria.

Regarding Vienna, I have not yet given up all hope; but you can be sure that here too my pessimism is every bit a match for yours. – From what you told me, on the other hand, I had assumed that the BBC had invited you to the *Lulu* performance; has this now come to nothing?

The structure of the variations you had intimated to me was familiar from Reich's analysis;[6] but what concerns me most is the question of whether it is *otherwise* all dodecaphonically composed (as was the original intention); or whether – no doubt with the most serious of reasons – you once again acted not on principle. Being myself deeply involved in composition once more,[7] in the very sparse time my new book[8] allows, I am faced with the antinomy at every second: that non-dodecaphony lacks constructive rigour and constraint; but that dodecaphony severely restricts all construction coming from the imagination, and constantly invokes the danger of rigidity. While I would never give voice to my doubts in public, I cannot keep them from you, the only one who knows that they are not reactionary or stemming from a lack of formal disposition on my part.

Křenek seems to be taking care of my songs in the most touching manner, and it is a strange feeling: he of all people, who after all came to them 'from without', is showing solidarity in a genuinely friendly manner; while our Steuermann himself remained peculiarly aloof, had *nothing but* objections (there are certainly enough to be made – but surely other things too in the songs), and did not ultimately believe in the whole undertaking – as a result of which it turned out in an entirely unconvincing manner.[9] – Is the singer good, young and not *too* unmusical?[10]

I hope you are working well. I myself am a little nervous owing to some troubling reports concerning the possibility of returning,[11] and am taking my mind off it by working three times as much. The other day I heard Mahler IX on the radio, and was once again deeply impressed by it – this has more to do with us than all the Stravinskys and Hindemiths put together.

Reich is to publish a part of the letter I wrote to you on 9 February.[12] You poor fellow – it seems to be your fate that you are not spared my essays at *any* opportunity ('I am spared nothing'), but I hope that it will not make you grow all too bored of your old and loyal bore

Teddie Wiesengrund

Original: typescript with Adorno's signature.

1 Adorno's essay 'Zur Lulu-Symphonie' appeared on 1 February 1936 in the issue of 23 dedicated 'to the memory of Alban Berg'; see *GS* 13, pp. 472–7.

2 Sir Adrian Boult (1889–1983) was director of the BBC Symphony Orchestra from 1930 to 1950.

3 Edward Clark (1888–1962), a student of Schönberg, was musical programmer at the BBC.

4 Translator's note: this phrase appears in English in the original.

5 In England, Adorno was living off the money that his father owned there, while the German authorities were made to believe that he had been granted an English scholarship. The rigid exchange regulations did not allow any transfer of money or capital abroad from Germany.

6 Berg's comments on the orchestral interlude between the first and second scenes of Act III (which at the same time forms the fourth movement of the *Lulu-Symphonie*) had evidently appeared in the lost pages of his letter of 8 March 1935 (no. 129).

7 There is no evidence of compositions by Adorno from his Oxford days; it could not be ascertained which plans he is here referring to.

8 This is the Husserl book (see letter no. 128, note 6), whose original title was 'Die phänomenologischen Antinomien: Prolegomena zur dialektischen Erkenntnislehre' (The Phenomenological Antinomies: Prolegomena to a Dialectical Theory of Cognition).

9 A reference to the premiere of the songs in Berlin, with Margot Hinnenberg-Lefèbre and Eduard Steuermann; see letter no. 87.

10 The Vienna-born mezzo-soprano Hertha Glatz (1908–1985) – later Herta Glaz – who had made her debut in Breslau, left Germany in 1933; in 1936 she moved to the USA, where she sang at the Metropolitan Opera between 1942 and 1956.

11 That same day, *The Times* had reported that Germans who had lived and worked abroad would be deported to concentration camps for 're-education' upon their return.

12 This never occurred.

ALBAN BERG VIENNA XIII/I
TRAUTTMANSDORFFGASSE 27
Austria

My dear Wiesengrund, I am sending a letter to Boult with this same
delivery concerning your attending the final rehearsal for the Lulu
symphony, which is indeed to sound in the Queenshall on the 20th,
and which I shall hopefully also hear. I had quite good reception for
Clark's Gurrelieder I[1] on Sunday: please extend my greetings to him –
I enjoyed it a great deal!

Regarding sale of mnscript: you will perhaps have a clearer view on
the maximum feasible price after consulting with Kolisch. Should you
be offered less than the sum mentioned, please ask me first. I cannot
bring myself to state a minimum price. Especially as I can see – *a sign
of the times:* – from the account for the 2nd half of 1934, which has
just arrived from UE, that I have earned the following in those 6
months: 306 Shillings 53 Groschen (i.e. 12 to 13 pounds!)

The Lulu score went out to you yesterday; hopefully it will arrive
without problems and not disappoint you.

Please extend my warm greetings to the Kolischs, and fond regards
to yourself from

Your Berg

Original: Postcard, stamp: Vienna 14.III.35. – Manuscript with sender
stamp.

1 Berg heard the radio broadcast by the BBC featuring the first part of
Gurrelieder on 10 March.

Frankfurt a. M.-Oberrad
19 Seeheimer Strasse.
23 March 1935.

Dear master and teacher,
a thousand thanks for your card and the score of the Lulu symphony,
which I received in London without incident. I heard the dress
rehearsal and the performance in London (returned yesterday) and

enclose the programme book,[1] containing an introduction by Herr Stefan that is even a match for our blessed friend Leopold Schmidt:[2] whereas the latter took the first bar of the Wozzeck passacaglia for the entire passacaglia theme (which would thus consist of only one note), Stefan took the term 'introduction', which naturally refers only to the first 8 bars, for a characteristic of the entire rondo, and thus speaks of this movement – the weightiest of the 5, at least within the setting of the symphonic version – as an 'introduction'. It hardly bears thinking about with what complete ignorance such characters dare to write about the most important music today – and if these are our friends, whom no god will protect us from, what should our enemies be like! (This is a case for 23) – The performance was carefully prepared, clear and utterly comprehensible in every detail, which I suppose is the most one can expect from a first performance, and one under – it has to be said – a rather dispassionate musician like Boult; at any rate, it proved entirely sufficient as an aid to imagining the work's *true* nature. Admittedly, Boult's achievement is not as great as it might appear at first glance. For the score, as with all your other works, is a miracle of *clarity*, and if one may speak of a 'development' since Wozzeck, it would seem to manifest itself most obviously in the work's clarity. I am not simply referring to the question of instrumentation (which had never been taken this far in any work since Mahler, not even Schönberg), which is the first to arise here, but equally that of the composition itself, which unifies in an almost paradoxical manner the greatest wealth with the greatest lucidity, almost simplicity, and it is precisely this paradox that bears the hallmark of the work's consummate mastery. I shall write a substantial essay[3] (in the very next few days, starting today) and send it to Anbruch and at the same time to you, and would be glad if you could expedite its publication somewhat; in it I hope at least to convey some of the things that first struck me, and in particular to concentrate on what is fundamentally *new* (also compared to your earlier works) about the Lulu music, i.e. what is 'characteristic' about it, which seems to me to arise from a uniform aspect, namely that of harmonic progression instead of a changing sound-world; and all other aspects are connected to this, also the orchestration (e.g. the accompanimental continuo group of harp, piano, and vibraphone: the vibraphone sounds enchanting). I hope this approach meets with your approval. Today I wish to tell you just two things: firstly, that the art of instrumental setting has enabled *sound* as a sensual phenomenon to attain such beauty as I had never heard before, a beauty that cannot fail truly to disarm the listener; Ravel's Daphnis et Chloë sounded utterly impoverished and banal after this. Then a private reaction: it was the very first bars that had the greatest effect on me. Perhaps it was because of the secrecy of first things, because it was in them that the atmosphere of the work first struck me, but perhaps ultimately for a more profound reason: Lulu's innermost secret, which is one of tenderness and beauty, and not, as some idiots write, one of 'elemental nature', seems to have been captured here, in fact I would say the secret of beauty itself: in these indescribable string chords with the flute above them lies the utterance of the whole promise that beauty offers us, all the joy, that joy that is not lived, never fulfilled and yet certain beyond any doubt, and which becomes manifest in the sight of human beauty – and that is: woman – and at the same time all the sorrow at its unattainable nature; that inconceivably exact pain that has never been put into words, only to be attained in music, that accompanies the first sight of true beauty; a secret touched in part only by Proust, which you have sought out in the cavities of Wedekind's masks, so to speak, and which is now preserved by the music as surely as the loneliness of great celebrations was preserved by Schumann. Do not scold me as a Stefan for thus insisting on the introduction, albeit the right one; this is not to take away a single one of the work's facets, and I dare say this only in the consciousness that, in perfect works, *every* tiny facet is a measure of the whole.

It was received with English courtesy, no especial degree of understanding (but *no* opposition); but this has *no* bearing whatsoever on the fate of the work; firstly, because it will be joined by the stage production – from which the variations can hardly be separated, and through which alone the horror of the final piece (the horns' staccati, which evidently refer to Jack, and which already frightened me in concert, to say nothing of Lulu's death chord) will fully transpire; but secondly also because the audience of the BBC concert, a thoroughly middle-class one, the typical audience for a metropolitan 'second' symphony orchestra, is absolutely nothing to go by. It had first been offered the extremely modest symphony by Malipiero,[4] then fed with Jascha Heifetz, who is, incidentally, not as bad as his name is good. – Otherwise, this much can be said with great certainty: this time, the sheer artistry of musical setting, without any harmonic concessions, has swept away all the antipathies normally covered by the expression 'disharmony', and with these probably the most influential ones. After the impression of the London performance, I can hardly doubt that there shall soon be a staged one.

Lyric Suite score: Cortot reacted negatively, and Rudi Kolisch considers it a mistake to have asked him at all. We have decided *not* to go to the Sunday Times, for the following reason: as the paper arranged an exhibition of autographs, it would unquestionably approach the matter from the perspective of the autograph market. This, however, would be unfavourable in several respects: firstly, because the autograph market is extremely bad, and one would only be able to get a

222

disproportionately small price; but then also with regard to your prestige. So the only option would be a rich art-lover who would not value it as an object (i.e. in market terms), but out of spontaneous interest. We are thinking of Christie (the man who runs and finances the Glyndebourne Festival).[5] But I cannot get to him until the return of Ebert,[6] with whom I am on excellent terms, and who will surely be helpful. I would therefore request that you remain patient in this matter until the end of April – I shall not be able to make any real progress over there before then. Rudi will also make an attempt in America. But naturally I do not wish to hold you back from taking the initiative yourself, and would take this opportunity to remind you of the Reinharts in Winterthur, who would prima vista be the available ones.[7] Little can be done here (i.e. in Frankfurt and Berlin), as, if the score were bought here, you would not be able to get the money on account of the exchange regulations, and would thus have to spend it in Germany, which would then disturb the disposition of your work – but if you consider it wise, I shall make an attempt here nonetheless. Please let me know.

As far as the trip to Vienna is concerned, your prophecy was of course accurate: it has come to nothing for all sorts of reasons. I need hardly tell you how downcast I am this time in particular. I would ask you sincerely to write to me of your impression of the performance and the music that will be heard on Monday as openly and clearly as possible (Křenek is of course partial, and with the best will in the world simply cannot have the necessary distance to assess the performance). And one more thing: should the performance, contrary to my expectations, be a success – this would probably be the right psychological moment to speak to UE (for those people blindly worship success). Would you then be so kind and – perhaps best of all together with Křenek – make the most of this moment and take steps to achieve the printing that they have been promising me for the last 6 years? The songs are now 7 years old – and thus sufficiently matured to be consumed, I should think. I would leave an arrangement of the terms entirely to you and Křenek: there is only one thing I would like to insist on, namely that the *whole* book be published, and do not wish to pay any subsidy – or rather: I cannot, because of the exchange regulations. But even aside from this, I would find it wrong and undignified in this case. I hope I am not burdening you all too much with my request. Not a note of mine has been printed – and when I look at what is being printed, I am seized by a most peculiar feeling.

Clark was sincerely pleased by your recognition. The Kolischs and I spent an evening with him

Fond regards to you both from your devoted

Teddie Wiesengrund.

Original: typescript with Adorno's signature.

1 No copy of the book could be obtained.

2 See letter no. 19 and note 8 there.

3 'Zur Lulu-Symphonie'; see the attribution in letter no. 130.

4 This is the *Sinfonia in 4 tempi come le 4 stagioni* (1934) by the Italian composer Francesco Malipiero.

5 The English businessman and patron John Christie (1882–1962), who had founded the Summer Opera Festival at Glyndebourne, his country residence in Sussex. See also Adorno's report on the first festival, 'Mozartfest in Glyndebourne' (*GS* 19, pp. 178–80).

6 Carl Ebert (1887–1980) had most recently been director of the Städtische Oper in Berlin; he was dismissed in March 1933, and emigrated in 1935. Among his productions were also some at Glyndebourne.

7 The patrons Werner and Oskar Reinhart.

133 WIESENGRUND-ADORNO TO BERG
FRANKFURT, 25.3.1935

Frankfurt a. M.-Oberrad,
19 Seeheimer Strasse.
25 March 1935.

Dear master and teacher,

I am very glad to be able to enclose the manuscript of the Lulu essay today. For this time, I presume to believe that I have said something meaningful about your music for the first time – as superficial as my knowledge must by necessity be after hearing the music only twice. Am I perhaps mistaken? I would be most grateful to you for your true opinion.

I have sent the essay to Anbruch on Reich's recommendation, and would be glad if you could give a little assistance to its publication there, as Heinsheimer was most ill-behaved towards me the last few times. The question of payment is unimportant. Should *Anbruch* reject it, I would make the essay available to Reich: in terms of the success of 'Lulu' in the publishing world, however, Anbruch seems more profitable to me. Perh. Reich can reprint the essay; a second essay would only appear to be new, being in truth a repetition, and the reprint would then be the more honest option (and I am not thinking of Redlich[1] –).

Reich was planning to make a few short articles on the London performance for Viennese newspapers from parts of my manuscript, and I would be most grateful to you if you could make the manuscript available to him for this.

The more closely I examine the work, the more profound its effect upon me!

You will understand that I am particularly sad not to be in Vienna tonight.[2]

Fond regards to you and Helene
Your devoted
Teddie W.

Original: typescript with Adorno's signature.

1 See letter no. 87 note 6. Translator's note: the German word *redlich* means 'honest', and is used by Adorno directly before the parentheses.

2 The concert with the two songs from Adorno's op. 3 took place on the evening of 25 March.

134   BERG TO WIESENGRUND-ADORNO
      AUEN, 4.7.1935

ALBAN BERG
'WALDHAUS'
IN AUEN BY
LAKE WÖRTHER
POST OFFICE VELDEN   4.7.35
AUSTRIA

My dear friend, your news was most distressing to us;[1] we know just *how* close you were to your 'second mother', and *what* you have now lost. Allow me to take you by the hand in the most sincere and friendly sympathy! And please also convey this to your mother.

You have now no doubt been through a great deal & I will not ask – how you are. But I would be most glad if you could write me a few lines again nonetheless & tell me of yourself & your activities & your plans

We have been here since 11 May & I am hard at work. I should finish *composing* the violin concerto commissioned from me by the American violinist Louis Krasner by the middle of the month:

Two parts with 2 movements each:

Prelude, scherzo (Allegretto Andante)

Cadenza, chorale (Allegro, Adagio)

Then I shall write out the score of it. – Hereupon music festival in Karlsbad (Lulu Symphony with Jalowetz)[2] & then back to the still outstanding 2nd half of the Lulu score. So I am 'supplied' with work until the end of this year. –

Once again, my dear fellow, our heartfelt condolences and – despite all you have suffered: a *good* summer!

Yours Alban Berg

Original: manuscript with sender stamp.

1 Berg had been informed by a printed mourning-card of the death of Adorno's maternal aunt. The pianist Agathe Calvelli-Adorno lived in the Wiesengrunds' house, and had great influence on Adorno's musical development; she had died on 26 June from the consequences of a stroke.

2 The ISCM festival took place from 1 to 8 September in Prague, not Karlsbad, for political reasons; George Szell – not Heinrich Jalowetz – conducted the *Lulu-Symphonie* there on 6 September.

135   WIESENGRUND-ADORNO TO BERG
      OXFORD, 17.10.1935

Dear master and teacher,

please accept this small analytical article on the lyric suite[1] as a little greeting and as an announcement of a forthcoming letter. It was written for the programme book as an introduction to the B.B.C. performance. Today I proofread the English text. It is abridged and (of course) simplified. I am therefore sending you the original (there is no duplicate). I really do not spare you anything. I had to write the analysis from *one day* to the *next* and had at my disposal only the orchestral version, not the whole work – which is *necessary*, in particular for an understanding of the Adagio. (Are you in agreement with my understanding of it as a 'development', rather in the sense of the 'Litanei'?).[2] Much is therefore incomplete, and the article's brevity did not improve matters. But I could imagine nonetheless that the essay might give you some small pleasure – not least for having been written exclusively for you, and not for the B.B.C. listeners –.

Should you find the English text too greatly disfigured, and if you consider it worth doing, then one could publish it in German. I shall leave it to your discretion where this might happen, just as I would ask you to view this manuscript as your private property.

Might I ask you in this context what became of the Lulu essay – whether you liked it at all? I never heard anything about it from you, and would be truly desirous to do so!

I hope you are well and at work. Is the concerto finished, and how far have you got with the Lulu score? – I have changed completely since Agathe's death. To put it in Kierkegaard's words, I have stopped living 'immediately' –.

Might I recommend Frau Else Herzberger to you, who will probably call you in the next few days?[3] She is the closest friend of my parents, has been a motherly friend of mine for as long as I can remember, and would like to make your acquaintance. She is no everyday sort of woman, and I could imagine that you might find her matter-of-fact[4] manner stimulating.

Fond regards to you and Helene

Your old

Teddie W.

Oxford

47 Banbury Road.

17 October 1935.

Original: manuscript written on page 4 of the original typescript of Adorno's essay 'Alban Berg: Drei Stücke aus der Lyrischen Suite, für Streichorchester'.

1 For the German original of the text, see GS 20.2, pp. 797–801. The English text was intended for the programme book accompanying the BBC concert on 23 October 1935, but appeared there only in a heavily abridged version – signed 'A.F.' – that did little more than combine Adorno's main motives and formulations. The concert also featured the Sinfonia from J. S. Bach's Church Cantata no. 174, Beethoven's Violin Concerto (with Carl Flesch) and the First Symphony by Brahms; the conductor was Adrian Boult.

2 See Arnold Schönberg, String Quartet no. 2, for string quartet and soprano, op. 10; the third movement is a setting of Stefan George's poem 'Litanei'.

3 It is not known whether Else Herzberger (see letter no. 8, note 9), who gave Walter Benjamin financial support on Adorno's suggestion, made contact with Berg.

4 Translator's note: this phrase appears in English in the original.

136 BERG TO WIESENGRUND-ADORNO
      AUEN, 2.11.1935

ALBAN BERG
'WALDHAUS'
IN AUEN BY
LAKE WÖRTHER
POST OFFICE VELDEN   2.11.35
AUSTRIA

My dear friend, I have so far refrained from responding to your kind letter (and article), as I was waiting to receive the *English* text. But

227

now I do *not* intend to wait any longer, but rather give you my warmest thanks, I find the article exceptionally good & it undoubtedly fulfils its purpose *entirely*. (& much better than a more extensive *analysis*) And everything is put very clearly & tactfully, so I am truly 100% happy. 'Tis a pity that you have not discussed the *whole* work in such a manner. Perhaps this can be made up for at some point (when the need arises); at any rate, I shall have you sent a *quartet* score by the Philharm. Verlag, which incidentally contains a detailed purely musical analysis by Stein.

But I am keeping your present article at the ready & hope to use it on the occasion of the next *orch.* performance of the lyr. suite for the programme book. Thank you, my dear fellow!

But I would also very much like to have the *English* version of your article. Could you not have the concert (or radio) programme sent to me. Please do not forget!

The idea of the Adagio as a development section is not bad at all – especially in the setting of the 3 middle pieces. It corresponds to my own understanding of the materials found there *as expositions on their 1st appearance* (particularly the trio in the 2nd (or rather the 3rd) movement). – The lack of *'sonata'* character that you quite rightly pointed out even remains despite the fact that the 1st movement is *formally* a strict (albeit short 1st) sonata movement, yet its *character* is not at all perceived as such, rather as a light intrada to what follows. –

Incidentally, I had good reception for the performance in London, also of the *speaker*, who was rather well informed. *Between you and me* the 1st movement was good, the 2nd amazingly accurate! but the 3rd much too fast. ADAGIO!!! (despite appassionato)

& as we are on the subject of the 'lyr. suite'. I. Should you by chance be asked, or even be in a position to influence the recording (*long* planned by the Kolischs):[1] this would be an enormous help to me – & I really do need *help* therefore II. Sale of the original sc. of the lyr suite (or 'Wein' aria) still most desirable. For my material circumstances are miserable & I do not know what to do in the next months [perhaps *English* students who want to study with me: in Vienna now or at Lake Wörther from May] For I cannot bring myself to sell the Waldhaus; because it is increasingly proving the *only possible* place of work for me. In the summer (diagonally across from the house where Brahms wrote his Violin Concerto) I wrote mine. In 3 months incl. the score. And now I am on Act III of the Lulu score (on the c. 500th 24-stave page!) But one cannot live off the *latter* (so prem. of the opera $^{1935}/_{36}$ missed again!) nor from the *concert* performances (of which the Lulu pieces will soon have had a dozen & so far none of them unsuccessful). After the 100% hopelessness in Germany comes 100% hopelessness in Austria, where I am not Catholic enough for the Catholics & not Jewish enough for the Jews (& that is all that counts at pres.)

So you can imagine *how reluctant* I am to go to Vienna. But I *must* on account of a few students – & the hope that I shall perhaps gain a few more. I should be there around 12 Nov.

Helene too fears the winter (mostly for climatic reasons) & is already pining for our Waldhaus, which is indeed the only source of joy in our lives. When will you pay it a visit – it really is a *particularly* beautiful thing.

Thank you again for your letter & for all the personal news that is always of great concern to your

Berg

Original: manuscript with sender stamp and a note in the margin of the first page in Adorno's hand: 'This is the last letter I received from Berg.'

1 Kolisch did indeed record the *Lyric Suite* with his quartet in the USA, the (New) Pro Arte Quartet.

Appendix I:
Letters from Adorno to Helene Berg 1935–1949

1   WIESENGRUND-ADORNO TO HELENE BERG
FRANKFURT, 28.12.1935

Frankfurt, 28 December 1935.

My dear Helene,
until the very last second, I was unable to believe that the unthinkable had happened[1] – still telegraphed Křenek after reading the newspaper announcement, hoping that it was a mistake. Now his response has dashed all my hopes.

I cannot find many words. This last blow has struck me so hard that my only wish is that I might soon join my beloved friend, to whom I owe my most precious moments as an artist and as a person. No longer permitted to revolve around him, my existence lies meaningless before me. I am with you in all my thoughts. There is no consolation, but if it means something to you that there is someone who shares your thoughts and feelings in every layer of his person, through and through, then let me tell you this much.

In everlasting friendship
Your Teddie Wiesengrund.

Original: manuscript.

1   Alban Berg had died on 24 December 1935.

231

Frankfurt a. M.-Oberrad
Seeheimer Strasse 19
16.4.1936.

My dear Helene,

if I have been silent for so long, then only for the reason that I did not wish to come to you before proving my right to speak as a friend. The death of a beloved person – and whom might I so call if not him – fills us with a sense of guilt; all the unfulfilled possibilities, all the missed chances, and even the smallest fault one might charge oneself with come between our memory of the departed and ourselves – and it often seemed to me as if I had murdered him, simply because I might not have been there at the moment when I could have helped him. Already brought down so far by Agathe's death,[1] I do not know how I should have survived his death at all if I had not had the chance to stand by him one last time in the only way that I am able: through the presentation and theoretical interpretation of his work. You can hardly imagine how grateful I am to Reich for asking me to co-operate with him on the monograph,[2] which I immediately did with the greatest fervour; every minute that I could steal from my big book[3] was devoted to the monograph, and so my part is already finished, six weeks before the agreed deadline. I need hardly tell you that this work belongs to you as much as Alban: please accept today, as a sign of this, the original manuscript of my part. Seven of the analyses and the notes for all of them were written by hand first; only the last, of the orchestral pieces (which seem to me in many respects his greatest work and which I therefore wanted to benefit from my accumulated experience of the others), was typed straight away; this is how I have collected them for you. I would only like to add that the analyses, in the state in which you are here receiving them, cannot be considered final drafts; while typing out the fair copy, I revised all of them thoroughly (also the last one) and changed many details. The copies I have sent to Reich and Křenek are fit for printing; I shall take out repetitions and suchlike when I check the proofs. But I have given you the original copy because I believe that its immediacy – for these pages speak in person to him, whose student I have been once again these last three months – could perhaps mean something to you that the more definitive form could not so readily.

Today I now also have the courage to speak to you of something else, something that does relate to the analyses, but at the same time concerns you in the most private fashion. I am referring to the events in connection with the Lyric Suite.[4] The essence of my analysis – which was written for an English publishing opportunity but ultimately not used there[5] – was still known to him and met with his approval, expressly in the manner in which I touched on the poetic accusation (it was precisely because of this difficulty that I had previously avoided writing about the Suite). I therefore consider it best to publish this reference to the poetic accusation in precisely the state in which he was familiar with it, and hope that it might also meet with your approval.

Indeed, this is now above all else your business. I knew of the H. F. matter from the first day on, and was – in a most unsuccessful way, I should add – his confidant and, if you wish, his accomplice. I had given him my most solemn oath never to speak to anyone about it, and remained true to this promise until the moment when I found out through Reich that you already knew. Now there would no longer be any justification for remaining silent – at the very least for his sake. The first thing I could think of after hearing the news of his death was: what should happen if Helene finds letters. But at that time I still believed (always thinking that I was the only one who knew about the events of 1926 [recte: 1925]) that I was bound to my oath of silence. What I then did seemed the only possible course of action. I am speaking of the long essay for '23'.[6] It is written for you alone – and is entirely ambiguous, calculated in advance in case you should hear about the H. F. business; and how very much the idea of such ambiguity is in his spirit! Everything in it: the passage about incurable loneliness, about real existence as material for the aesthetic, about cunning, loyalty, disloyalty – all this was intended not only to present his being, but also to explain, in anticipation, his behaviour to you; please do not consider it immodest of me to request that you read it again with this in mind. I know that some people took exception to the 'indiscretion' of the essay. In your case, such a misunderstanding is out of the question; but everything in that essay that sounded more private than I would risk elsewhere, and more aloof than I would have loved – all this came only from thinking of you, and from my wish to help you and Alban after his death.

What is most important to me, however, and my reason for speaking of the matter at all, is this: the various private motives underlying that essay do not serve your consolation, but are rather, I am entirely convinced, *true*. You may consider my position at that time to have been questionable, and I do not wish to defend it; I think there is nothing that I would not have been prepared to do for him. But even then, at the age of 22, one thing was clear to me: that the H. F. business was *not* paramount for him; that she was not in a position to challenge his relationship with you; and that it was far more a case of his loving H. F. in order to write the Lyric Suite than of his writing the

Lyric Suite out of love. This admittedly touches on a secret that is perhaps harder to bear than any 'infidelity', namely that the artist in Alban's sense (and I know I am his kindred spirit in this) simply cannot live an immediate life: but from the first moment, this secret made the experience seem different to me than how it appeared to him. Do not think that I am adopting the position that 'Goethe was wrong about this' – except in the sense that Goethe (Tasso, whom I speak of in the analysis of the Suite) can *only* be wrong as an empirical existence. It is clear from his own words and actions that this is not merely impertinent conjecture on my part (he knew from the first day that he could never leave you for H. F., and, I am sure, was in essence glad that she also never considered it on account of the children). When I think back to these events today, it almost seems to me as if his innermost motive was fear: the fear of a person who spent his entire life-force on the objectification of *squandering* his life – which is, after all, only there to be squandered by the likes of us. It is entirely in keeping with this that H. F. was a romantic error – she is a bourgeoise through and through, who was once touched by the chance to be different, yet without being herself able to fulfil it. And he was, besides everything else, a thousand times too astute not to see that she was not his equal, as clearly as he saw that you were his equal – an equality that manifested itself in the two of you like the mythological model of the Heavenly Couple. I never spoke openly to him about it, but the meaning of his later silence regarding H. F. seems clear enough. Nothing would be more wrong – let me say it again, in all profound seriousness – than to think that the somewhat dramaturgical relationship with H. F. could even have approached the sphere in which you and Alban belonged together. You are as much aware of this as I am; but perhaps there is some sense in uttering it this once so clearly and seriously as to remove all shadow of doubt.

Here I also have something concrete in mind: the fate of the Lyric Suite score. You are being urged, supposedly in accordance with Alban's wishes, to give it to H. F. I would advise you most urgently, with all my knowledge and all my conscience, not to do so. For all sorts of reasons. I shall name only two. Firstly, Alban had asked myself and Kolisch repeatedly and with great urgency to arrange a sale of the manuscript. Would this be conceivable if he had intended for H. F. to receive it at some point? Does this not, on the contrary, show his desire to rid himself of the only real tie to her – the score? Would surrendering the score then not go directly against his innermost intentions? But furthermore: for you, the most musical of women, the score is of inestimable vitality. For H. F., it would be a museum piece and a fetish; not only can she not read a bar of it, she probably cannot even understand it. I do not wish to prevent you from sacrificing the score: but from sacrificing it wrongly. It belongs in your hands, under your gaze that brings it to life; it is too precious to satisfy the narcissism of a woman merely bored to death. Forgive me for speaking bluntly; but relinquishing it would immortalize his relationship with H. F. in a way that seems to me, as his friend and yours, an injustice towards him and towards you. The obvious and unprecedentedly barefaced manner in which attempts are being made to snatch the manuscript from you is a further reason not to have anything to do with it.

I have much to ask and much to say: above all concerning the completion of Lulu and your future. I shall spare you all that today, but would ask that you write to me as soon as you are able; from the end of next week I shall be in Oxford, 47 Banbury Road. I am glad that you are travelling to Barcelona to hear the Violin Concerto;[7] I hope to attend the performance in London,[8] and shall write to you immediately thereupon. One final thought: would it not be possible for us to see each other in the summer? Please let me know of your arrangements, I shall do the same.

Fare thee well, Helene. Ever and wholly yours
Teddie.

Original: typescript with Adorno's signature.

1 Adorno's aunt Agathe Calvelli-Adorno had died on 26 June 1935.

2 Willi Reich, *Alban Berg: mit Bergs eigenen Schriften und Beiträgen von Theodor Wiesengrund-Adorno und Ernst Křenek*, Vienna, Leipzig and Zurich, 1937. English translation: T. W. Adorno: *Alban Berg: Master of the Smallest Link*.

3 See letter no. 128 and note 6 there.

4 Adorno later described these – in the penultimate version of his recollections of Berg, which he decreed should not be published during his own lifetime or those of any persons directly involved – as follows:

> Berg had numerous affairs, which never went well, however; the unhappy end was part of the composition, so to speak, and one had the feeling that these liaisons were a part of his productive apparatus from the start, that they were – entirely in keeping with Austrian humour – desperate, but not serious. At the time of my studies with him, he was involved with Hanna [Fuchs-Robettin], Werfel's sister; in this context he used me as a postillon d'amour, taking my frequent visits to Prague to see my friend Hermann Grab as a pretext; I played my part clumsily, never spoke to Hanna alone, while the entire business was arranged so conspicuously that her husband became suspicious. The affair was hopeless from the start; on the one hand, it was burdened with an incredible pathos, while on the other hand, Berg was no more willing to leave his wife than Hanna was to leave her husband and two children. He con-

ducted the affair with infinite secrecy: officially to prevent his wife from finding out, but in truth probably because he loved secrets in their own right; he gave me all manner of functions within this system of secrets; from the very first day he had told me the whole story. The dedication he wrote in my score of the three Wozzeck fragments, 'the fragments of your Alban Berg', referred to the fact that he considered himself broken apart by the constraint of self-denial; but I think he had rather less difficulty recovering from the matter than it seemed to me at the time. The Lyric Suite, a work of programme music based on an unknown programme, turned the whole story into music through countless allusions, though without allowing any of these allusions – which also included the dedication to Zemlinsky and the citation from his Lyric Symphony – to impair the work's quality in the least; on the contrary, this highly seductive work drew its élan precisely from that source. I shall note only one of the allusions: in the second movement, the first theme represents Hanna, the second her husband, the third – composed of two contrasting elements – the two children. The characteristically repeated note C corresponds, according to the old solfège system, to a double *Do*, and the older Fuchs child was called Dodo. Any hermeneutician who took on the Lyric Suite would have enough work for a lifetime. The Allegro Misterioso is a play with the initials AB and HF. The analogous aspects of Leverkühn's music, which generally has more in common with Berg than Schönberg, are modelled on these games. They also border on his taste for numerology and astrology. As he knew my opinion of such things, however, he almost never spoke openly of them to me. If Helene is now holding séances to contact his spirit, he would presumably not have denied the undertaking his consent. (*GS* 18, p. 490f.)

5 See letter no. 135 and note 1 there.

6 The first version of Adorno's recollections of Alban Berg appeared under the title 'Erinnerung an den Lebenden' (Recollections of the Living) in the Vienna music journal *23* of 1 February 1936. Adorno revised and extended the text in 1955 to form the version cited above, which openly presents the *poetic accusation*. Adorno produced a third version, in which all private elements were removed, for his Berg monograph of 1968 (see *GS* 13, pp. 335–67. English translation: T. W. Adorno: *Alban Berg: Master of the Smallest Link*).

7 The Violin Concerto was premiered by Louis Krasner and Hermann Scherchen, in the presence of Helene Berg, on 19 April 1936 at the ISCM festival in Barcelona.

8 Adorno attended Berg's memorial concert on 1 May 1936 at the BBC, where Krasner and Webern performed the Violin Concerto; see Adorno's report in *GS* 20.2, p. 802f.

Oxford
47 Banbury Road
21 November 1936.

My dear Helene,
a thousand thanks for your letter, which was a source of great joy and comfort to me. I was already worried that my manuscript had been lost, and though objectively it would hardly have been a loss, as Dr. Reich is after all in possession of the final version (which has been improved in countless details), it goes without saying that these thoughts belong to you in the state in which they first came into being, namely in the first manuscript, and it would therefore have pained me if I had been prevented from giving you this sign of loyal attachment and devoted friendship as I had planned. I therefore had the postal service research the matter,[1] and find the signature of the housekeeper – how this word alone conjures up the time in Vienna, the happiest of my life!![2] As far as the subject matter is concerned, you are perhaps better off reading the analyses in the final version, which should be in print now. It not only reads better, but is also, I hope, a marked improvement on the first. The first is really intended more as a symbol than something of functional value. Without these analyses – and without the months of immersion in his work that they required – I would not have been able to cope with his death. So I even owe it to him that I survived him. –

Concerning the analysis of the Lyric Suite: I would not like to change anything, for a very simple reason that you will no doubt also find entirely convincing. The analysis of the Lyric Suite is the only one that he lived to read (it was originally intended for the London radio broadcast). And he not only approved of it, but in fact particularly appreciated the reference to its 'poetic' content.[3] This is entirely clear from a letter he wrote to me, which is currently in Reich's possession.*[4] What is more, the analysis contains nothing 'personal'. On the contrary: I think that I have sufficiently objectified these aspects through the term 'latent opera' that nobody will look for private motives. – As far as the assessment of the experiences with H. F. and all related matters is concerned, I am – as you know – entirely in agreement with you.

I must still apologize for not responding to the letter and the card you sent me this summer. The reason is quite simply that they arrived

---

* But you will surely agree with me that we should not remove the one passage in the book that he specifically expressed his agreement with. Any misunderstanding is out of the question.

here only after I had left Oxford, and were not forwarded to me. When I returned, it was of course much too late. – But it would have come to nothing even if I had received them in time, as the Austrian who had initiated the matter left me completely in the lurch, despite all his grand words and his Lords. Please forgive me: I truly made every effort. Are you considering renting out the Waldhaus again in the summer? Please let me know. It will be much easier to arrange things in the longer term.

The book I am currently writing is seemingly of a rather specific nature, on phenomenology; but it in fact pursues very fundamental philosophical aims.

I should be glad to hear from you soon; but if you do not care to write, then none could understand this better than I.

Yours
in old loyalty and warmth
Teddie Wiesengrund

Original: typescript with Adorno's signature.

1 Adorno's letter had only reached Helene Berg in autumn 1936, as she writes to Adorno on 5 November: 'Dear Teddy, your retrieved letter of the 16.4. (!) only reached me very recently. The housekeeper received the delivery during my absence from Vienna, and – as incredible as it sounds – had <u>forgotten</u> it! It only came to light through the inquiries of Dr. Reich and the postal service.'

2 Translator's note: the original word is *Hausbesorgerin*, a specifically Austrian term.

3 Translator's note: the original term *dichterisch*, as opposed to *poetisch*, refers not to poetic and aesthetic matters in general, but specifically to poetry and writing.

4 The reference is to Berg's letter of 2 November 1935 (no. 136), which Adorno had lent to Reich.

4   WIESENGRUND-ADORNO TO HELENE BERG
    FRANKFURT, 23.11.1949

Theodor W. Adorno
Frankfurt a. M.
Liebigstrasse 19, III, c/o Irmer   23 November 1949
Germany, American zone

Dear Helene,
having returned to Europe a few weeks ago, I feel a profound need to rekindle our contact, which has been so long and so tragically inter-

rupted. It has never been clearer to me than it has been in recent times how strongly I am bound to Alban and you – the two of you and the world that I associate with fundamental happiness are one and the same to me, and I want you to know that I feel as close to you today as otherwise only in Hietzing or Hütteldorf. And it would mean so very much to me to know how you are – how you survived the unspeakable. I would also like to hear about Smaragda[1] and your brother,[2] and would be deeply grateful if you could write to me soon.

As for myself, I shall tell you today only that I survived the end of the world reasonably well, thanks to the Institut für Sozialforschung and my friend Horkheimer, who had me come over in good time. I expect you know that I am married to Gretel Karplus. My parents also managed to escape a few months before the war started; my father died 3 years ago in New York following a stroke, my mother is still living there as an 84-year-old. We emigrated to California in 1941, and worked intensely and undisturbed in Los Angeles – I also composed a considerable amount. At the moment I am here, standing in for Horkheimer as professor for social philosophy during the winter semester.

Today, I am now also writing to you for a particular reason, one that seems to me the most important for both of us: the orchestration of the missing parts of Lulu. I know that Schönberg refused to do it. Webern was also against it when I last saw him in England (probably 1936); and I have been told that you are not generally in favour of the plan.

If I now strive to change your mind with all due seriousness and responsibility, you must believe that I am guided by nothing other than concern for the work and for Alban's intentions. I myself, to clarify the matter well in advance, neither wish nor am able to take on the task.

As far as Schönberg's rejection[3] is concerned, first of all, I am convinced that his motives – despite the one serious argument he advances – are not of the purest sort. We often spoke of his jealousy, you, Alban and I; I had occasion to observe it in its basest manifestations, and I have no reservations about claiming that the thought of cutting off Alban's deciding work from posterity through his refusal is a tempting one to him. And in conversation with Webern, I also encountered a form of coldness that was able only with some effort to mask itself as respect before the fate one must accept. He said, with his air of native cunning, that a work such as Schubert's B minor Symphony is also incomplete, yet lives. But this is a sophistic analogy. There is a *fundamental* difference between a symphonic work and an opera. Anyone with even the slightest understanding of theatre, which is by its very nature dependent on an audience, knows that an unfinished opera, outside of memorial or festival performances, could not live.

God knows that I honour the idea of the fragment, but in an art form whose aesthetic substance cannot be separated from a certain drastic materiality, a fragmentary reproduction would be an impossibility, even if it survived the worldly demands of the theatrical world. And I would stake my life on the fact that Alban would have approved of my intention. No one who knew his quick-witted, ingenious concern for the practicability of everything he wrote – the counterpart to his unconditional and uncompromising imagination – could doubt that he would have considered an unperformable opera an absurdity, and looked upon his work, as one with unfinished orchestration, as lost. I believe that a respect for this element of his persona focused on *realization* demands for Lulu to be completed, without allowing any of all this to lead one astray. I do not have the words to express how serious I am about this.

There can be no issue of desecration, as the original short score exists – as far as I know, it has even been duplicated[4] –, so the slightest infidelity would be avenged by history. And if Webern claimed in the end that the composition was not really complete, but in some sections only sketched in the principal parts, then I refuse to believe this before I have seen, nay: studied it with my own eyes. Berg told me unequivocally of the composition's *completion*; in a letter to me, he wrote that the big scene at Casti-Piani had turned out 'quite especially well'[5] (which would be inconceivable in the case of an unrealized sketch) – and above all: twelve-tone composition does not allow such a generalized sketching with missing subsidiary parts etc. One should not believe anything to the contrary.

Now, I am all too aware of the incredible difficulty, arduousness and responsibility of such a task. No one person can carry it out. *The orchestration of Lulu is only possible collectively.* And this is precisely what I have in mind.

My Paris friend René Leibowitz, whose name you are familiar with, is not only a musician of the very highest order, not only versed in the style in a way that is without equal today; not only bound to the cause by the most passionate love. He has also gathered together a group of musicians fanatically devoted to Alban, who, with him, would solve the matter together. I asked him straight out in Paris a few weeks ago, and he confirmed it. It would be particularly important to draw on the co-operation of one of his students, Duhamel (the son of the poet), who knows every note by Alban and would devote years of his life to the matter. I therefore wish to recommend, in the most convincing manner available to me, that you entrust Leibowitz and his group with the task.

It could finally be argued that there is plenty of time yet for such a matter, and that one could see to it one day, much, much later, when

Alban has 'become entirely historical' (itself a ghastly notion). I also consider this argument false. There is never enough time for the things that matter. The world we live in has taken on the tempo of catastrophe; it would be naïve to simply trust its course – it can all fall to ruin. And, to speak of more concrete matters: the tradition of our music lies in the hands of very few people, among whom Leibowitz is the most important. If it is interrupted, the instrumentation of Lulu will no longer be possible, as no one will understand the sense and language of such an instrumentation any more. But if those few people still directly familiar with it succeed in completing the instrumentation, then this can itself save the tradition.[6] The extreme importance of which calls for no further words.

It would probably be best for you to contact René Leibowitz directly. His address is: 17 Quai Voltaire, Paris. Should you for some reason be unwilling to do so, however, then I would naturally be prepared to ask him officially myself, with your consent.

And: please write to me soon, and at length.

Yours

In old loyalty and devotion

Teddie

Original: typescript with Adorno's signature.

1 Alban Berg's sister Smaragda Eger-Berg (1886–1954).

2 Franz Josef Nahowski had died in 1942.

3 See *Lulu/Alban Berg: Texte, Materialen, Kommentare*, ed. Attila Csampai and Dietmar Holland, Reinbek, 1985, pp. 244–8.

4 The reference is presumably to the photocopy of the short score owned by Universal Edition; further copies of this photocopy, which seems to have been made shortly after Berg's death, are unknown.

5 See Berg's letter of 18 November 1933 (no. 120), which Adorno is citing from; the work's completion, however, is not confirmed there, but suggested in letter no. 127: '1. I have not yet finished orchestrating "Lulu"', and perhaps stated clearly in the lost part of letter no. 129.

6 It was not René Leibowitz, who died in 1972, but Friedrich Cerha who reconstructed Act III (see Friedrich Cerha, *Arbeitsbericht zur Herstellung des 3. Akts der Oper 'Lulu' von Alban Berg*, Vienna, 1979); it was in this version that the work was first performed at the Paris Opera on 24 February 1979.

Appendix II:
Other Correspondence

1   ALBAN BERG TO BERNHARD SEKLES
    VIENNA, 27.7.1925

ALBAN BERG, VIENNA XIII/I
TRAUTTMANSDORFFGASSE 27 $^{27}./_7.25$
(AUSTRIA) TEL. R 84–8–31

To Herr Bernhard Sekles

Frankfurt $^a/_M$

Most honoured Herr Direktor, I feel it necessary (– now that the season has ended –) to mention your student Theodor Wiesengrund & I think that you may also find it of some interest to hear about him.

In the last few months as my student, he has written some splendid songs & a set of variations for string quartet that I was really *most satisfied* with. He is now working on a big string trio,[1] which equally promises to be good – in fact, I would even say important. All this leads me to believe that we are here dealing with a truly great talent, one that still – as far as I have been able to assess within this short time – shows much scope for development, and that, I believe, we can expect great things of him. And it was clear from our first meeting that he 'knows the ropes' very well; I would have expected nothing else, of course, after the excellent musical training he was given by you, honoured teacher. And so I indeed have every cause to congratulate you most sincerely on this student, who also happens to be an excellent fellow.

Please accept this, and allow me to convey my deepest respect
Your most devoted Alban Berg

Original: manuscript.

1 Only one movement of this has survived among Adorno's belongings.

2 ALBAN BERG TO HANS W. HEINSHEIMER
  VIENNA, 12.12.1928

Copy

Alban Berg, Vienna, XIII.
Trauttmansdorffgasse 27   12.12.28

Dear Doctor Heinsheimer, *I cannot write the article for Anbruch!*
Believe me, the mere thought of causing you, and Anbruch and UE disappointment and inconvenience, this thought alone would have prevented me from such a cancellation. But if you consider that my own disappointment is yet greater, having abandoned unfinished a piece of work that I brooded over for months, worked on for weeks, and whose conceptual solution I desired, and still desire more urgently than I ever have with a composition, thus never to reach the resolution and appeasement of that great tension within me . . ., if you consider this, dear doctor, then you too will have to admit that my refusal is no frivolous one, and must have good reason: I can only write the article you desire if I have the opportunity *to destroy Casella!* If I were to evade this, the article would be quite abysmal, and U. E. can no more expect that of me than I could expect the chance from U. E. to destroy Casella. And after brooding for some time on other people's suggestions and my own feeling that this polemic must be carried out *objectively*, I can only say to you today: the more objective, the more devastating! The more right I am, the more ridiculous Casella would appear!
My natural disposition enables me to write only where I am stimulated by the opportunity for satire. But an article like that could only turn out like the one against Pfitzner or harsher still: and this, sadly, is impossible in the present case. But perhaps Casella will publish his article elsewhere (if *you* refuse to print it) – although by now there is no longer any need for such an introductory article on his Kalafatti music, so I would not expect anyone to publish it – *then* you can be sure I would unleash my counter-article entitled 'Faddish Truths'* somewhere!

---

* with the subtitles: Back to . . .
    The Atonal Intermezzo
    Social Reordering and Music

But perhaps – if you do consider it necessary to publish the Casella article in Anbruch – perhaps Wiesengrund will reply himself. At any rate, dear doctor, I would ask you to pass on the copy of this letter I have enclosed to him.

And – if you are able – do not be cross

Yours with warm regards

Enclosed: The Casella article with translation
4 Scarlatti books
1 Kalafattiana score
1 Shostakovitch score

3   HANS W. HEINSHEIMER TO WIESENGRUND-ADORNO
    VIENNA, 1.10.1929

Duplicate of the letter from Herr Dr. Heinsheimer of 1 October 1929.

Dear Herr Wiesengrund,
thank you for your letter of 25 September; I am pleased, first of all, that you agree with my suggestion for the November issue. Herr Berg still seems not to have decided whether he will let us have the abridged lecture or not. But he will return to Vienna this week, and I shall speak to him then. Křenek received your letter, and is in agreement. He will write the essay. I would ask you to send us the Haba essay soon with your annotations, so that we can decide whether it can be included in the November issue.[1]

I would think it best not to request anything else from Gutman now, otherwise we shall have too much material again in November.

And now, dear Wiesengrund, I must discuss a fundamental issue that is central to our further work. It has become clear, as I already implied in my previous letter, that the new Anbruch has not had nearly the effect that we had all expected and hoped for. I do not intend to mention merely that the number of subscribers, instead of increasing, has in fact dropped, and that we indeed have fewer subscribers today than in former times. In addition to this, the response from the intellectual world has not been at all strong enough to warrant the great material sacrifices that the journal has demanded of us this year. It was not only the press whose reaction to our efforts left so very much to be desired – a somewhat wider circle of musically interested people and experts equally failed, as I observed time and again, to engage with the efforts, formulations and working methods of the journal in a genuinely positive or pleasing manner. During this year we have drifted very much into an abstract, theoretical and one-sided

245

approach, despite all our attempts to create a balance. But it has also become apparent that not even the people with whom you, dear doctor, are primarily concerned in your efforts, namely Schönberg and his closest circle, have really found the journal satisfactory.

But for the publisher, the situation was, and is, as follows: we might have been able to justify and get away with the great sacrifices resulting from a perhaps indirect, but certainly noticeable, stance *against* a large part of our most important and successful authors (e.g. Kaminski, Casella, Kodaly, Jaromir Weinberger, to mention but a few) if the journal had met with a genuinely powerful resonance as the intellectual organ of the publishing house, so to speak. Unfortunately, however, it has become apparent that these very authors whom we must value most highly in the current situation are increasingly taking *offence*, and that the publisher's foremost reason for subsidizing Anbruch so generously, namely that it provides a forum for its prominent authors that serves their interests, has been increasingly forgotten. For there can be absolutely no doubt, honoured Herr Wiesengrund, that the 'stabilization' of music which you have understandably fought against has become *a reality*, in a way that still seemed unthinkable a year ago. If we consider, on the one hand, the unbelievable success of a primitive popular opera like 'Schwanda', and see, on the other hand, what eminent difficulties a piece like 'Mahagonny' has to battle against, despite a personality like Klemperer, if we draw the right conclusions from the events in Baden-Baden,[2] without any prejudiced or blinkered view, then I must say, quite clearly, directly and openly, that a publishing house such as our own, faced with such an entirely unusual situation, can absolutely not afford the luxury of pursuing a policy in its journal *whose importance for the general public and potential for success are decreasing day by day*. In this context, let me give you a drastic example. I am sure you know Alexander Jemnitz's opinion of Kodaly, and the disputes he has with him, and I am convinced that you must value Jemnitz and his music more highly than the works of Kodaly. But what does the wicked world do? It completely and utterly *ignores* the published works by Jemnitz, despite thorough propagandistic efforts, while Kodaly's music has become an incredible success, in the sectors of orchestral and choral music in fact an almost unparalleled *world success*. I could give you an entire list of similar cases. But now, U. E. must finally draw practical conclusions from these signs that are so incredibly important to our house and completely unambiguous in their message. We must at all costs return to a broader stance in Anbruch. We must engage with works and personalities that we have utterly neglected, regardless of whether these are now in keeping with the intellectual and individual insights of the editors. We must recognize the signs of the times exactly as such, even if they are less to our taste, or in the long term perhaps seem wrong or indeed worth fighting against. We simply cannot adhere to such an ultimately one-sided editorial policy in the current situation. It will be necessary to involve a wider circle of employees. It will be necessary above all to devote much more attention to the house authors and works and, to put it quite clearly, the interests of the house than has been the case during this last year. Obviously, this cannot be done in a mindless or overly commercial way. On the basis of these reflections, however, we shall under no circumstances be able to permit the publication of your suggested 'Reaction' issue. Nor shall we publish 'Problems of Reproduction', but rather turn our attention to more important matters. I have already discussed a number of plans and ideas with Herr Direktor Hertzka on this subject.

I am completely aware, dear doctor, that these thoughts are quite substantially different to your own aims and intentions, and, in whatever form our working relationship may continue, the current arrangement, which has allowed you a certain independence of editorial direction, will have to change significantly. Due to the execution of our whole administrative programme, it will also no longer be possible to guarantee you a sum of 100 Marks per issue, as the combination of an increased royalty account and the reduced number of subscribers during this last year has left us with a severe deficit, which we must overcome at all costs in the coming year.

I would prefer, my dear Herr Wiesengrund, not to make any practical suggestions yet about how we might continue our work together in a fruitful fashion, but rather for you first to let me know what your thoughts are on these matters, and whether you are at all interested in still participating in an editorial and advisory capacity under these clearly altered circumstances, or would now prefer to work for the journal merely as an external contributor once again. I would ask you to give me a statement on the matter quite soon. Quite aside from the issue of our collaboration, I would also generally be interested to know your thoughts on what I have written here.

Yours with sincere greetings,
Heinsheimer

1 See Alois Hába, 'Casellas Scarlattiana – Vierteltonmusik und Musikstil der Freiheit' (Quarter-tone Music and the Musical Style of Freedom), *Anbruch*, 11 (1929), pp. 331–4.

2 In July 1929, Brecht's *Lehrstück* (Didactic Play), which was later entitled *Badener Lehrstück vom Einverständnis* (Baden Didactic Play on Consent), was performed during the Chamber Music Days in Baden-Baden, with music by Paul Hindemith; Heinsheimer is evidently referring to the scandal that ensued in scene 3, which involved a political provocation of the audience.

77 Panton Street
21 November 1933   Cambridge

Dear, most honoured Herr Berg,

Dr. Wiesengrund-Adorno has already written to me, and on Sunday I discussed the matter with Prof. Adolf Rebner from Frankfurt, who knows him very well. Rebner is in London with his two sons, and had the great kindness to play for us (together with Wolfgang) on Sunday evening at King's College. It is lucky that Wiesengrund is not in financial difficulties, as he could at least live in England as a private scholar.

The whole situation is extremely difficult. Here in England, we have the best will to help Jewish refugees, and the English Jews are doing everything they can. But in England there is terrible unemployment among native musicians, especially the average ones – this is primarily a result of the mechanization of music, as in all countries, and also of the general economic crisis. Therefore, orchestral musicians and all the 'little people' of the music world have joined forces against all foreigners. Higher-ranking artists feel obliged to remain loyal to these co-operatives etc. and agree with them, out of the feeling that better-off artists should support and defend their poorer brothers. This is why the authorities (Home Office and Labour Office), as well as people like my very good friends Sir Hugh Allen (director of the Royal College of Music in London) and Sir John McEwen (director of the Royal Academy of Music), are unwilling to take on any German-Jewish teachers in their institutions. In the summer, when we heard about Schönberg's sorry situation in Paris, Arthur Bliss said to me: 'the Royal College should have invited him immediately to hold a master class at the College, just as the University of Oxford immediately invited Albert Einstein – it would not only have been a fine gesture, but also a wonderful intellectual and artistic stimulus for the institution and its students.'

But from the directorate's perspective, it was impossible; if Allen had dared, he would have had the whole gang of co-operatives against him. I cite this only as an example. Herr Curt Prerauer, répétiteur at the Berlin opera, is in London, and looking for a post; I tried to get the Old Vic to employ him, but the ministry was entirely unwilling to permit it as long as English pianists are unemployed.

Rebner will be in the same situation. And musicians like Rebner and Prerauer are still better off than scholars, critics, etc. like Wiesengrund, Paul Bekker, Kathi Meyer and all the others who are coming to me. Excellent minds, but the whole music life in England is organized so utterly differently than in Germany that such people cannot find any place here at all. The posts are simply not there. What can an umbrella-maker do in the Sahara? Or a ski instructor in Venice?

I asked a philosopher colleague about studies in aesthetics at Cambridge. In my subject, musical aesthetics is out of the question; my students have to learn harmony, counterpoint, fugue, score-reading, figured bass and general music history, and for these disciplines we already have enough teachers.

Among specialized philosophers ('Moral Science') there are only very few who study aesthetics at all, and these are mostly connected to the English department – that is, they tend more towards English literary criticism.

In Oxford and Cambridge, almost all students work towards an examination after three or four years; it is not like in Germany, where one writes a dissertation and submits it at some point or other. The only people doing dissertations at our institution are a relatively small number of 'research students' who have already graduated here or at another university.

So Wiesengrund would not have any opportunity to hold lectures on musical aesthetics at our institution. But if he has money and can live in England as a private man, why should he not live here for a few years, in London, Oxford or Cambridge, or wherever he likes, settle into society here, continue his own studies and research, compose, if he likes, and in particular learn good English, so that he can gradually write for English journals, or write a book – as he pleases.

He would have to be prepared to become quite definitively English, and to no longer be German. After about three years in England he could also take on English citizenship, if he wanted.

The trouble with the Jews is that they are almost all egotists and careerists. I have been observing for a long time, especially with 'German' Jews, that they think only of their own careers, not about the musical welfare of all. (Webern, on the other hand, is a fanatical altruist; he sees his own talent as something that he can and must give to others; and Scherchen is also an altruist.) Consequently, all Jews want to live and work in a capital city. Now, Germany has had a surplus of musical production for years, and Austria even more so; this is why you (as also Kodaly and Bartok etc.) take it for granted that you can earn your money primarily in Germany. You [note in Berg's hand: '(The Jews?)'] are indeed Hitlerians, as you consider Germany, Austria, Switzerland, Holland, Scandinavia, Czechoslovakia and perhaps even England as belonging to 'Germany'!!! And as the Jews are particularly talented musicians, and all want to live in the capital, almost all music in Austria is concentrated in Vienna. For otherwise the musical idealists would have tried years ago to make Innsbruck and Graz (for example) into significant musical centres, as Oxford and Cambridge are in England. And then your students would sing madrigals and motets, like ours, instead of making Nazi propaganda! And the workers would sing Bach and Handel, instead of proletarian choir music, which I am occasionally sent from Germany – a music that only mirrors present hardship, rather than enabling these people to find a musical heaven in which they can think of higher things for an hour. I am, as you know, no admirer of Mahler, but it is at least better for the workers to sing Mahler than that 'proletarian music'.

And this 'proletarian music' (e.g. Weill's 'Bürgschaft', a work that I otherwise regard highly for purely musical reasons) was in any case a snobbish pose; no real proletarians came to the opera, only petit bourgeois people in ill-fitting dinner jackets! And felt very modern; and did this then spur them on to do anything practical for the poor?

I do not know how things are in America; but in the European countries, I think that your works, as also those of Schönberg and Webern, are received better in England than on the continent (except perhaps in Czechoslovakia?) Things are improving very slowly, but surely here, and in the whole country, not only London; there is now much more music flowing through the whole of England. We do not have anyone world-famous, either composers or virtuosos (and virtuosos do not grow here at all); but I am now observing an extraordinarily widespread love of good music in England.

The fact that your works, and those of other highly important composers, are only performed comparatively rarely here is because they were written for German circumstances. I hear that 'Wozzeck' is being given a concert performance by the B.B.C. People are very enthusiastic about it; but it is a shame that it is not being staged: artistically speaking, it is nonsense to put on the work without staging. But we lack the organization for a staged performance. Kodaly's 'Psalmus Hungaricus', on the other hand, which fits well into our music organization, is being sung everywhere.

The complications that have come about through Hitler are terrible; here in England we hear about it every day, and I have to write a letter in German every day! Recently a German friend of mine came over; he is the purest blonde Aryan, and the ideal of a Nazi, but he married a Jew, and so he had to give up his work at the gynaecological clinic in Freiburg.

Now I must tell you a story. When I was chairman of the directorial board of the Philharmonic Society (I have now retired, as each member must after so and so many years), we wanted to arrange a performance of the Piano Concerto by Toch, and tried in vain to convince the piano virtuosos to play it. We went to Horowitz, but he only wanted to play the Tchaikovsky – the B flat minor. Finally we got

Gieseking, who had given the premiere in Germany. But Gieseking did not want to play it; said that he had no time to learn it – which was rubbish, as Toch told me that Gieseking could learn the work within 8 days. But G. behaved rather unpleasantly, and made a very bad impression on the Philharmonic committee through his National Socialism.

In the end he played the Concertino by Honegger and the old Burlesque (!) by R. Strauss. I took Toch to the concert; he told me that G. did not want to play his work in London, as he would be boycotted in Germany if he had done that, or something like that.

And now the really amazing and funny thing. Gieseking received a great deal of applause after the Burlesque (which he of course played brilliantly); sat back down at the piano and as an encore played a transcription (presumably his own) of the song 'Ständchen' by Strauss, which naturally delighted the audience, as all singers like Elena Gerhardt and Elisabeth Schumann sing it to great success. Toch turned to me and asked me, quite naively: 'Do you know what that is?' 'But of course, "Ständchen" by Strauss!' Toch did not know it. Afterwards, G. played a further encore, 'Golliwog's Cake-Walk' from Debussy's Children's Corner. The same question from Toch.

I also discussed with him the possibility that he (Toch) could give a private piano recital at Cambridge; I suggested playing a few classical pieces, so as not to deter the audience too much, and works of his own. Then I asked, 'Do you also play modern pieces by other composers?' 'No'. And quite simply 'no', without any further words, without the slightest apology!

It seems that, for him, no music exists outside of his own works. And this I find typically Jewish.

What are such people to do in England, where we all have to *work together* to keep music alive?

Yours with warmest regards,

Edward Dent

Original: typescript with Dent's signature; music collection of the Österreichische Nationalbibliothek, F 21 Berg 655/5. – Partial publication in: *Alban Berg Studien*, ed. Franz Grasberger and Rudolf Stephan, vol. 2: *Alban Berg Symposium Vienna 1980*, Vienna, 1981, p. 184f. (Eva Adensamer, 'Bergs geistige Umgebung: Briefe aus seinem Nachlass').

Translator's note: the original letter is in German.

Bibliographical Listing

For the list of Adorno's compositions, all finished works, both published and unpublished, are given; a separate category contains all incomplete, planned and lost works (or those merely mentioned) referred to in his letters. Berg's unrealized plans – as improvised and provisional as they may have been – have been listed in this manner. Indirect allusions have not been included.

I Adorno's Compositions

1 Completed Works

First String Quartet

First String Trio

Four Poems by Stefan George for voice and piano [*Vier Gedichte von Stefan George für Singstimme und Klavier*] op. 1

Four Songs for middle-register voice and piano [*Vier Lieder für eine mittlere Stimme und Klavier*] op. 3

Huck's Entrance Song [*Hucks Auftrittslied*] from *The Treasure of Indian Joe* [*Der Schatz des Indianer-Joe*]

Movement for String Trio

Second String Trio

Seven French Popular Songs arranged for voice and piano [*Sept chansons populaires françaises arrangées pour une voix et piano*]

Six Bagatelles for voice and piano op. 6, no. 2

Six Short Orchestral Pieces op. 4

Six Studies for String Quartet

Three Piano Pieces

Three Poems by Theodor Däubler for four-part female chorus [*Drei Gedichte von Theodor Däubler für vierstimmigen Frauenchor*] op. 8

Tomcat's Lament [*Totenlied für den Kater*] from *The Treasure of Indian Joe*

Two Pieces for String Quartet op. 2

2 Planned, Incomplete and Lost Compositions

Chamber songs

Incidental music to Jean Cocteau's *Voix humaine*

Piano Concerto

Piano pieces

Piano Sonatina

String Trio

The Treasure of Indian Joe (lyrical drama)

Third movement for the Two Pieces for String Quartet

Three large orchestral pieces

II Adorno's Writings

1 Completed Texts

Against Epistemology, trans. Willis Domingo (Oxford: Blackwell, 1982) [*Zur Metakritik der Erkenntnistheorie: Studien über Husserl und die phänomenologischen Antinomien*]

Alban Berg: Master of the Smallest Link, trans. Juliane Brand and Christopher Hailey (Cambridge: Cambridge University Press, 1991) [*Alban Berg: Mit Bergs eigenen Schriften und Beiträgen von Theodor Wiesengrund-Adorno und Ernst K_enek*, ed. Willi Reich, Vienna, 1937; contains material reworked from Adorno's original contributions to the Berg monograph]

'Alban Berg: On the Premiere of "Wozzeck"' [*Alban Berg: Zur Uraufführung des 'Wozzeck'*]

'Alban Berg's Early Songs' [*Alban Bergs frühe Lieder*]

'Atonal Intermezzo?' [*Atonales Intermezzo?*]

'Bartók Performances in Frankfurt' [*Bartók-Aufführungen in Frankfurt*] (concert review)

'Berg: Clarinet pieces' [*Berg: Klarinettenstücke*] *See Alban Berg*

'Berg: Concert Aria "Der Wein"' [*Berg: Konzertarie 'Der Wein'*] *See Alban Berg*

'Berg: First String Quartet' [*Berg: Erstes Streichquartett*] *See Alban Berg*

'Berg: Lyric Suite' [*Berg: Lyrische Suite*] *See Alban Berg*

'Berg: Orchestral Pieces' [*Berg: Orchesterstücke*] *See Alban Berg*

'Berg: Seven Early Songs' [*Berg: Sieben frühe Lieder*] *See Alban Berg*

'Berg: Songs on Poems by Hebbel and Mombert' [*Berg: Lieder nach Hebbel und Mombert*] *See Alban Berg*

'Berg: Three Pieces from the Lyric Suite for String Orchestra' [*Berg: Drei Stücke aus der Lyrischen Suite für Streichorchester*]

'Berg and Webern – Schönberg's Heirs' (published in English), in *Modern Music* 8, no. 2 (1931), pp. 29-38

'Berlin Memorial' [*Berliner Memorial*] (opera and concert review)

'Berlin Opera Memorial' [*Berliner Opernmemorial*] (opera review)

'The Concept of the Unconscious in the Transcendental Doctrine of the Soul' [*Der Begriff des Unbewussten in der transzendenten Seelenlehre*]

'Concerning "Anbruch": Exposé' [*Zum 'Anbruch': Exposé*]

'Contemporary Chamber Music: First and Second Evenings in the Society for Dramatic and Musical Culture' [*Zeitgenössische Kammermusik: Erster und zweiter Abend im Verein für Theater- und Musikkultur*] (concert review)

'Controversy about Gaiety' [*Kontroverse über Heiterkeit*] (with H. H. Stuckenschmidt)

'Critique of the Minstrel (Ad Vocem Hindemith: A Documentation)' [*Kritik des Musikanten (Ad Vocem Hindemith: Eine Dokumentation)*]

'Hanns Eisler: Duo for Violin and Violoncello, op. 7 no. 1' [*Hanns Eisler: Duo für Violine und Violoncello, op. 7, Nr. 1*]

'The Instrumentation of Berg's Early Songs' [*Die Instrumentation von Bergs Frühen Liedern*]

Kierkegaard: Construction of the Aesthetic, trans. Robert Hullot-Kentor (Cambridge, MA: MIT Press, 1993) [*Kierkegaard, Konstruktion des Ästhetischen*]

Paul von Klenau: Die Lästerschule (opera review)

'Little Quotation Compendium' [*Kleiner Zitatenschatz*]

'The Lulu-Symphony' [*Zur Lulu-Symphonie*]

'Mahler Today', trans. Susan H. Gillespie, in *Essays on Music*, ed. Richard Leppert (Berkeley and Los Angeles: University of California Press, 2002) [*Mahler heute*]

'Metronome Markings' [*Metronomisierung*]

'Motifs', trans. Rodney Livingstone, in *Quasi Una Fantasia: Essays on Modern Music* (London: Verso, 1998) [*Motive*]

'Motifs II' [*Motive II*]

'Motifs III' [*Motive III*]

'Motifs V: Hermeneutics' [*Motive V: Hermeneutik*]

'Night Music' [*Nachtmusik*]

'The 1929 Volume of "Anbruch"' [*Zum Jahrgang 1929 des 'Anbruch'*]

'Oblique Retrospect' [*Schräger Rückblick*]

'On the Posthumous Works of Frank Wedekind' [*Über den Nachlaß Frank Wedekinds*]

'On the Social Situation of Music', trans. Wes Blomster, in *Essays on Music*, ed. Richard Leppert (Berkeley and Los Angeles: University of California Press, 2002)

[*Zur gesellschaftlichen Lage der Musik*]

'On Twelve-Tone Technique' [*Zur Zwölftontechnik*]

'The Opera *Wozzeck*', trans. Susan H. Gillespie, in *Essays on Music*, ed. Richard Leppert (Berkeley and Los Angeles: University of California Press, 2002) [*Die Oper Wozzeck*]

'Problems of Opera' [*Opernprobleme*]

'Ravel'

'Reaction and Progress' [*Reaktion und Fortschritt*]

'Recollections of the Living' [*Erinnerung an den Lebenden*]

'Scherchen Music Festival Review' [*Scherchen-Musikfest-Kritik*]

'Schönberg: Five Orchestral Pieces op. 16' [*Schönberg: Fünf Orchesterstücke, op. 16*]

'Schönberg's Wind Quintet' [*Schönbergs Bläserquintett*]

'Schönberg: Serenade op. 24'

'Schönberg: Suite for Piano, Three Woodwinds and Three Strings op. 29 and Third String Quartet op. 30 [*Schönberg: Suite für Klavier, drei Bläser und drei Streicher, op. 29, und Drittes Streichquartett, op. 30*]

'Schönberg: Variations for Orchestra op. 31' [*Schönberg: Variationen für Orchester, op. 31*]

'Schönberg: Von heute auf morgen op. 32'

'The Situation of the Song' [*Situation des Liedes*]

'The Stabilized Music' [*Die stabilisierte Musik*]

'Three Conductors' [*Drei Dirigenten*]

'The Transcendence of the Real and the Noematic in Husserl's Phenomenology' [*Die Transzendenz des Dinglichen und Noematischen in Husserls Phänomenologie*]

The Treasure of Indian Joe (libretto) [*Der Schatz des Indianer-Joe*]

'Anton von Webern'

'Anton Webern: On the Premiere of the Five Orchestral Pieces op. 10 in Zurich [*Anton Webern. Zur Uraufführung der Fünf Orchesterstücke, op. 10, in Zürich*]

'Why Twelve-Tone Music? [*Warum Zwölftonmusik?*]

2 Planned and Lost Texts

'Berg: Analysis of the Piano Sonata op. 1' [*Berg: Analyse der Klaviersonate, op. 1*]

'Berg: Chamber Concerto' [*Berg: Kammerkonzert*]

'Berg: Der Wein: Concert Aria with Orchestra [*Berg: Der Wein: Konzertarie mit Orchester*]

'Fragments on the "Ring"' [*Fragmente über den 'Ring'*]

'Neo-Classicism in Music' [*Neoklassizismus in der Musik*] (radio interview with Heinrich Strobel)

'Otto Jokl: Sonatine for Piano op. 21' [*Otto Jokl: Sonatine für Klavier, op. 21*] (introductory lecture)

'The Philosophical Content of Psychoanalysis' [*Die philosophischen Gehalte der Psychoanalyse*] (two presentations)

'Problems of Instrumentation' [*Instrumentationsprobleme*]

'Schönberg: Analysis of the Wind Quintet op. 26' [*Schönberg: Analyse des Bläserquintetts, op. 26*]

'Second Wozzeck Essay' [*Zweiter Wozzeck-Aufsatz*]

III Berg's Compositions

1 Completed Works

Adagio from the Chamber Concerto (arrangement for violin, clarinet and piano)

Chamber Concerto for Piano and Violin with 13 Wind Instruments

Concerto for Violin and Orchestra

Five Orchestral Songs on Postcard Texts by Peter Altenberg [*Fünf Orchesterlieder nach Ansichtskartentexten von Peter Altenberg*] op. 4

Four Pieces for Clarinet and Piano op. 5

Four Songs for Voice and Piano op. 2

Lulu

Lyric Suite (arrangement of the second, third and fourth movements for string orchestra)

Lyric Suite for String Quartet

Piano Sonata op. 1

Schliesse mir die Augen beide (Storm), 1st setting

Schliesse mir die Augen beide (Storm), 2nd setting

Seven Early Songs

String Quartet op. 3

Symphonic Pieces from the opera 'Lulu'

Three Fragments from 'Wozzeck' [*Drei Bruchstücke aus 'Wozzeck'*]

Three Orchestral Pieces op. 6

Der Wein/Le Vin Concert Aria with Orchestra (Baudelaire/George)

Wozzeck

2 Planned Compositions

Baudelaire songs

Der Dybuk (plan for an opera)

Plan for a symphony

'Und Pippa tanzt' (plan for an opera)

IV Berg's Writings

1 Completed Texts

'Arnold Schönberg, Chamber Symphony op. 9: Thematic Analysis' [*Arnold Schönberg, Kammersymphonie, op. 9: Thematische Analyse*]

'Binding Response to a Non-Binding Questionnaire' [*Verbindliche Antwort auf eine unverbindliche Rundfrage*]

Credo

'The Musical Impotence of Hans Pfitzner's "New Aesthetic"' [*Die musikalische Impotenz der 'neuen Ästhetik' Hans Pfitzners*]

'Why is Schönberg's Music so Difficult to Understand?' [*Warum ist Schönbergs Musik so schwer verständlich?*]

Wozzeck lecture (1929)

2 Planned Essays

Casella article

'On Schönberg's Chamber Symphony' [*Über Schönbergs Kammersymphonie*]

'On Schönberg's "Pelleas und Melisande"' [*Über Schönbergs 'Pelleas und Melisande'*]

259

Index

Aber, Adolf 143
Achron, Joseph 96
Achsel-Clemens, Wanda 49, 122
Adorno, Theodor
  academic career
    crisis points 78–9, 174–5, 184–5
    music or philosophy? 44
    postgraduate at Oxford 211,
      215, 216
    prepares for qualification 31, 35,
      55–6, 67, 78, 92–3, 109
    seeks Cambridge post 197
    thesis problems 114–15, 118–19,
      152
    Vienna Circle and 197, 198
  applies for critic's post 143, 150
  Berg's death 231, 232
  in California 239
  car accident 115–16, 117, 118
  film projects 194–5, 196
  hears Lulu in London 220–2
  ill health 30, 46, 91–2
  introductions 3–4
  joins Anbruch 9–10
  leaves Anbruch committee 159–61,
    164–8, 245–7
  loss of aunt 226
  on Lulu 220–2
  marriage to Gretel Karplus 239
  musical compositions
    counterpoint studies 195, 196
    Four Poems by Stefan George 129
    Four Songs for middle-register
      voice 110, 111, 117, 118, 119,
      125–8, 130, 133, 165, 214–15

    libretto for Tom Sawyer 194
    publishing 128, 133, 181
    Seven French Popular Songs
      86–7
    Six Bagatelles for voice and piano
      67, 68
    Six Short Orchestral Pieces vii,
      135, 136
    String Trio 243
    Two Pieces for String Quartet 3,
      60, 67, 86, 87, 88, 91, 243
  Nazi politics and 202, 203
  operation 98, 101, 103, 109
  romantic involvements 9, 70, 76–7,
    109, 111, 197, 207
  stagnant in music 184–5
  studies with Berg vii–viii
  writings
    Against Epistemology 216
    Alban Berg 31
    'Atonales Intermezzo?' 135,
      143–4, 168
    on Alfredo Casella 155, 166
    'Die Instrumentation von Bergs
      Frühen Leidern' 148, 151–2,
      154–5
    introduces Lyric Suite 226, 227
    on Kierkegaard 162, 174–5, 198
    on Lyric Suite 237
    on Mahler 52
    'Nachtmusik' 55, 59, 63, 72, 76,
      77, 86
    'On the Social Situation of Music'
      190–1
    recollections of Berg 31, 235–6

Adorno, Theodor (*cont*)
  writings (*cont*)
    Reich monograph on Berg 232,
      235
    on Schönberg 13, 15, 22, 71, 73,
      98–100, 104
    'Die stabilisierte Musik' 108,
      110, 111
    on Webern 54–5, 56, 57, 203
    on *Wozzeck* 39, 41, 43–4, 46,
      158, 169, 170, 172
Alban Berg (Adorno) 31
Albert, Eugen d'
  Der Golem 82
Allgemeiner Deutscher Musikverein
  182
Altenberg, Peter (Richard Engländer)
  7, 15, 16, 22
Anbruch (journal) ix, 9–11, 31
  Adorno leaves committee 159–61,
    164–8, 175
  Adorno's *Wozzeck* article 51
  conductor portraits 71
  Heinsheimer to Adorno 245–7
  Lulu essay 224
  restructured 128, 141
  Schönberg and 166, 168
  Webern essay 57
anti-Semitism
  in Austria 199, 228–9
  Dent's letter 248–51
  effect on music 201–3
  Prague's view of Berg 85, 89
Aravantinos, Panos 162
art, truthfulness of 37–9
Austria
  Engelbert Dollfuss and 206
  ethnicity in 199, 228–9
  German culture and 200

Bach, David Josef 86, 87
Bahr, Hermann 119
Bareuther, Herbert 104
Baudelaire, Charles 92, 93, 95, 206
Békessy, Imre 66
Bekker, Paul 248
Benjamin, Walter 227
  on Hofmannstal 63, 64
  'Karl Kraus' 186, 187
  opening of *Wozzeck* 33–4, 35–6
Berg, Alban
  Adorno's birthday wishes for 207

Adorno's studies with vii
on Adorno's quartet 91
affair with Hanna Fuchs-Robettin
  233–6
Akademie der Künste 178
asthma 10, 24, 122, 155
ethnicity 228–9
fiftieth birthday 205–7, 210–11
financial position 211–12
Hauptmann's *Und Pippa tanzt*
  43–5
health of 24
ill health 17, 81, 191
last letter to Adorno 227–8
Nazi Germany and 200, 201
portrait of 178–9
sells scores 213–14, 216–18, 222–3
works
  Allegretto gioviale (1st movement
    of *Lyric Suite*) 25, 26
  Chamber Concerto 79, 80, 86,
    95, 96, 97, 103, 119, 189–90
  Four Pieces for Clarinet and
    Piano 169, 172
  Lyric Suite 15, 91, 93, 95, 97,
    107, 110, 140, 226–7, 233–6
  Piano Sonata op. 1 212
  recordings 228
  Seven Early Songs 116–18,
    122–3, 126, 140–1, 146, 212
  String Quartet op. 3 31–2, 48
  Symphonic Pieces 212, 213
  Violin Concerto 213, 225, 228,
    235
  'Wein' aria 155, 175–6, 181,
    191, 216, 218
  see also Lulu; *Wozzeck*
Berg, Helene (*née* Nahowski) 18, 22,
  53, 229
  Adorno's consolation 231, 232
  burned in explosion 191, 195, 200
  neck cyst 104, 105
  nickname for 61, 62
Berliner Zeitung am Mittag 143–5
Bernhardt, Sarah 47
Blei, Franz 119
Borchardt, Rudolf 207, 209–10
Born, Claire 123
  sings Berg's Seven Early Songs
    146–7
Boult, Adrian 210, 217, 221, 227
Brand, Max 157

Brecht, Bertolt 247
Büchner, Georg
  Woyzeck 32, 202, 203

Calvelli-Adorno, Agathe 18, 225,
  226, 232, 235
Carls, Ludwig 194
Carnap, Rudolf 197, 198
Casella, Alfredo 65, 66, 82, 143–4,
  145
  Adorno's essay on 166
  Berg declines to respond 244–5
  La Giara 82
  'Scarlattiana' 134, 135–6, 137
Cerha, Friedrich 241
Christie, John 223
Claassen, Eugen 198, 199
Clark, Edward 217, 219, 223
Claudius, Matthias 50
Coates, Albert 65
Cocteau, Jean 175, 177
Connor, Herbert 69
Cornelius, Hans 31
Cortot, Alfred 214, 215, 222–3

Däubler, Theodor
  'Verloren' 117, 118
Debussy, Claude 251
Delden, Maria van (Liselotte
  Reifenberg) 101, 102
Dent, Edward 197, 198, 199, 201,
  205–6, 209
  letter to Berg about Jews 248–51
Dick, Marcel 48
Döblin, Alfred
  and Karl Kraus 10–12
Doblinger Publishers 185
Dranishikov, Vladimir 105
Dreyfuss, Carl 94, 195
Dreyfuss-Herz, Ellen 73, 90
Dubislav, Walter 197, 198
Dubost, Jeanne 122, 123

Ebert, Carl 223
Eger-Berg, Smaragda 239–41
Ehrenburg, Ilya 61
Eisler, Hanns 10, 79
Eisner, Stella 171
Elkan, Benno 74, 76
Engel, Carl 213
Engländer, Richard (Peter Altenberg)
  7, 15, 16, 22

Felber, Erwin 160, 162
Ferand, Emmy 82, 83
Frankfurter Kammermusikgemeinde
  21, 23, 76
Franzos, Karl Emil 202, 203
Frey, Walter 96, 97, 100
Fritsch (R.) Film Inc. 194
Fuchs-Fayer 150
Fuchs-Robettin, Hanna viii, 54
  Berg's affair with 6, 233–6, 237
Fuchs-Robettin, Herbert 6
Furtwängler, Kurt 71

Gál, Erna 98, 100
Gál, Hans 182
General German Music Society 182
George, Stefan
  'Litanei' 226, 227
Germany
  censorship 194
  effect of Nazism 200–1, 208,
    248–9
  failed Steierische Heimwehr coup
    188
Geyer, Stefi 95, 96, 100
Gielen-Steuermann, Rose 190
Gieseking, Walter 251
Glatz, Hertha 219
Glyndebourne Festival 223, 224
Goethe, Johann Wolfgang von 206,
  209, 234
Goldbeck, Frederick 141, 142
Grab, Hermann viii, 9, 11, 25,
  49
  in Prague 21
  pretext for affair 235
Graener, Paul 190
Graf, Herbert 160, 163, 183
Greisle, Felix 86, 87
Gropius, Manon 213
Grosz, Wilhelm 76, 77

Hába, Alois 247
Hartleben, Otto Erich
  'Liebesode' 116
Hauptmann, Gerhart
  Und Pippa tanzt 43, 46, 112–13
Hauptmann, Karl
  'Nacht' 116
Hauser, Kasper 63
Heger, Robert 122, 123, 131
Heifetz, Jascha 222

Heinsheimer, Hans 9–10, 11, 22, 86, 137
  and Adorno 159–61, 164–5
  Berg on Casella article 244–5
  as editor 55, 60, 144
  letter edges Adorno out 245–7
  against Willi Reich 173
  and *Wozzeck* 34
Herbert, Kurt 140
Herbert, Walter 135, 136, 194, 218
Herlinger , Růžena 123, 150, 152, 164, 171
  sale of 'Der Wein' aria score 218
  'Der Wein' aria 175–6, 191
Hertzka, Emil 10, 17, 18, 22, 145, 147, 150, 161
Herzberger, Else 227
Hindemith, Paul 107, 185, 200–1, 218
Hinnenberg-Lefèbre, Margot 128, 131, 133, 159
  performs Adorno's songs 137, 138, 140
Hirsch, Paul 60
Hirschland (pianist) 35
Hofmannsthal, Hugo von
  Der Schwierige 186
  'Der Turm' 63, 66, 67
Hohenberg, Paul
  'Schöne Sommertage' 116, 117
Holl, Karl 3, 5, 21, 71, 73
Holle, Hugo 182
Horenstein, Jascha 123, 140
Horkheimer, Max 177, 239
Hubermann, Bronislav 200, 201
Husserl, Edmund 219
  Adorno's *Against Epistemology* 215, 216

Ihlert, Heinz 201, 203
Institut für Sozialforschung 239
Internationale Gesellschaft für Neue Musik 45

Jalowetz, Heinrich 48, 49, 195, 196, 200, 225, 226
Jarnach, Philipp 182
Jemnitz, Alexander 110, 246
Johansen, Sigrid 33, 35, 149
Jokl, Otto 185
Jüdischer Kulturbund 202, 203

Kahn, Erich Itor 202, 203
Kapp, Julius 22
Karplus, Margarete/Gretel (later Adorno) 111, 192, 193, 197, 239
Kastner, Rudolf 120, 121, 143
Keller, Gottfried 10
Kestenberg, Leo 150
Khuner, Felix 93, 106, 190
Kierkegaard, Søren
  Adorno's thesis on 162, 174–5
Kleiber, Erich 27, 65
  Berg's Seven Early Songs 145, 147
  Berg's Symphonic Pieces 213
  forced out of Germany 208
  opening of *Wozzeck* 32, 33, 34
Klein, Fritz Heinrich 14, 15, 17, 28, 31
Klemperer, Otto 60, 120, 143, 246
Klenau, Annemarie von 8, 153
Klenau, Paul von
  Michael Kohlhaas 200, 201
  suggests song settings 116, 117, 118
Kodály, Zoltán 246, 250
Kolliner, Else 61, 62
Kolisch, Rudolf 48, 75, 82, 92, 168
  Adorno's Four Songs 128
  Berg's Chamber Concerto 96, 103, 105, 106
  Frankfurter Musikfest 107, 108
  Lyric Suite 141
  programmes Adorno's op. 2 86
  useful connection 214, 216
Korngold, Julius 48, 49, 156
Koussevitzky, Serge 213
Kracauer, Siegfried viii, 130
  Ginster 127, 136, 138
  travels in Italy 14, 15
Krasner, Louis 213, 225, 236
Kratina, Valeria 82, 83
Kraus, Else C. 96, 106
Kraus, Karl 7, 8, 137, 189
  and Matthias Claudius 50
  and Alfred Döblin 10
  Offenbach celebration 156–7
  response to Walter Benjamin 186
  on Shakespeare 202, 203
  truth of art 37, 39
  Die Unüberwindlichen 130
Krauss, Clemens 29, 30, 60
  Berlin Opera 208, 210

Der Golem 82
Wozzeck 158, 162
Křenek, Ernst 133–4, 137
  Adorno's songs 214–15, 223
  loyalty 218
  monograph on Berg 232, 235
  Preussner's article on 160, 162
  'Verloren' 213
  hears *Wozzeck* with Adorno 149
Krips, Josef 197, 199
Kurzmann, Rita 212

Lange, Hans 3
Lebert, Anna (*née* Nahowski) 18
Lebert, Arthur 16, 18
Lehmann, Lotte 122, 123
Leibowitz, René 240–1
Lenau, Nikolaus
  'Schilflied' 116
Library of Congress 213
Lopez-Vito, Maria Luisa 4
Lothar Stark-Gesellschaft 196
Löwenthal, Leo 78, 80
Lukács, Georg 9, 11
Lulu (Berg)
  Adorno on 220–2, 224
  Berg's finances and 193, 211–12
  or 'Pippa'? 111–12
  posthumous orchestration 239–41
  production planned 196
  progress of 128, 131, 138, 152,
    158, 188, 199
  Symphonic Pieces 212, 217, 218,
    220–1, 225, 226
  text 162–3
  twelve-tone technique 215

Mahler, Gustav 218, 250
  Adorno's book on 52
  Das Lied von der Erde 186
  Third Symphony 29
Mahler-Werfel, Alma viii, 6, 66, 167
  and Soma Morgenstern 104
  Prague *Wozzeck* performance 85,
    89
Malipiero, Francesco 222
Mangeot, André 214, 215, 216
Mann, Thomas
  Felix Krull 9, 11
Marx, Josef 38
May, Karl 156
Mengelberg, Josef Willem 141, 142

Meyer, Kathi 248
Meyrink, Gustav 8
Milhaud, Darius
  Le boeuf sur le toit 82
Modern Music (magazine) 178–9
Moholy-Nagy, László 162
Morgenstern, Dan 200
Morgenstern, Soma 9, 11, 29
  Adorno's *Wozzeck* article 43, 44
  Frankfurt and 110
  on 'Gedeikitztes' 62
  and injured Adorno 116
  and Alma Mahler-Werfel 104
  'Personenwaage' 68
  struggles with text 152
  suffers from silence 69, 70, 74, 75
  travels 58, 108, 109, 200
music
  Berg's unfinished works 239–40
  jazz 60
  metronome markings 42, 55
  'New Classicism' 65
  variation theory 28
  see also twelve-tone technique

Nahowski, Franz Josef 241
National Socialist German Worker's
    Party (Nazis) 178
Nemeth, Maria 197, 199
Nessy, Julia 212

Offenbach, Jacques 156–7, 162
Oppenheim, Gabrielle 70, 121,
    124
Oppenheim, Paul 70
Ostrčil, Otakar 85

Pabst, Georg Wilhelm
  Pandora's Box 194
Pisk, Paul A. 176, 178, 213
Pisling, Siegmund 78, 80
Prerauer, Curt 248
Preussner, Eberhard 160, 162
Pringsheim, Klaus 39, 41
Proust, Marcel 127
Pult und Taktstock 34
  Adorno's *Wozzeck* article 43–4, 46
  metronome questions 42
  Schönberg issue 98, 100
  Stein edits 11

Quer, Jens *see* Schönberg, Arnold

Radlov, Sergei 105
Ravel, Maurice
  Daphnis et Chloë 221
Rebner, Adolf 4, 248
Recka, Erna 178
Redlich, Hans Ferdinand 141, 142,
  160
  meaning of name 225
  as mediator 164
Reger, Max 69, 70
Reich, Willi 173, 178, 207–8,
  210–11, 218, 224
  monograph on Berg 232, 235
Reifenberg, Benno 101
Reifenberg, Liselotte (Maria van
  Delden) 101, 102
Reinhardt, Max 186
Reinhart, Oskar 105
Reinhart, Werner 96
Réti, Rudolf 45
Riemann, Hugo 171
Rilke, Rainer Maria
  'Traumgekrönt' 116
Rosanska, Josefa 106
Rothschild, Fritz 48
Rückert, Friedrich 94
Rudinsky, Arthur 96
Ruyneman, Daniel 159

Salmhofer, Franz 87
Schäfke, Rudolf 69
Scheler, Max 119, 122
Scherchen, Hermann 4, 63, 96,
  249
  Berg's Chamber Concerto 103
  Berg's Violin Concerto 236
  as conductor 71
Schlaf, Johannes
  'Im Zimmer' 116
Schlick, Moritz 197, 198
Schmid, Josef 35, 36
Schmidt, Leopold 33, 34
Schnéevoigt, Georg 65
Schneiderhahn, Franz 65
Schnoor, Hans 143
Schoen, Ernst 172
Schönberg, Arnold viii, 248
  Adorno and 110, 195
  analysis of Variations for Orchestra
  183
  Anbruch and 160–1, 166, 168
  Jens Quer pseudonym 39, 41

Modern Music article 179–80
'Problems of Harmony' (lecture) 94,
  95
Pult und Taktstock 98, 100
refuses *Lulu* orchestration
  239–40
school of 28
Suite op. 29 12–13
teaches in Boston 200
truth of art 37–9
twelve-tone technique viii
works
  Four Pieces for Mixed Choir
  op.27 26, 99
  George songs op. 15 133
  Gurrelieder 146, 148
  'Litanei' (String Quartet no. 2)
  226, 227
  Pelleas und Melisande op. 5 94,
  95
  Piano Pieces op. 11 45
  Piano Suite op. 25 22
  Quartets 71–2, 110, 119
  Serenade op. 24 21
  Suite op. 29 26, 58, 72, 119
  Variations for Orchestra op. 31
  183
  Von heute auf morgen op. 32
  161–2, 163
  Wind Quintet op. 26 64, 131
Schreker, Franz
  Der Ferner Klang 150, 151
Schumann, Robert 180
Schützendorf, Leo 33, 35
Sekles, Bernhard vii, 3, 4, 32
  '10 Küsse' 51, 53
  Adorno on 29
  Berg's letter to 243
Seligmann, Anita 110, 111–12
Seligmann, Milton 111–12
Seligmann, Walter Herbert 111–12
Sievert (artist) 162
Sigmund-Freud-Institut 104
Simon, Heinrich (Heinz) 101, 102,
  169
Slezak, Leo 71
Starke, Ottomar 72, 73
Stefan, Paul 9–10, 38, 168
Stein, Erwin 9, 11
  borrows from Adorno 55
  publication of Adorno's Four Songs
  128

questionnaire 22, 23–4
receives Adorno's songs 132
Stein, Fritz Heinrich 182
  piano reduction 57, 58
Steinberg, Hans Wilhelm (William)
  82, 83, 164, 185, 202, 203
Steuermann, Eduard viii, 9, 96, 97,
  218
  Adorno's songs 128, 137, 140
  Adorno's *Wozzeck* article 44
  Anbruch and 160
  Berg's Chamber Concerto 103,
    105, 106, 190
  Berg's fiftieth birthday concert
    212
  irate 6, 7
Stiedry, Fritz 190
Stokowski, Leopold 95, 96, 210
Storm, Theodor W.
  'Nachtigall' 116
  'Der Schimmelreiter' 194–5
Strauss, Richard 251
  controls Germany's music 200
  Fanfare for Brass and Timpani 54
Stravinsky, Igor 207, 218
  Berg delighted with 68–9
  disappoints Berg 48, 49
  Else Kolliner on 61, 62
  Oedipus Rex 120
Strindberg, August 83
Stuckenschmidt, Hans Heinz 34, 143,
  150
Stutshevsky, Joachim 48, 92, 93
Sundell, Stina 106
Sutter, Otto Ernst 102
Swinburne, Algernon Charles 206
Szell, George 226
Szendrei, Alfred 160, 163
Szenkar, Eugen 60, 61
Szymanowki, Karol 160, 162

Talich, Václav 213
Tasso, Torquato 234
Tillich, Paul 177
Toch, Ernst 182, 250–1
Toscanini, Arturo 150
Turnau, Josef 65, 66
Twain, Mark
  Tom Sawyer 194
twelve-tone technique viii, 25, 28
  Adorno's use of 67, 141
  Adorno's writings on 86, 119

Berg on 57–8
Lulu and 215, 240
Schönberg's use of 71–2, 99,
  110
Stein borrows Adorno on 55

Ullstein 143, 145, 147
Urbar 150

Van Geuns, Co 65
Veselá, Marie 149, 151
Vienna Circle 197, 198

Wagner, Richard
  Parsifal 29
Wallerstein, Lothar 82, 160, 163,
  164
Walter, Bruno 186, 200, 201
Waterhouse, Lady 214
Webern, Anton von viii, ix, 35, 36,
  122
  Adorno's writings on 54, 60, 203
  altruism 249
  Anbruch and 160
  as conductor 54, 63, 71, 170,
    171–2
  fiftieth birthday 200
  Five Orchestral Pieces op. 10 56,
    64
  Modern Music article 178, 180
  and Nazi Germany 200
  objectivity of art 37
  success 65, 66
Wedekind, Frank 186–7, 188, 189,
  194, 222
Weill, Kurt 140, 143, 207, 250
Weingartner, Felix von 208, 210
Weisman, Julius 120, 121
Weissmann, Adolf 22, 23, 143, 150,
  156
Werfel, Franz 39, 66, 85
  Paulus unter den Juden 104, 105
Westphal, Kurt 141, 160, 163
  essay on Schönberg 168
Wiener Streichquartett 48
Wiesengrund-Adorno, Maria 17, 32,
  90–1
  on Adorno's car accident 115
Wilde, Oscar
  Salome 47
Wlach, Leopold 212
Workers' Symphony Concerts 87

Wozzeck (Berg) viii, 14, 60, 79
  Adorno's later experience of
      149–51
  Adorno's lecture on 170
  Adorno's writings on viii, 39, 41,
      43–4, 46–7, 169, 170, 172
  Berlin production 94, 95
  Bruchstücke 97
  Brussels production 189
  chords 72
  Darmstadt production 180
  Frankfurt production 158, 164,
      166, 167, 176
  and German politics 208
  Erich Kleiber and 147
  London performance 208, 210,
      212, 250
  Alma Mahler-Werfel and 85, 89
  metaphysical perspective 50–1
  Oldenburg production 139
  opening performances 24, 32–4
  Prague controversy 83–9
  in Russia 105, 108, 109
  sale of score 216
  Rudolf Schäfke's essay on 69
  score at American National Library
      212
  twelve-tone music 28
  Vienna production 158, 162

Zeitschrift für Musik 3
Zemlinsky, Alexander von 6, 49,
      83
Ziegler, Heinz 86
Ziegler, Oscar 96
Zillig, Winfried 66